Electronic Commerce Relationships: Trust by Design

Electronic Commerce Relationships: Trust by Design

Peter Keen
Craigg Ballance
Sally Chan
Steve Schrump

Prentice Hall PTR
Upper Saddle River, New Jersey 07458
www.phptr.com

Library of Congress Cataloging-in-Publication Data

Electronic commerce relationships : trust by design / Peter Keen ... [et al.].
p. cm.
Includes index.
ISBN 0-13-017037-2
1. Electronic commerce--Security measures. 2. Business enterprises--Computer networks--Security measures. 3. Internet (Computer network)--Security measures. I. Keen, Peter G. W.

HF5548.32 .E372 1999
005.8--dc21 99-046370

Editorial/Production Supervision: *Joan L. McNamara*
Acquisitions Editor: *Michael Meehan*
Editorial Assistant: *Diane Spina*
Manufacturing Manager: *Maura Goldstaub*
Marketing Manager: *Bryan Gambrel*
Cover Design Director: *Jayne Conte*
Cover Design: *Kiwi Design*
Cover Photo: *John Terence Turner/FPG International*
Composition: *Ronnie K. Bucci*

Prentice-Hall, Inc.
Upper Saddle River, NJ 07458

The publisher offers discounts on this book when ordered in bulk quantities.
For more information, contact

Corporate Sales Department,
Prentice Hall PTR
One Lake Street
Upper Saddle River, NJ 07458
Phone: 800-382-3419; FAX: 201-236-7141
e-mail: corpsales@prenhall.com

Printed in the United States of America

10 9 8 7 6 5 4 3 2 1

ISBN 0-13-017037-2

Prentice-Hall International (UK) Limited, *London*
Prentice-Hall of Australia Pty. Limited, *Sydney*
Prentice-Hall Canada Inc., *Toronto*
Prentice-Hall Hispanoamericana, S.A., *Mexico*
Prentice-Hall of India Private Limited, *New Delhi*
Prentice-Hall of Japan, Inc., *Tokyo*
Pearson Education Asia Pte. Ltd.
Editora Prentice-Hall do Brasil, Ltda., *Rio de Janeiro*

Contents

Acknowledgments

The authors wish to thank the following professionals for their independent review, challenging comments and valuable input:

Tanya Alves of PriceWaterhouseCoopers, Toronto; Rosanna Au of Royal Bank of Canada; Florin Berca of Information Systems Audit and Control Association; Cindi Bonnette of the Federal Deposit Insurance Corporation; James Bruce of Office of the Superintendent of Financial Institutions, Canada; Ashley Dafel of The Canadian Institute of Chartered Accountants; Henry Jablonski of BCE Emergis; Erik Luysterborg of Deloitte & Touche, Brussels; Dr. Al Marcella Jr. of Webster University; Peter Tashjian of HKICS; Bryan Walker of The Canadian Institute of Chartered Accountants; Mike Williams of Deloitte & Touche, London, U.K.

Introduction

In the last week, you almost certainly used your credit card in a restaurant, but you didn't follow the waiter through the door to double-check that he or she didn't imprint the card twice or photograph your signature. You trust the system. But you may be one of the 60% of people who report when surveyed that they are not yet comfortable giving their credit card number to make a purchase on the Internet. You probably made a cell phone call last week, too. Cell phone fraud is many times higher than credit card fraud. But again, you trust the cell phone system more than you trust the Internet.

Electronic commerce (EC) represents the future of commerce, with the Internet the most obvious driver. Just in the past five years we have seen companies like Dell, Schwab, and Cisco extend their customer relationships—their traditional commerce—into this new style of business and quite literally make billions of dollars in doing so. We have seen a far more cautious shift in consumer behavior, but just about every business person and most consumers accept that at some point, EC will be as much a part of their everyday life as are credit cards and cell phones. Ask them when that will occur and their answer will basically be, "When we can trust it?" Ask the customers of the Dells, Schwabs, and Ciscos why they use EC and the answer will be, "It is a better way of doing business for us and we trust it." Ask them why they will trust it, they will say, "Because it is reliable, we feel safe in providing information, any problems are quickly recognized and responsibly dealt with, and we don't worry." Then, we trust the relationship. It removes our fear of the unknown.

Raw technology was the enabler of EC—the complex of transmission links computers, "standards," that created first value-added networks (telecommunication-based transaction systems for groups of trading partners) and Internet Commerce (trading systems for anyone in the world). The technology is now all in place. And it can only get better and cheaper. It's no longer the differentiator for EC.

Trust is now the currency and differentiator. Whereas in the early days of EC growth came from skills in building and managing networks and developing information systems, it now comes from building and maintaining trust and sustaining relationships. Just as a decade ago managers needed to be sure their firm had the skills and resources to design the technology base, today, EC is about designing the trust base. This is what our book is about. It is not about trust in itself: its importance, social impacts, or honesty, sincerity and the like. It's about designing trust: system frameworks and tools for ensuring that your organization's EC technology base becomes the platform for the comprehensive continuing and growing trust relationships that will determine its future business health.

What is EC? Just two years or so ago, the answer might have been a "fad—Internet hype" or "online transactions" or "paperless business." There's still no real definition, but it's more and more equated with an essential element for ensuring business innovation and even industry survival. In other words, EC is now very much moving into the mainstream, not lurking on the periphery of business. It's already turned the rules of competition upside down in such industries as securities trading, travel reservations and sales, PCs, and book and music retailing, and has profoundly changed supply chain management in manufacturing, retailing, and distribution.

That means it must be in the mainstream thought and practice of those business professionals whose job it is to ensure effective design of EC services and, more relevant to our book, to ensure the reliability and safety needed to build customer trust. EC professionals must provide the same degree of organizational controls taken for granted in nonelectronic commerce: security, financial controls, audit trails, privacy, integrity, and confidentiality. EC is not going away—it is very much here to stay. In business-to-business commerce, there are more than a dozen firms, each selling more than a billion dollars of goods a year via the Web. Cisco, the telecommunications equipment manufacturer, gets 70% of its revenues that way. In 1998, one of its customers bought $100 million of its products *without a single human contact.* Dell Computer not only gets 70% of its revenues from a combination of Internet and phone call center sales, but has destroyed the business model of Compaq, the leader in the personal computer market. Charles Schwab similarly has put at risk the business model of Merrill Lynch, a superbly successful and well-managed company, within its traditional industry. More than half of Schwab's 1999 business came from online trading.

The picture is less clear in the consumer market. Amazon, Yahoo, Excite, eBay, and other Internet stock "plays" may or may not turn out to be viable businesses five years from now, but they have in effect invented entirely new industries, with customer and revenue growth rates in the 50–150% per year range. America Online has turned a company described by a journalist as America's "most dysfunctional" firm into an online equivalent of Wal-Mart. Perhaps the breakthrough point for consumer EC was the Christmas 1998 period. Online retail sales increased by a factor of four over the same season in 1997. But, customer satisfaction halved! The dissatisfaction related to trust and safety: outages, weak links between the online software interface and inventory management, order fulfillment, customer service, payment, and security processes.

Better audit, control, and monitoring processes would have avoided many of these problems. Neat Web sites and great prices don't in themselves add up to reliable, safe, and trustable commerce. EC changes so many rules of the business game.

So, how do you yourself deal with it as a business opportunity for your company and client? What approaches to your work are most effective in applying forms of paperless commerce? Answering this question is what motivated us to write this book: to provide a practical guide for you to manage your business evolution into the electronic world of the future. Our goal is to help you make sound business decisions that will apply EC and its technologies for your benefit.

Our approach is simple: EC, whether via the Internet, electronic data interchange, value-added industry networks or even electronic mail, is basically about the systematic design of trusted relationships. Again, of course, that's what commerce has always been about: handshakes, keeping your word, writing contracts, ensuring informed consent, and the like. But, equally obvious, in the electronic ether, there is no face-to-face contact (look you in the eye and shake hands), very few regulations about commerce protection, and immense uncertainties, all of which add up to customer risk. Cut the risk, build the trust, and cement the relationship.

This book is designed to help you achieve these through:

- a no-nonsense approach to the key trust design issues surrounding EC, such as risk mitigation, control, audit, and security
- an interpretation of where EC technology is and where it is going, so you can anticipate the trust design agenda

Trust is the very foundation of commerce and EC doesn't change that. What EC does, though, is challenge many of the trust assumptions and processes that paper commerce now takes for granted, even those are often vulnerable, though built up over as much as centuries and supported by law, professional expertise, and experience. The mere fact that in the paper world, we have become accustomed to processes that consider paper to be irrefutable proof doesn't really respond to the fact that there are still bogus bonds and worthless contracts. If someone displays their broker's license on their office wall or gives you a business card that says J. J. Jones, CPA, you wouldn't automatically check this out.

Paper documents are powerful. We have become accustomed to them, because we either know the broker or CPA or assume the paper is valid; the business card opens up the relationship. Perhaps we should be more prudent; certainly, there are many con artists exploiting our trust in licenses, receipts, business cards, and the like. But we feel in general that we are in control, and that if something goes wrong, we know where to turn. If things look funny, we back off and don't give the party our business. In the EC world, we often have to decide to give our business and hence our trust *before* the fact rather than after. That's why so many of us decline the EC invitation to give our credit card number or fill out a form on our personal computer screen that asks for "private" information, yet we happily fill out almost the same form to apply for a department store credit card. EC removes paper and in doing so can remove a sense of confidence and familiarity. How do we find new ways of restoring that sense?

In Chapter 1, we begin our journey for controlling EC by exploring the very basics of trust concepts and issues. Trust is such a commonsense concept and so central to our lives, yet it's hard to even define except in vague terms. We start the journey by zeroing in on the pragmatics of trust.

In Chapter 2, we specifically approach the question of the risk issues in trust relationships and provide suggestions as to how to mitigate these risks on an ongoing basis. One of the most obvious effects of EC is that it accelerates the business process to a degree that there is literally no time to intervene if anything looks out of order. When companies aim at a "one-click" Web service, they mean that there can be no "Excuse me a minute" or "Do you mind if I get a little more information from you"—it's point, click, and go. Things that might have taken days or weeks in the paper commerce world now take minutes or seconds. What does this acceleration mean to the business process and for traditional controls? Chapter 2 provides answers. We also place these risks in the context of the roles and responsibilities of the business and IT manager—what needs to be looked for and what can be done about it.

How to control these risks is the central theme of Chapter 3. We see a direct relationship between the value of control processes and the success of a trust-base business relationship. That may seem a contradiction; "control" suggests bureaucracy, suspicion, and distrust. But consider the everyday use of notaries to "control" the validity of a signed document. Bureaucracy? No, it's a service in the interests of all parties that makes it easier to do business, not more difficult. In fact, creating and managing an effective control process can be seen as a *marketing* tool for the success of a firm planning to move its business over to EC-based technologies. For us, control on behalf of the customer creates a service advantage. Audit trails, security, backup, reliability, privacy, data integrity, confidentiality, and the other components of control build a trust bond, which is the theme of Chapter 4.

Chapter 5 is about security, which is the most cited concern about not using EC, yet many companies are using EC tools like the Internet with few worries about it. Does this mean these firms don't care? Have they resolved these concerns through technical tools? Or is there something else? What do we mean by security, and more important what tools should be applied under what circumstances? For us, security is more than just procedures and software/hardware protections. These are only a part of the story, which is about business planning. Our study on the Secure Electronic Transaction (SET) standard, which has been adopted by all the major credit card issuers (but has yet to be widely embraced and proactively implemented), clearly focuses on the need to look at the total picture and the key issues for EC before implementing a technological solution.

Chapter 6 is an exploration of EC itself: its roots and its components.

Because we see EC as being as much about relationships as about technology, the purpose of security, audit, and control is to make those relationships safe for all parties. (For this reason, we use the broad term "safety" to cover the full range of security, audit, and control procedures, software, standards, firewalls, audit trails, and the like in the rest of this chapter.) That shifts them from being specialized responsibilities of a technical or accounting function in the organization to their becoming an integral part of business planning and business management.

That they rarely are reflects what we will call in Chapter 7 the systems *defense* approach to business safety in computer systems and networks. We define a business *enhancement* strategy that augments systems defense and builds safety into the design of EC relationships.

EC puts more and more of a firm's cash flow online. There has always been a conflict in telecommunications between access and control. The relationship elements—communication, speed, convenience, variety of transactions, provision of information, and opening up the system for more and more users and uses—pushed toward open access; that's long been the ethos of the Internet and a major factor in its success and diffusion. Anything that gets in the way of these elements limits the relationship. The control elements are required for reasons of safety, regulation, protection of proprietary information, privacy, and ensuring an accurate record and audit trail. The challenge is to ensure that these augment, not intrude, on the relationship.

All this leads to a rethinking of where internal control, audit, and security should be targeted. EC is creating a new age for business and management. Approaching controls and audit processes in traditional ways no longer provide the level of assurance needed for the successful management of an organization. This is why in Chapter 8 we have developed an EC-specific approach to audit and control that looks at adding business value to a role that has been largely handled as administrative.

EC changes external processes and demands. Regulatory and tax agencies are profoundly affected by electronic processes, and governments are responding with new laws and expectations. What are the key issues and where are they going? EC is still bereft of a great deal of formality in law, which creates uncertainty and risk for business managers in trying out a new process or EC technology. We review a number of key regulations and their impacts on the business community in Chapter 9.

Finally, in Chapter 10 we describe where future trends lead, what the likely scenarios and solutions are: how you plan for what you can't predict. Our final chapter is about the future—that means it's about uncertainty. Our goal is to help you make *change* an ally, not a threat, by focusing on what we see as the most likely developments in EC over the coming years. "Likely" does not mean "definite"; it is close to impossible to predict anything in the field of EC, though, of course, there's a growing industry of expert opinions and forecasts, especially concerning the growth of Internet commerce.

We make no direct predictions, though we give our own best estimates of trends. We do this so that we can highlight opportunities for you to look out for and to assess their implications for risk reduction, security, audit, and control. We classify these trends into categories of likelihood: inevitabilities, strong probabilities, possibilities, and unknowns.

EC is a dynamic interaction of *electronics*: technology; *commerce*: relationships, markets, services, industries, and competition; *context*: social and political forces; *economics*: capital, investment, revenues, and margins. We can only guess at what these will lead to. Throughout this book, we present our personal views. Whether or not they turn out to be prescient or misguided and whether or not you agree with them, several points seem incontestable:

- The future will see a rapid loss of traditional control points and security mechanisms.
- Many of the most likely developments in the technology and its applications will transform the nature of commercial relationships.
- The pace of change is such that it inherently means an increase in uncertainty.
- All this adds up to a challenge, a threat, and an opportunity.

We hope that as you finish our book, you see EC as your opportunity.

1

Electronic Commerce and the Concept of Trust

DEFINITION OF TRUST

Trust is the foundation of commerce.

You simply cannot have commerce without it. Sometimes it's law, contract, and regulation that generate the trust; examples of this are the "truth-in-lending" law for mortgages in the United States, or the "lemon laws" many states have passed that protect consumers when purchasing a car. Sometimes it's a company policy, such as a money-back guarantee or the store automatically accepting the return of goods. Sometimes it's personal reputation or an established long-term relationship.

Trust determines the *space* for future interactions between parties. Distrust closes down possibilities—trust opens them up. The trust factor opens up or closes down the pace and nature of electronic commerce (EC) growth. Today, EC is well beyond the take-off stage but is still not widely established as part of the mainstream of business process. There's a lack of regulatory and legal protections in many areas, especially in consumer transactions over the Internet. We have limited experience in how to define contracts in the electronic environment. Companies do not yet know what policies to set, and there's a lack of long-term history of relationship and no face-to-face contact. Every story about fraud on, say, eBay's Web auction site, or breakdowns in e*Trade's online securities trading services contributes to customer concern, just as familiarity and frequency of use of credit cards online is reducing many customers' worries: In 1998, most surveys indicated that around 60% of people using an online service would either log off or lie if asked to give private information.

In the business-to-business sphere, there are far more established mechanisms for ensuring trust. The precursors of Web commerce—value-added networks that offer electronic data interchange services, bank payment networks, and industry supply chain relationship networks, for instance—have built up legal and technical protections, offer specialized software and services, and also are very sophisticated in their control and audit processes. That's because their users demand these: Many of them will not move to the often cheaper and more far-reaching Web commerce until they are sure it fully meets their trust criteria. It's no exaggeration to say that trust, more than technology, drives the growth of EC in all its forms.

This book is about designing trust mechanisms for EC especially concerning payments over the Internet. We see this as a source of competitive advantage. Our first chapters look at the nature of EC. We start with a straightforward definition of trust: confidence in the business relationship. We extend this definition to include some definitions of risk and focus in the relationships that are directly handled through computers and telecommunications. Together, all these create and maintain the trust bond: security, safety, honesty, consumer protection laws, contracts, privacy, reputation, brand, mutual self-interest, and many other factors. We want to help you build them for EC.

Trust is so multi-faceted that it can be hard to view it as a design issue. Instead, we generally think of it in common sense terms and observe the mechanics of trust design only when they break down or are missing. It's hard, for instance, for many managers to accept that you can create trust relationships with dishonest people; they pride themselves on being able to tell if someone's honest by looking them in the eye and testing their handshake. That's what con men love, of course. It's equally hard for many of us to insist on a written contract with a housepainter who is so nice and has done so much excellent work for us before. In the world of EC, it's increasingly bewildering to determine if a document is valid, if the law protects you against an error made by a Web supplier, or even if the supplier is who he describes himself as being.

None of this is new in principle, of course. Business, since the beginning of time, has been based on some form of trust. Looking back to the very first transaction—which may well have been the exchange of animal pelts or food for shelter—there had to be some level of trust between the exchanging parties before the deal could proceed. Later on, it was trust in the currency of exchange; that the seashell or iron bar the seller received had real value. (That the dollar is called a "buck" was because a major exchange item in barter was a deerskin. In many instance, that was a more-trustworthy currency than the bills issued by the flood of banks that grew up and often vanished in the early years of colonial America.)

The cavemen didn't have receipts and purchase orders, so there was no opportunity to use documents as instruments in commerce. Those were trust based—trust that an invoice for goods already delivered would be paid, trust in a letter of credit issued by a bank that enables a manufacturer to release goods for unloading at a port. In today's world of EC, it's trust that the sender of an electronic data interchange (EDI) transaction is the party claimed on the message, that your credit card numbers won't be stolen, that your Internet transaction is private, and many others.

Trust, therefore, seems to have developed from the simple concept that "I won't steal from you if you don't steal from me" (an interesting concept, especially in modern business ethics). As society and commerce have evolved, the concept of trust has become more complex and something that is not easily defined or quantified. It has now moved from the face-to-face relationships to often anonymous movement of logic bits. The implications of this shift are essential to the success of EC. Whether at a personal or corporate level, the need to understand and define "trust" in this new context becomes the point from which all future EC transactions extend.

Trust, not technology, paces EC change.

Take the emergence of the Automated Teller Machine (ATM), for instance. The technology, reliability, and performance issues were ironed out by the late 1970s. As ATMs proliferated, the resistance to them in the consumer market baffled bankers. With the ATM, one of the first true applications of EC, a bank's customers could have access to their account and money, 24 hours a day, 365 days a year. The benefits, surely, were obvious. The missing element turned out to be related to whether the consumers *trusted* the ATM system, not the underlying technology or institution. The typical consumer was reluctant to commit to banking electronically—with a machine instead of a human. There were entire conferences devoted to the question of how to break the "33% Barrier," relating to the one third of most customers who were early adopters of nearly everything, and how to convince the remaining two thirds to become users of the system.

Until the early 1980s, the ATM had a struggle justifying its existence. One of the authors of this book was asked by one bank to review its ATM investment, which most of the top management team viewed as a blunder for which someone should be fired! This was yet another technology "bleeding edge" fiasco. They saw it as a technology solution looking for a problem. No, it was part of a new way of doing business that rested on a new type and degree of customer trust. At some point, the trust question was resolved. The banking community was, over time, able to create or *design* trust for its users. First, it improved security and built a track record of operations. It made the ATM both easy and safe to use. As more and more people tried it out, its reputation grew, along with its convenience. New laws, policies, and procedures handled lost cards, contested transactions, and password management.

The same historical process has occurred with credit cards. Today, we perhaps are overtrustful in giving our card numbers and expiration dates over the phone or leaving them on file with a travel agent. We do this because we trust the "system." One of the key trust design mechanisms here was the change in U.S. Federal laws to limit customer liability for misuse of a credit card to just $50. Previously, it was open-ended, and you were liable for all or any charges incurred up until the moment you realized it had been lost or stolen and reported this to your bank (of course, in the pre-800-number days, if you found this out on Saturday evening, the rest of the weekend was spent in a panic.)

Would we have 1-800-FLOWERS, Domino's Pizza, and telephone ordering of goods as such a routine element of our own everyday life if the old laws still applied? Would the technology of call centers and catalogs have taken off so fast and far?

According to many surveys, over half of us don't trust the Internet and won't use a credit card to make purchases over it. Yet it's more secure than using the phone; in fact, there seems to be more cell phone fraud than Internet fraud. Even though the Internet is more *secure*, by using encryption techniques, people don't feel *safe*. Credit cards took off, like ATMs, when new trust design mechanisms encouraged people to try them out and as the security and reliability translated into a sense of safety and confidence. It's not enough for a company to say, "But trust us—we're honest!" Say, "You can trust us because we know what we're doing and that means you don't have to worry about us being honest. By the way, we're also *very* honest."

Designing trust demands going beyond the often simplistic view of it as just values: integrity, honesty, and sincerity. It's much more complex than this; it's a discipline and skill. There are some very basic questions for which managers need answers in order for trust to become the base for building a competitive identity and organizational advantage:

- What are the dynamics of *trust in action*, that is, in everyday commercial operations? How can a firm design for trust for all the parties in the relationship—in both buyer and seller?
- What are the *costs and risks* associated with conditions of trust and of distrust and what are the dangers of overtrusting and undertrusting?
- What organizational *structures and processes* facilitate trust? How do you build a trust advantage through "service and operations?"
- How do we build *effective partnerships* between parties who are often at the same time competitors to combine trust and self-interest?
- How do we best handle the dilemmas of *balancing trust with suitable monitoring, surveillance, and protection* against dishonest employees and outside parties?
- How do you trust *people you've never met*? (One of the key issues for the emergence of EC and the Internet)
- What changes must be made in *formal procedures* for contracting, sharing of information, and project coordination?
- *What is the management agenda for building the trust advantage*?

THE BASICS OF TRUST

Managers can't begin to answer these questions without asking the overriding one: *What exactly is trust*? It's so easy to talk about, so hard to pin down. It's a topic widely studied in business, political science, sociology, psychology, medicine, philosophy, law, and economics. It's not an exaggeration to summarize the basic conclusion in all these fields as "trust is becoming more and more important but we still can't really say what it exactly is."

There are many ways of defining trust and thus many perceptions of it. This leads to an overall picture of confusion, ambiguity, conflicting interpretations, and absence of reliable principles. For many business practitioners, trust is mainly equated with *behavior*: reliability and predictability. Can I really count on you? This view is well grounded in their own organizational experiences: Businesses are interested in results, not motives. For others, it's more equated with personal *traits*: attitude, confidence, and interpersonal skills; here, the emphasis is on individual intentions. Can I really believe you?

Trust is thus variously defined in both theory and practice in terms of interpersonal skills, self-trust, reliability, rationality, faith, psychological states, self-confidence, competence, expectations, and good will. So, at one extreme are the views of trust as a personal and interior response. If that is so, then there's minimal scope for viewing trust as a formal element in relationship design, in that there's nothing you as a firm can do: Either your customer or employee perceives you as trustworthy or he or she simply doesn't. At the other extreme of conception, trust is merely about rational assessments of reliability, in which case it's a redundant concept. If it were either of these extremes, it wouldn't be so central to the language of everyday life and be moving so rapidly to the center of business life and EC. Our view of trust focuses on reliability rather than on honesty and sincerity. The key to trust is to balance collaboration and control—President Reagan's famous quip about his view of how to handle nuclear disarmament with the USSR is subtly deep in its insight: "trust but verify." In the context of EC, it often needs restatement as "verify, so you can trust."

We often take trust for granted in relationships. It's generally automatically viewed as a fairly simple commodity and a positive virtue. Yet, the very notion of trust as good and distrust as bad are open to challenge. Distrust may also reflect personal competence as a trustor and a caring about standards; the widely reported increase in distrust of politicians may thus be more a matter of citizens being more aware of the standards they expect in performance, more knowledgeable about what's going on, and more concerned about trust breakdowns, rather than indicating some radical decline in the standards of public life. We sometimes acknowledge the legitimacy of distrust by paying someone to handle situations for us and take on the trust burden. We get a signature notarized or select a broker who is "licensed," for instance. The more complex a transaction is, the more likely it is we choose this approach, even when it may be cheaper to do it ourselves. The most obvious example is selling a home. The 6–8% commission to brokers may seem unreasonable for the little work they do, especially when you can list the house yourself on the Internet and thus handle the entire sale through EC. Most of us are uneasy about doing this, not because of the purchase element but those elements that center around trust and verification: inspections, title search, contract conditions, escrow, and the like. When real estate dealers talk about someone being a fizzboo (FSBO: "for sale by owner"), they don't mean it as a category but as a shorthand for "poor idiot."

Complexity compounds the reliance on others to ensure reliability, safety, and surety. The use of "direct exchange" trust (barter or similar activities) has now widely extended into "intermediated" trust, where a third party acts as a broker between the buyer and seller. Very little "barter" or direct business happens anymore. Most of us in our personal or business lives use a form of intermediated trust to conduct our business and ourselves. We use money, whether in the form of legal tender (coin and cash), a check, bank draft or money order, or a credit card. We are comfortable with the process of trusting the forms of payment and exchange that are common today. However, as EC becomes more pervasive, we have to reexamine our expectations and criteria for what we trust and can accept for payment.

For example, if you were offered payment in an unfamiliar or highly unstable currency, you may say "No, I don't want that kind of money—pay me in local currency." If you live in the United States, the trust and confidence you have in your local money and in the backer, the U.S. Government, may be well placed. On the other hand, if you were in Russia, where payment in rubles is "required," but not always desired, the Government's backing of the currency doesn't create a similar level of confidence and trust. How does one conduct commerce when the currency can't be relied on? Simple. You seek one that you can. In the Russian case, there is an enormous percentage of commerce that is conducted (illegally, from the government's view) in U.S. dollars. Even though the U.S. dollar is a foreign currency, a Russian business has trust in the backer and in the value and the stability of the currency. As long as a token of exchange is trusted, it's used. If the trust disappears for whatever reason, it stops being used. The most famous instance of this truism was the tulip bulb mania in Holland in the Seventeenth century. Bulbs were like gold, selling for as much as $60,000 in today's currency equivalent. Then, the bubble burst, and they became just bulbs. They were the very same bulbs as the day before but now were bulbs not money.

This comparison is of more than historical and anecdotal interest. It illustrates one of the major problems of EC today: what financial instruments will be accepted as trustable exchange tokens. There have been many efforts to create new forms of electronic currency through micropayments, smart wallets, digital cash, and e-tokens. None of them has succeeded to date and in early 1999, one of the most promising innovators, Digicash, declared bankruptcy just a year or so after it was being hailed in the business press as the harbinger of the new economy's handling of payments.

Trust is fragile, hard to build, and easily lost. With EC, there are so many areas of fragility: payments, contracts, security, and financial and legal recourse. The converse of this is that when trust is iron-strong as it is today across the world for U.S. hundred-dollar bills, the domain of commercial relationship expands in size and possibilities.

TRUST AS A FOUNDATION FOR EC . . . .

EC is now rapidly creating the introduction of new tools for conducting business and payment, which in turn generates new demands that often are not adequately catered to by established tools. The extreme example of the latter here is that there is absolutely no way you can really trust "news" you get off the Internet or be sure that the copyright of anything you list can be protected. This is creating many problems in journalism and publishing. In mid-1999, a well-known professor in political science issued a broadcast e-mail message to the academic community, stating that a "fact" he had published was simply untrue. He operated by the established trust mechanisms of researchers and the research process. The fact had appeared in another professor's Web article. But that professor was a fake identity, and the fact a deliberate libel. Anyone familiar with the often arcane rituals of academic refereeing, citations, peer review, and copyrighting can see how the Net at the very same time opens up the creation, dissemination, and sharing of knowledge—that is, increases academic intellectual commerce—while destroying many of its trust foundations.

That must not happen for EC for the obvious reason that if it does, there won't be any commerce. A direct analogy here is with Value-Jet, the airline whose safety record was revealed after a plane crash as less than stellar. Trust died and so did its business. Luckily, it's far easier to protect and validate business assets and transactions than it is to do the same for academic intellectual capital and copyright. The issues, though, are the same. Charles Schwab's online securities trading service is one of the major 1998–99 successes of EC on the Internet. Yet, in a context where the basic drive of this new industry that now amounts for over 25% of all trades has been price, Schwab dominates the market at a commission of $29.99 versus as low as $6 for other players. Talk to any Schwab customers and they'll quickly tell you they pay the premium because of the firm's superbly responsive processes for handling outages, errors in trades (including the customer's), and customer "care." They feel they are paying for peace of mind and the confidence that they will be looked after.

Building peace of mind and confidence is what makes technology into EC. The trust paces the technology's impact. After the ATM, the plastic-card-based payment systems that relate to credit card systems are now becoming payment tools for "direct debit." Direct debit works similarly to the ATM, except that instead of the card removing cash from a machine, charged to your checking or savings account, it is used at a terminal at a merchant location, where a purchase is charged against the buyer's account and credited directly to the merchant's, even if each of the parties deals with different banks. Again, this is as much a trust extension of the commercial interaction as a technical one. The next step is the use of a "smart," or "stored-value" card, which has a microchip embedded in it and can store money in an electronic "cash" format. Again, the technology is stable and reliable, but the issue of trust—along with relevance to the consumer, ease of use, and costs—will decide the stored value card's fate.

Another issue of trust exists in the management of supply chain relationships, one of the central forces in EC. When a manufacturer begins a relationship with a supplier, there are a multitude of components that require levels of trust, from both the supplier and customer perspectives. There must be trust in the component quality, consistency, on-time delivery, and so on. But there's also a need for trust in how breakdowns in the supply line will be handled. Commerce is fundamentally built on recurrence: repeat business and established relationships. Think of your own relationship with credit card firms, car manufacturers, airlines, or retailers. Probably 99 of every 100 interactions you have with them are completed with no mishap. It's how they handle number 100 that establishes your *future* trust in them.

Remember the great Tylenol scare of the 1980s, where a still unknown sociopath tampered with several bottles of Tylenol (putting cyanide in them) and created an enormous concern for the manufacturer as to what the source problem was—not to mention the public outcry and impact on sales. Was it in the manufacturing process or had the cyanide been added afterward? An army of people was mobilized to discover the problem, resulting in the conclusion that the product had been tampered with *after* manufacture. We now can "trust" the fact that Tylenol, like virtually all other consumable medical products, is now sold in tamper-resistant containers. Perhaps more importantly for the maker's trust relationship, the company took immediate and complete responsibility for recalling the product, at significant expense. It didn't deny responsibility, even though it wasn't responsible. The Tylenol case is widely taught in business schools as a model of leadership. We comment on it here as an example of trust as part of the business brand; Johnson and Johnson gained brand identity for the product because of this added trust premium.

EC faces many problems analogous to the Tylenol example, even if not as dramatic and far-reaching in their implications. Electronic transaction systems are designed for recurrence. They aim at levels of reliability in the 99.999% range. They are convenience factories. They reduce the costs of processing a credit card transaction to pennies and the time to a few seconds. They make it easy for a retailer to handle millions of inquiries and thousands of purchases smoothly and simply.

But they are too-often poorly positioned to handle exceptions. This is shown in the experiences of customers in online shopping during the 1998 Christmas season. Sales were up by a factor of four over the same period for 1997, indicating that a new critical mass of buyers has been tapped. This success was offset by a *halving* in levels of satisfaction. The *New York Times* summarized the situation in January 1999 as "Online Customer Service? It's Pathetic!" The failures were almost all ones of poor handling of customer queries—other surveys show that only about 15% of companies responded to e-mail messages within a day—dealing with incorrect shipments and informing customers if an ordered item was out of stock. Given that many purchases were last-minute Christmas gifts, the last of these was particularly annoying, indicating poor coordination between marketing and production/order fulfillment.

In business-to-business EC, the situation is generally far better, largely because it builds on a larger body of experience, but the same issues apply. EC is about *commerce* first and foremost. It is a system of (1) technology service access and processing tools; (2) processes behind the technology to ensure excellent completion of the commercial transaction; (3) sales, credit, service, and account management support; and (4) trust mechanisms, including policies on refunds, security, and many other tools unique to EC. These make up a system; neglecting any one puts the others at risk.

The Trusted System

All these lead to the essential issue that emerges from EC: What is the effect of EC on my own business and on me as an individual, and how do I establish a level of confidence and trust in it? Conversely, what is the effect of my EC operations on my customer's business, and how do I establish a base of confidence and trust? It helps to step back and take a more abstract look at the dimensions of trust in answering these two intensely practical questions.

Trust has become more and more central to business for four reasons that have nothing directly to do with morality and ethics:

1. Complexity: The more complex your environment, the more you have no choice but to trust, because you can't understand and do everything yourself.
2. Interdependence: The more people, steps, and intermediaries involved, the more you have to depend on others whose competence and behaviors directly affect the outcome.
3. The trust economy: The evolution of business over the past 40 years has been to make different forms of trust the differentiator: Trust in the product for the 1970s, trust in the transaction for the 1980s, and now trust in the relationship.
4. Telecommunications networks in general and the Internet in particular: Telecommunications, especially, the Web at the same time increases complexity, coordination, and relationships while removing many of the established trust mechanisms of commerce, increasing the risk to all parties and hence requiring entirely new mechanisms and practices.

Each of these forces in itself raises the salience of trust, but their interaction is what is making trust the new currency of business. The following applies to just about every firm that has more than 50 or so employees and to many firms that are even smaller:

Complexity

The company's business environment is more and more uncertain. Prediction, even in the short term, is difficult, and the firm must be ready to respond to business changes quickly. Cycle times have become shorter and shorter. Customers' expectations are growing ever higher, and they demand ever-increasing levels of service. Organizational structures must be kept flexible, with more emphasis on cross-functional processes and teamwork. It is harder and harder in many areas for the company to locate skilled staff; "intellectual capital" is recognized as the prime asset in an environment of change and complexity, with the "learning" organization a new priority. In other areas, the firm has moved through a sometimes almost-continuous flow of downsizing and outsourcing, with all the disruptions, policy issues, human resource concerns, and impacts on both victims and survivors. Regulation, environmental issues, and healthcare management consume more and more time and resources.

The nature of competition is changing, with many new and nontraditional players from outside the industry and many global entrants. Channels of distribution are becoming more complex and varied, including phone service, the Internet, and electronic procurement. Customer and market segmentation pose new challenges, with no more "average" customers. Information technology, previously delegated to the firm's information services function, is now a central element in almost all elements of operations, with many business executives feeling uncomfortable, whether they understand the issues and risks or not.

This company—an increasingly typical one—can respond effectively to the demands of complexity by loosening its controls over employees and encouraging and facilitating collaboration, teams, and real employee empowerment. Managers have to trust their subordinates more than ever. There's no time or expertise to monitor them or review their decisions. Instead, we all have to ask, "Who knows how to get this done?" In other words, "Who do I trust to get it done?"

Interdependency

The firm is involved in a number of partnerships and alliances, to handle shared sourcing, joint development, and distribution. It is a member of industry associations, consortia for regional development, and other shared interest groups. Key customers and suppliers work together on many issues, to the extent that they cooperate in the morning and compete in the afternoon. They jointly share information and plan functions that were previously the domain of each individual party; those shared functions include inventory management, quality control, and forward planning for materials and distribution. The company has a number of long-term outsourcing projects underway, which require continuing review and adjustment as the original business conditions and contract agreements must be adapted to changing situations. In high-tech and engineering-dependent firms, there is constant movement of staff within the industry, with both frequent sharing of intellectual property through licensing agreements and frequent legal skirmishes about protection of patent rights and of proprietary information when key employees move to a competitor. In many instances, competitors have to work together, because customers demand it as a condition of contracts in such areas as telecommunications and information systems integration.

Is this what some have called "Coopetition"—cooperation with competitors? It's the basis of the business game in Silicon Valley. As the Chief Operating Officer of one of the leading business-to-business EC players told one of the authors in early 1999, "You're only as strong as your weakest ally and you're kidding yourself if you think you can go it alone." And as another top manager in the Valley told him, "It's a real bitch when you know that you and your nearest competitor have no choice but to trust each other or you're both in trouble."

The Trust Economy

We are rapidly moving toward a trust economy that has progressed through three eras: Product, Service, and now Relationship. All of these pose heavy trust demands. The firm is challenged to make its products fully trustable: quality, warranties, after-sales service, and so forth. It must achieve ever-increasing levels of trustable service: guaranteed delivery time, fast turnaround, reduction in error rates, convenience, security, and availability. Increasingly, it is looking to establish stronger ties with customers and suppliers. as many service and product elements become commoditized. The customer is no longer an anonymous statistic. The more commoditized the product, the more important that service becomes as the premium item. (You don't phone Domino's Pizza because it offers the world's best cheese.) The more commonplace a service is, the more important the relationship becomes as the differentiator among the many providers.

In the 1970s, consumers lost trust in the quality of American manufacturing: cars, consumer electronics, and household goods. Toyota, Sony, and other Japanese firms were the gainers. Total Quality Management, invented in the United States and applied in Japan, created a trust premium for them and a decade-long catch-up race for their U.S. competitors. In the 1980s, ATMs, 800 numbers, and credit cards generated a convenience society and a new trust advantage; you could be sure you could get cash in Swedish krone through an ATM in Stockholm, pay for your hotel in Paris, and order pizza from Domino's. You don't have to worry about traveling anywhere in most of the world if you have your credit card and know the phone number for calling the country using your AT&T, MCI, or Sprint calling card.

So, you now take product quality for granted when you go to Circuit City to buy a VCR. Indeed, you could pick one at random and trust it's reliable. Even if it turns out to have some problem, you can return it for any reason within 30 days. You can pay for it by credit card and indeed could order it over the phone without even seeing it. We now take product quality and convenience in transactions as a given of everyday life. This trust had to be worked at to build and keep. Even now, banks, retailers, airlines, and credit card firms vary widely in how well they live up to their service promise. But all in all, ours is a convenience society with very high standards of quality in most types of services and products.

What happens when all leading competitors have excellent quality and convenient, reliable transaction handling? These features then lose their premium value. Trust in relationship becomes the differentiator. That is now the case in financial services, airlines, retailing, and manufacturing. It's the very basis of EC, in that it depends fundamentally on relationships, not transactions, as the basis for long-term success. If a company offers only transactions, it's simply an online convenience store that can compete only on price. The buyer can use a search engine to locate the lowest price, which puts pressure on the company to cut its own price. Just as customers see its price, so do competitors. It's a no-win game to be in. Also, the cost of acquiring customers is so high at present, that without repeat business, the company won't be around for long; in April 1999, the customer acquisition cost for Amazon.com was over 20% of revenues.

This is why Amazon's entire strategy is based on building repeat business through providing impeccable service, encouraging collaboration with readers and authors, first adding CDs and videos and then other products that its customer base trusts Amazon to sell, and always keeping customers fully informed about the status of their orders. Charles Schwab & Co., Cisco, Dell, and the other firms who have made their name an EC brand follow the same strategy: build and cement the relationship. By definition, relationship means trust. These are the trust brands of the new online economy.

Telecommunications Networks

Between 40 and 80% of the firm's cash flow is now online, through electronic data interchange for procurement, customer–supplier supply chain logistics, distribution, customer information and service, electronic payments systems and cash management, production planning, reservation systems, engineering design, inventory management, and a wide range of other functions. When the telecommunications network is down, so is much of the business. The firm has 800-number customer service links. It is investing in Internet operations that today may be small-scale or experimental but in the case of firms like Cisco and General Electronic, some companies handle billions of dollars in transactions. It has intranets and extranets and uses global data communications networks, "value-added" industry networks, and many others. Many of its operations are remote from the firm's main locations. Customer service may be handled out of Ireland or Omaha, the telemarketing centers of the world. Back office processing of, say, insurance and healthcare claims are routed via Mauritius. Programming teams in India link to the firm's computer complexes in New Jersey.

Reservation service operators work in centers in Europe and Texas, with calls routed to them as customer time zones demand. Many employees work as much from their homes as from the company's location, with their laptop and modem as key tools of business. The firm talks increasingly about the "virtual organization" to describe the use of telecommunications to make operations time, and location-independent.

One distinctive aspect of these telecommunications-dependent services is that the customer sees every failure—the firm can't hide it inside the corporate building and race to fix things before the customer finds out. One major "outage" can offset a hundred flawless transactions and badly damage confidence in the relationship. In late 1998, the online security trading services like e*Trade, Datek, and Schwab had grown at such a rate that their systems were overloaded, and there were a number of delays in executing trades and many crashes. Customers rapidly switched accounts—gave up on the relationship—and in many instances were willing to give up the major advantage of online trades, the low commission fee, in return for a better guarantee of service. Trust is again the differentiator when many providers can give the same basic offers and transactions.

Just-In-Time Practices

Complexity, interdependence, the trust economy and telecommunications combine and build on one another. The result has been to make time the basis of competition and logistics management. Look at a business practice that has been directly affected by the application of EC processes: In seeking better control and management of their inventories, companies implement "just-in-time" (JIT) processes along their entire supply chain, removing processes, steps, and stores. This means, in many cases, the cost of storage and support of the inventory is offloaded to the first-tier suppliers, so in order to maintain their commitments, and therefore trust, they have to eat costs of storage and risk "out-of-stock" positions. As well, many of the obligations and risks are transferred to the supplier to make sure the buyer is not left out of stock—with severe penalties for nonperformance. The supplier base, which tends to be smaller organizations, starts to have great difficulty in carrying the cost of its own inventory for production as well as its customers, and many will go out of business. Some, but not many, will try to apply the same principles to their own, second-tier, suppliers, but like so many other realities in business, there isn't always sufficient leverage to make the next tier of suppliers become part of the electronic supply chain.

The result? There may not be overall savings to the entire system in the early applications of JIT—in fact, there may be a slight increase in the cost—largely due to smaller companies having a higher cost of funds to maintain the inventory. This is an issue that has been challenging the North American auto industry, and it has necessitated the Big Three auto manufacturers to mandate the participation of second- and third-tier suppliers to participate in the electronic trading process, thereby stimulating further expansion of the applications of EC. There are many similar effects that trust has on the business process, such as evaluated receipt settlement (ERS), vendor managed inventory (VMI), and others, which are discussed in later chapters.

Customers don't want to put suppliers out of business, so this early win–lose approach that marked the evolution of supply chain management in the days of electronic data interchange networks has gradually moved toward a collaborative win–win strategy. Chrysler illustrates this: The car maker over a 10-year period moved from a relationship with many hundreds of suppliers, which was essentially based on playing them off against each other in order for Chrysler to gain contractual and performance advantages, to one of a tighter collaboration with a smaller number. This new collaboration rested on long-term trading partner agreements, encouragement to offer suggestions about how to improve supply chain processes with a sharing of benefits, and mutual involvement in design and development. In so many ways, EC succeeds by building sustained relationships with suppliers and customers. That takes effort and involves risks.

ADDRESSING NEW RISKS

The expansion of EC is creating a series of risks that, while not unique to the phenomenon of EC, have impacts that need to be addressed in new ways. For example, the Internet has created entirely new channels of delivery for services *to* the consumer and is seen as an opportunity for great mutual benefit and revenue generation. At the same time, access needed to support a valuable customer service opens doors of entry that were previously nonexistent: The customer gains direct access to the firm's information and processing assets. That access can't be casually allowed. The systems need protection. We now have barriers to electronic entry, commonly called *firewalls*, to prevent unauthorized entry to host systems or other sensitive data systems. This creates the need for definition and provision of formal policies as they relate to the use of the Internet or other EC-enabled systems. EC demands new rules of commerce.

These elements must be assembled into a policy based on the elements of:

- disaster recovery/business continuity
- resources
- information security policy
- network security policy
- e-mail policy
- Internet policy
- Outsourcing policy

Each of these categories has specific management responses and appropriate solutions need to be developed on that basis. For example, it is critical that policies related to external e-mail reflect the fact that information content and source can be outside the organization's control, and therefore an internal policy is ineffective. Sometimes, it may mean accepting the risk that the organization is exposed and that there is no real solution to be applied.

From these components, the basis of a trusted system emerges, and the ability to reliably support EC develops. The EC community is genuinely concerned about the issues of reliability and control, which generally relate to issues surrounding security and access. Research on the subject of EC supports the issue. In its study of the Internet and EC in North America, The EDI Group of Oak Park, IL found that message security was a key factor for businesses to use electronic messaging, the top concerns being related to audit trail, message validation, and authenticity of the trading partners. Key issues in the management and control of all business transactions, not just electronic ones but also the questions of "how" and "when," become more important as we progress into the electronic business world.

Ultimately, the establishment of trust in EC will be as a result of:

1. **Resolving the personal or interior response to trust:** Creating the perception that the system is trustworthy and can be used with confidence. This has happened with the acceptance of the ATM and many other similar automated delivery channels that have become popular over the past several decades. It doesn't necessarily happen overnight, but it can, and can lead to the acceptance of parallel forms of electronic delivery. The Canadian Interac debit card's point-of-sale system is a clear example of this. In 1986, virtually all of the bank ATM systems were linked together into a common, shared facility for the domestic market. Almost any Canadian bank customer with an ATM access card could obtain cash from any other bank's ATM. In the early 1990s, the same concept was applied to the direct debit process, where, as mentioned before, cardholders could charge their account for a purchase right at the merchant site, using their ATM personal identification number to provide authorization. The system has been a tremendous success: Transaction volumes for December 1996 for debit exceeded credit card and all other forms of payment. Since then, volumes have consistently eclipsed other forms of noncash payment and will likely exceed actual cash transactions in the foreseeable future. Consumer acceptance occurred much more rapidly than for the ATM, mainly because the perception of a trustworthy system had already been established.

2. **The exterior view of trust:** In essence, ensuring that the reliability of the systems and processes are impeccable and that there are well-described and managed systems performing the tasks they are designed to. This has yet to be fully accomplished in most applications of EC and is critical for the success of the acceptance of EC from an interior view. Designing trust means implementing processes that not only impart control, security, and reliability, but also can be seen as being implemented by those who are being asked to use the technology. In other words, actions speak louder than words.
3. **Finally, there has to be true value to the parties in the exchange process:** For EC to be successful, the value and return to the participants have to be equitable and accessible. The Internet provides a vast delivery channel that may well be accessible but is not necessarily equitable. If the products and services do not reflect the expectations of the consumer in terms of price, performance, ease of access, or whatever, then consumer faith in the channel will not result. This is a critical issue for the use of the Internet in business EC channels as well. Issues of safety and reliability can be offset to some extent by vastly lowered costs of operation, but there is an urgent need for the issues of certainty and management that will reenter the requirements matrix.

ACTION ITEMS FOR IT MANAGERS . . . .

Effective management in the EC-driven business world requires a complete understanding of where the risks and concerns may be, followed by an effective strategy to deal with any areas of uncertainty or doubt. Although the use of technology can resolve these issues, it must be seen as a point of philosophy and business process that enables the technical components to be used effectively. Ultimately, the successful manager will structure his or her approach to EC trust based on the following steps:

- understanding the business environment
- categorizing and responding to specific areas of concern
- monitoring the relationship

Understand the Business Environment

What is the actual business process, and what can be improved? This means looking at each function within the organization and developing a matrix of the business needs. From this step, it is now possible to ask the key question, "What areas represent exposure that are not addressed in normal business practice?" In other words, what are the unique trust factors in EC that need to be addressed?

Categorize and Respond to Specific Areas of Concern

After analyzing the key elements in the business process, and once the appropriate tool for the job has been determined, an appropriate policy should be determined for applying techniques and levels of control commensurate with the level of trust required. In other words, one must determine how much risk and impact are involved before deciding how to trust. This is especially true of high-value, high-impact relationships that can typically create a mutual dependency, even if trust is hard to establish. This was true of the so-called Cold War of the 1960s and 1970s. The basis of trust in this case was in fact a high degree of distrust but was held in check by a process called mutually assured destruction (M.A.D). If one side were to fire its weapons, the other side could be trusted to fire its weapons instantly, without hesitation. This would represent the most extreme level of distrust, leading to an extreme control.

At the other end of the spectrum, the family business, passed on from generation to generation, can often (but not always) be seen as the ultimate trust relationship. Others who do business on a verbal promise and a handshake are also at this end of the spectrum. In EC, it is the electronic equivalent of handshake that needs to be sought in order to create growth and expansion. But it is the risk of M.A.D. that creates the checks and balances.

Monitor the Relationship

Throughout this book, we describe a variety of concepts and processes that can assist you in developing an approach to manage the EC trust relationships you wish to build. Creating trust is dependent on factors that are specific to your own situation. Whatever your specific circumstances, you need to revisit the process on a regular basis to ensure the relationship deserves the level of trust you give it. Sometimes staff or management changes or government/regulatory changes affect the level of trust afforded a relationship, and such a review is needed to ensure things don't get out of hand. Also, a regular review of all your business relationships and exposures needs to be included in your overall business process review, along with the mission-critical components of quality, price, and availability that are the usual components of business.

2

The Dark Side of the Force: The Risks of Electronic Commerce

RISKS COMMON TO ALL DISTRIBUTED NETWORKS . . .

Trust and risk go together; one is the concomitant of the other. With EC, the good side of the Force—to borrow an analogy from Star Wars—is the trust-centered invitation to a long-term relationship. The dark side is that there are dangers everywhere: Some include Darth Vaders, villains deliberately aiming to sabotage a system through viruses or commit fraud and theft. Most of the risks are problems of omission rather than commission. That doesn't make them any less damaging.

Telecommunications-based services are inherently risky for the one simple reason that underlies every aspect of their use as part of commerce: the conflict between access and control. The more you open up access, the more you give away control. By definition, commerce means access. By definition, risk management means control. How to balance these two conflicts is the topic of much of this book. In this chapter, we look at the risk side. EC has in general been able to ensure reasonable degrees of control through "closed" networks, such as the industry-specific value-added networks (VANs) that have managed payments in banking (SWIFT, CHIPS, CHAPS, Fedwire, and many others), insurance (IVANs), and many other industries. The World Wide Web, which has become the base for more and more EC, is the ultimate in access; anyone, anywhere can not only access it but set up a presence on it as a merchant, information resource, individual, or, of course, potential crook or commercial incompetent. VANs protect against risk by limiting who can be part of the Web's activities, imposing procedures and tightly guarding against known sources of risk. The banking networks, for example, not only provide specialized security mechanisms across the entire network entry points, transmission links, and processing systems, but also establish agreements on exactly how electronic transactions are settled by the parties. It's far harder to accomplish on the Web, where no one is in full control, in the interests of preserving the full access that makes the Internet truly a world wide "web."

The Internet is the largest distributed network ever. Distributed networks have made the medium used to transmit information irrelevant. The transmission link may be a fiber optics cable, a wireless radio wave, a cable television link, or a satellite beam. Anything that can be digitally encoded—that is, personal information, business information, financial information, video, photograph, phone call, radio program—*any* information product—can be transmitted far easier and faster than ever before. Increasingly, it can be accessed by more and more types of devices: The Internet Protocol (IP), that is, the base of the Internet, allows any IP device to communicate with any other, without either needing to know what or where the other device is. Coffee pots and cameras have for a decade been Internet addresses. Now, cellular phones, printers, fax machines, TV sets, and even cars are IP addresses (somedevice@someplace.something). More and more of these devices are outside the traditional security points of corporate networks and value-added services. Consider the new-generation digital cell phones with built-in Internet browser, e-mail, fax, pager and messaging system, or the famous Palm Pilot, which now comes in versions with wireless Internet access. These are new extensions that distribute the reach of EC computing services even further than before—and also compound the risks and problems of control. In the wake of distributed networks came misdoers of all varieties, intent on adverse exploitation. It has been stated that the computer is the greatest villain wreaking havoc within the network domain. The computer is a universal machine, capable of copying any other machine's software and information, and while linked to a network can easily retransmit to any number of destinations, can be infiltrated, and can also be used to create sophisticated software that damages or steals from other computers.

The reach of business process automation has evolved from the basic solo functions on a computer to complex distributed processing models, such as funds transferred from one bank to another, to the worldwide linking of all of these plus links of many networks to each other via the Internet. Distributed networks have allowed a business process to span multiple independent systems—often in separate facilities, cities, or countries—contributing to a common goal. However, despite all of their virtues, distributed networks do have their share of risks. Like other information systems, distributed networks' risks revolve around information privacy, integrity, and availability, except that the related risks multiply. It's important for managers to understand that it's the degree of distribution that creates risk hazards. You can quite easily protect a single "stand-alone" personal computer from viruses or intrusions, but even there it gets harder and harder. Early 1999 saw a flood of new threats, including the Chernobyl virus, which used the widespread Microsoft Word software package as a hiding place from which to launch its attack and wipe out the PC's disk storage. In North America, almost everyone who uses the Internet and e-mail also installs virus scanning software. That was not the case in many countries. Taiwan was reportedly very hard hit by Chernobyl.

There are scams everywhere now: e-Bay, the massive online auction system, had to adjust its trust mechanisms in 1999 to address the gaps in its processes that enabled crooks to set up identities and sell goods, disappearing as soon as they received the money, without sending the goods, of course. Beware if you're a professor who gets an innocent e-mail from a "student" asking for information about your family as he or she is studying from your books. The student wants information about your family, especially your mother's maiden name, your date and place of birth, your middle name, and so on. This is, of course, just the information someone needs to commit credit card fraud.

We could list many other such examples. We list the ones above that happened to one of the authors in a single month, April 1999. These are not the tip of an iceberg—at least you can *see* an iceberg.

Limitations of Traditional Risk Management

As human beings, we routinely establish defense mechanisms that protect us from undue or accidental peril. We enroll in self-defense classes, vaccinate against disease, obtain insurance, and so forth. It's a natural, often instinctive, reaction that we rely on to ease or soften the effects of threats. Distributed networks are no exception to this natural defense mechanism. Risk mitigation deals with threats through the establishment of defense protections—characterized as a threat-driven approach. This threat-based (also known as a compliance-based) approach results in controlled and structured security programs that are rigidly enforced. In dealing with distributed systems, compliant-based approaches have advantages and disadvantages. The advantages include:

- being composed of well-established, understood, and unambiguous requirements
- standardized requirements that are easily monitored and audited
- analysis and evaluation of unique environments to determine needs and countermeasures that are not required

The disadvantages include:

- all systems are treated alike, with all countermeasures implemented, whether required or not
- the line of business has no control in determining reasonable risk acceptability
- the implemented system does not respond to rapid changes in technology and evolution

The limitation with a traditional threat-based approach (and the defense mentality) is that it assumes that all possible threats associated with an implementation are contained within and defended against the known body of defined countermeasures. Given the rate of change of technology and the complexity, this is a very shortsighted view. It can work well for hermetically sealed systems following strict and limiting design policies, but that's just not reality. The hyperaccelerated rates of technological change and techniques for delivering solutions are inappropriate conditions for these traditional methods. Furthermore, this approach demands that associated resources and expenses must be expended to defend against all known threats, whether or not the countermeasure is applicable. This is like being forced to buy a home alarm and a safe, when all that is needed is a padlock.

New Awareness

EC extends distributed systems with the ability to perform transactions involving the exchange of goods and services between two or more parties. Although not visible to the average person, EC is pervasive and substantially contributes to the global economy. Consider the exchange of trillions of dollars every day on stock exchange trading floors and international commodity markets; currency markets that only exist as bits and bytes stored on bank systems and circulated around the world at light speeds on fiber optic networks; ATM machines that are always online and credit card networks validating thousands of purchases a second. Indeed, EC is fundamental to the global economy, and with millions of people and organizations continuing to sign up with Internet service, it was only a matter of time before we see a burgeoning of the consumer and business-to-business trade.

Relationship Management

EC has extended the traditional model of distributed systems to a social space without precedent. These networks form relationships that are everywhere and nowhere, infinitely flexible and scalable, which range from a handful to thousands. And therein lies the distinction from traditional information exchange over distributed networks and EC relationships. Those were tightly bonded. These are wide open.

For EC to reach its potential in balancing the expansion of relationships with the management of trust-related concerns, many complex issues need to be addressed. Key ones include finding acceptable methods for authentication and protection of information (privacy and integrity), accommodating needs for performance and reliability of transactions, and creating the requisite means for resolving disputes.

Although there have been great strides in the use of EC, these initiatives are largely limited today to well-bounded and highly defined partner relationships. For EC to extend beyond these bounds, systems and policies must allow the creation of trusted, dynamic, and *ephemeral* relationships. Essentially, EC is the formation of dynamic relationships through the embodiment of player interaction through technologies, policies, and methodologies. The principal players include customers, suppliers, partners, and intermediaries.

The challenge with EC is the appropriate formation and management of these relationships. These relationships can be characterized as business-to-business, business-to-consumer, and intraorganizational. Business-to-business involves the buying or selling of products and services between organizations, the exchange of transactions and information relating to back-end processes between suppliers, partners, or channels (electronic data interchange, procurement services, payments, logistics, and so forth.). Business-to-consumer relationship building focuses on the consumer as the channel for selling the products and services. The dynamics of these relationships are explored in Chapter 7.

Management of these relationships begins with the definition of the information flow between the respective players. Information flows are composed of discrete business functions which, when combined, establish business transactions. In the case of a secure electronic transaction (SET), the emerging technology standard and tool for ensuring secure credit card transactions over the Internet, the information flows/business functions for a purchase request between a cardholder and a merchant includes request, response, purchase request, and purchase response. Other types of transactions include cardholder/merchant registration, payment authorization, credit, credit reversal, and so forth. It is these transactions that define the relationships between parties. And as such, to manage the relationship effectively requires appropriate mechanisms to manage the transactions. As described earlier, this can be accomplished through technical or non-technical means. This aspect is further illustrated in the SET study in the appendix.

Expectation Gap Between Parties to EC

EC is certainly a substantial improvement over traditional paper-based commerce in terms of speed, cost, accuracy, and simplicity. The automation of collaborative business processes over networks has provided customers with greater choices, decreased the cost of processing business transaction, expanded marketplaces, facilitated just-in-time production and payment, and the list goes on. We mentioned earlier that one Cisco customer made $100 million of orders with the firm online and without a single human interaction. Cisco documented over $500 million in administrative cost savings for 1997 alone from the substitution of online for face-to-face, mail, and telephone transaction handling. Study after study show that the buyer reduces its procurement costs substantially too. But, although EC may impart many benefits, it does not come without a challenge.

Managing expectations between parties is perhaps the greatest of the challenges. The following list includes elements that typically contribute to expectation gaps (if not well managed):

- the definition of structured messages (EDI format, electronic forms, contacts, and contact rules, design specifications)
- account, account databases, and accounting rules
- transaction and function definitions
- intermediaries (information filters, translators, trusted third parties)
- decision support models

In some instances, these gaps are being addressed by comprehensive EC standards, such as those for handling structured messages, standards such as EDIFACT, ANSI X12, and CSIO, and so on. Over time, each of these elements will become more universal, and industry standards will emerge to close these gaps and mitigate the risk of misplaced trust in EC relationships.

The need for the establishment of standards is nothing new. In the late nineteenth century, the typewriter had a profound impact on the management of information. Although the industrial economy burgeoned—through mass production, mechanization, and uniformity or manufacturing—the information superstructure remained essentially a manual endeavor. The bookkeepers and clerks maintained all records and correspondence with pen and paper. Over time, the size and complexity of industry made the handwritten process obsolete. The scale of information management in the industrial economy dictated standardization: Heterogeneous accounting systems and file libraries soon gave way to standardized management practices, policies, and forms. The typewriter created uniform and instantly legible text. Information in the form of typewritten documents became a discrete resource that could be quickly prepared, ordered, stored, and quantified. In addition, the typewriter keyboard layout became standardized and today we take the typewriter layout for granted on the personal computer keyboard, which postdates the typewriter by more than a century.

Today, the scale of EC dictates standardization, which will in return contribute to narrowing expectation gaps.

Breach of Trust and Reputation Risks

Today, trust with respect to traditional commerce is well supported by legal vehicles. The world's legal texts are replete with commercial privacy and intellectual property statutes. However, this is not the case with EC: It lacks the required formal business and legal structure to properly protect its transactions, which can result in a less-than-predictable business relationship.

EC relationships cannot simply be taken for granted. For instance, if confidential information falls into the wrong hands, who is to blame? Was the system breached, and where was it breached? What were the consequences—the theft of documents or other valuable data, destruction of data, corruption of data, destruction of network integrity, denial of services, and/or tarnishing of reputation? Could the information have been sold by one of the EC players? If so, is that allowed? Because EC solutions are composed of many players' entities, a tenuous relationship is formed between each player, in essence creating a "web" of trust. Given that business transactions span multiple players, breaches in a single trusted relationship can easily cascade to all players. If but one strand is broken, the entire web can be compromised. The repercussions from such an incident can result in financial, and more importantly, reputation risks.

The challenge is how a trusted EC solution can be created and maintained. The objective is to reinforce the trusted relationships such that they can endure the transgression of adversaries, technological glitches, and ignorance. To achieve this, organizations must establish clear security processes, policy, and practices. Safety translates into reputation. Failures in security are failures in meeting the implicit and explicit commitment in the relationship. Processes as described in the previous section must be implemented to close the expectation gap among the participants of the EC solution. This first step limits the scope to well-understood business transactions only.

Policies and practices establish commonly understood and accepted rules that define accountabilities and conduct for each of the players involved in an EC transaction. Depending on the risks, these policies and practices can be either generally understood or legally binding. The following common topics need to be addressed: community and applicability, enrollment, local security, technical security, operational, and legal policies. They should be viewed as risk-reduction exercises rather than defense exercises.

Community and applicability policies define who the various players are and their respective roles in the EC solution. This exercise establishes a common understanding of what role each player plays in the fulfillment of business transactions. Respective accountabilities can then be formed with guidelines for accepted practices, which are ratified among all of the participants.

Enrollment policies define how new players can participate in an EC solution. The very nature of EC is a continually expanding relationship base. Each of these relationships contributes to the overall trust of the EC solution. As such, rules for registration, expiration, and reregistration must be defined and ratified to avert the risk of relationships being ruined.

Local security policies are nontechnical security policies for managing physical, procedural, and personnel controls. The EC community will be composed of players, each with distinct local security policies. This introduces issues of subjectivity and inevitability and an overall lack of trust in the system. As such, sets of principles must be defined, agreed on, and implemented by the various players. These practices will be defined in relation to the distinct communities.

Technical security policies focus directly on the information technologies themselves. Technical security controls for computer equipment, network security, encryption, and so forth, must be defined. The degree to which these controls are defined and implemented is directly related to the potential risks. Again, these controls will be defined in relation to the distinct communities.

Operations policies are specifically concerned with the respective responsibilities of the players involved in each business transaction. Because the operating entity of any EC solution is composed of constituent players, a common operating policy, just as a single organization, must be defined, implemented, and monitored.

Legal policies simply help to bind the various participants to the conditions of the policies. Because language in itself is ambiguous, in those circumstances, where the risks are high, it is good practice to involve the legal community. Liabilities are then clearly articulated and allocated among the various players.

By following these guidelines, organizations can substantially raise the level of trust between the various players as well as in the EC solution itself. In unprecedented times, neglecting to do so may result in conditions that may not only damage the EC endeavor but the organization as well. For example, consider a financial institution that prides itself on its rightfully established trust—often over a period of 100 years—decides to participate in an EC solution to exchange information. Let's assume that the nature of the business is to offer banking services over the Internet through a third-party provider. The financial institution applies great due diligence in defining and interfacing with the third party, a relationship providing access to sensitive customer information. Furthermore, the third party utilizes Web hosting services from yet another organization such as an Internet service provider (ISP) or facility management organization. However, the third-party service provider does not apply the same data security standards while building a link with the Web hosting facility. It is later discovered that the link between the third-party service provider and the Web hosting facility is compromised by an unanticipated flood of customer information. Although the financial institution is not directly responsible for the mishap, it is ultimately accountable, and its reputation can be damaged. The luxury of using client data will quickly evaporate if your organization does not give customers a reasonable certainty that you are securing their data properly. To your customers, all intermediaries, third parties, and outsourcers are transparent. They don't know which party is at fault and, in this instance, they'll view the financial institution as at fault. The risk of losing you customers does not reside in your control environment but in those extended environments where you have no direct control.

These guidelines can be used for not only creating an EC solution but also for evaluating what EC solutions should be considered, with regard to the risks your organization faces.

TECHNOLOGY-INDUCED RISKS: WHAT'S NEW . . . .

Inexpensive, reliable computing and networking technology represent a double-edged sword for the beneficiaries of EC. On the one hand, there are virtues of conveniently and quickly conducting business transactions over a purely electronic infrastructure enabled by a widespread adoption of technology; on the other hand, this technology carries with it new flavors of risk that are simply not applicable to transactions conducted in a completely physical infrastructure. As human agents are replaced with electronic ones, the possibility of electronic attacks, complex failures, or short-lived but expensive intrusions increases dramatically.

Process-Oriented Technical Risks

New technology-induced risks present in the EC world fall into four broad categories:

1. *Exposures related to automated transaction and message handling:* New risks stem from vandals using computers and mailing lists, to make brute-force attempts to deny service or to break security measures, and send many parallel requests that result in an electronic theft of goods or services.
2. *Multiple, unknown network intermediaries:* Without the end-to-end control of a VAN common in the EDI world, EC transactions on the Web are passed through any number of uncontrolled intermediate sites. In addition to the inherent integrity issues, intermediate networks may add latency (a delay created by message processing overhead) or lose data, contributing to poor quality of service or a "false-negative" perception of remote system failure.
3. *The mystery of the black-box software components* that are integrated at the system's endpoints. The interactions between components may not be known or thoroughly understood. Conditions such as capacity, or interface limitations in individual components may induce failures in ways that are not known. Furthermore, these failures easily ripple through several layers of applications until they appear in a system that is monitored or audited regularly. Catastrophic failures, such as the crash of an application or the entire system sitting on the desk of someone in the global trading unit of a financial institution, for example, is an obvious case that may rate as more than a nuisance. But if the cash transfer system used by the Treasury employee is consistently prone to miscrediting, electronic funds transfer (EFT), payments under periods of intense load, the end-to-end integrity of the system is in jeopardy.

4. *Misunderstood, unclear, or simply nonexistent processes for handling problems of an electronic nature*: What happens to encrypted documents when the original sealer (and sole possessor of the decryption key) is fired or dies? How is the use of removable media such as floppies or Zip drives monitored, discouraged, or audited to prevent the introduction of viruses, overlaying out-of-revision software components, or the extraction of sensitive material?

Bill Friel of the U.S. Secret Service points out the gross magnitude of electronic financial crimes: Whereas a typical bank robbery nets about $10,000 in cash, a successful electronic theft averages $650,000. Without the obstacles of transporting cash and gaining entry to a protected physical area, electronic crimes can be committed repeatedly, rapidly, and involve large sums of money.

The risks of EC, however, are not limited solely to potential theft or fraud cases. As a business becomes more dependent on electronic processes, the predictable, reliable operation of those elements is a prerequisite for day-to-day functions. An operational failure caused by an unrepaired system crash, a prolonged denial of service attack, or a combination of performance problems leading to an effective network data flow shutdown, can be as catastrophic as physical disasters such as earthquakes or floods. The remaining sections highlight some of the risks introduced in EC, focusing on those that offer the best return on investment in risk reduction.

Public Communications Paths

On the surface, the use of public networks for EC seems to be the root of most security concerns. Limit the exposure of data over unsecure or unknown channels, and risks are most certainly reduced. However, securing a public communications path only makes the electronic process about as reliable as a telephone- or facsimile-based system, and a host of other technology-related risks remain. Furthermore, EC processes can suffer due to excessive network delays, network traffic loss, and denial of service attacks that have few, if any, physical transaction analogs.

The Telephone Standard

Using a telephone or facsimile-originated transaction as a benchmark, what are the risks to be avoided to reach a similar level of comfort with EC? When initiating a transaction via fax, the sender needs to be sure the recipient is present or can have the fax routed to him or her; there is a risk of eavesdropping with an uninvolved party reading the outgoing or incoming fax. A denial-of-service attack, in which the receiving fax machine is put out of service with an endless stream of garbage transmissions, is possible but highly unusual. Moving the fax machine to a different telephone line is a quick and simple solution. Denial-of-service attacks via telephone-based systems are also rare, because the caller's telephone can only initiate one transaction at a time. Taking down an entire bank of incoming lines requires a large number of "war or demon dialers" and outgoing telephone lines at the attacker's site. How can EC transactions be brought to the same plateau of well-understood, characterized risks? The primary difference in the two infrastructures is that telephone and fax systems use an effectively "sealed" system (at least within the United States and Canada; wiretapping and interception are much more prevalent in Europe), whereas public networks, the Internet, and corporate networks are porous and easily observed by uninvolved parties. Most of the protection mechanisms outlined below are explored in more detail in Chapters 4 and 5.

Evaluating Network Risks

Electronic business infrastructures, such as those based on the Ethernet standard over distributed networks have the wonderful property of being relatively isotropic: They appear the same, with the same data availability and bandwidth, from nearly any point in the network. This flexibility is the root of the internal risk in corporate networks and the more general risk in public networks: A network can be tapped or monitored from any access point with equipment as simple as a PC. Using freely available "sniffer" (eavesdropping) software that copies packets/data from a network interface adapter/card, nearly any user can examine traffic crossing the local information highway. Wide-area networks or private lines that extend beyond the building may be exposed in a basement wiring closet. Any intruder with basic wiring skills can run an extension of the digital line to a collection device. All of these threats, however, can be managed and controlled using encryption, rendering any data retrieved, monitored, or extracted from the network useless except to the intended recipient. Choosing the right combination of encryption technologies and implementation layers is treated in Chapter 5.

Impersonating another user or host on the network, commonly known as "spoofing" or "masquerading," rivals the ease of network data tapping as a top security concern. A remote user may guess (or steal) user identification and password information from a valid user. A remote host can borrow (or steal) the IP address of a well-known server and intercept traffic destined for the real machine. Spoofing can result in unauthorized access to target systems. User spoofing is an authentication problem discussed in a later chapter, and host spoofing may be dealt with using other, higher-level authentication mechanisms specific to each application. In 1995, spoofing made the headlines in *USA Today*, citing "High-Tech Crooks Crack Internet Security."

Denial of service covers the physical disabling of equipment or the flooding of communications networks by waves of message traffic. Required services or resources are systematically attacked to render them useless. Denial of service can be accomplished through malicious applications (viruses and worms) or by exploiting application services that directly affect the components of the operating environment. One such attack is known as the "ping of death." Ping is a simple and innocent Unix function in which a message sent to a host is echoed back (the name is taken from sonar). The automation of this function to systematically ping a single host proves to be an effective method for consuming all host resources. The 1998 Internet Worm demonstrated the impact of denial of service. Robin Morris, a graduate student at Cornell University, released code that reproduced itself on one machine after another. The code continued to multiply on host after host, swamping each in turn until the Internet was basically at a standstill. Curiously enough, Morris attempted to send an e-mail suggesting a fix; however, it never made it through the congestion. The cost of testing and repairing was estimated at over $100 million. The establishment of a perimeter around services (e.g., firewalls) is an excellent deterrent for these attacks.

Breaches in communications and data security are attacks on end-users' data and the software managing that data. Breaches lead to the unauthorized access (copying, damaging) of confidential data, whereas breaches in the software that manages data exploit the so-called trap doors in programs—secret hooks (conscious) or holes (errors) left by programmers. Trojan horses, which are seemingly innocuous programs that conceal damaging content, are used or replace existing programs. An excellent example is when in 1993 Panix Public Access Internet system in New York City was broken into and all users' IDs and passwords were recorded. In this example, the intruder exploited a security hole in the Unix SENDMAIL. Appropriate encryption and perimeters aid in defending against such common attacks.

Performance as a Risk

Communication can be simply defined as moving information between source and destination. All EC applications involve an element of communication. In an environment where all components and devices are controlled by a central authority, issues of communication are rare. However, EC systems require the use of public networks or decentralized networks—which are not controlled by one group. Additionally, the use and expectations of Internet communications as a medium in EC are growing by leaps and bounds. That strains the ability of service providers to keep up with the demand and when that happens, the reality of meeting these service expectations is simultaneously lowered. The risks of communication service provisioning, although not immediately apparent, can hamper the widespread deployment of EC solutions. The primary factors for this are the inability to provide economically consistent sustainable bandwidth and support for real-time information flows.

Sustained bandwidth is the measurement of a consistent rate of exchange of information from a source to a destination over a period of time. In this respect, present-day communication services are typically referred to as "best effort." They do not guarantee continuous information flows at any specific rate. The only way one can guarantee bandwidth and the desired service levels would be to control each and every network link into the desired service. This is costly and highly improbable to be successful given that EC services are meant to exploit a large number of endpoints. The automotive industry has attempted to solve this issue by creating standards that ISPs must abide by to insure a level of telecommunications quality. The resulting network, referred to as the Automotive Network Exchange, is an example of how industry is contending with this real issue.

Real-time information flow relates to transaction end-to-end timing and latency properties. These properties are of particular interest because of the precedence that has been set by systems such as credit card processing and ATM banking—without fail, ATM debit transactions are immediately posted to customers accounts. Although best-effort networks cannot meet such demands, they nonetheless can support real-time transactions but in an unpredictable manner. This becomes a question of serviceability and customer expectations.

One possible solution is to build a closed network, where all technical and communication uncertainties can be effectively controlled. However, this limits flexibility and realistically cannot successfully meet the demands of the mass market. At present, the only solution available is to understand the limitations of current communication services. Just as we described above, the expectation gaps between all parties will have to be managed.

In the future, carriers (local exchange carriers, interexchange carriers, cable operators, satellite, and so forth), manufacturers (modems, networking technology, switches, information servers, software developers, and so forth), and service providers (Internet and online) will have to collaborate to reach a high level of communication service with sustained bandwidth and real-time capabilities. That will take many years, given the costs, quality of existing infrastructure, and the competitive pay-off for providers (for instance, there's little incentive for them to upgrade services in small towns or help semi-developed nations build EC capabilities).

Automation Amplification

The universality of networks, specifically the Internet, has provided an effective medium in which countless computer systems can exchange information. The conscription of business functions onto these networks has redefined our perspective of execution—where once transactions lived outside the seconds, they can now thrive only within the seconds. Furthermore, the global Internet has allowed for well over 20 million processors to be attached, introducing the possibility of unparalleled cooperative processing.

Considering that one of the world's most powerful computer (Janus) only contains 9,216 Pentium Pro processors, such prodigious computing power has yet to be experienced. Even though the benefits are already manifesting themselves, we must take care not to be subverted into believing that there are no associated risks. Amplifying automation capabilities amplifies complexity hence risk and, of course, amplifies the ability of parties to use these new tools for subversion, not commerce.

Theft of Goods and Services

Automation does not discriminate between good and bad actions. Unfortunately, this behavior introduces the potential of automated attacks on EC solutions. One major concern is the potential for automating theft of goods and services. Photocopiers may have simplified the replication of printed information, but they also provide thieves with the means to effectively bootleg them as well. Automation attacks can be very subtle intrusions that exploit weaknesses in process, such as access (weak login, impersonation), approvals (loans, mortgages, credit cards, and so on), and purchasing (credit card fraud). Two common methods for executing an attack are known as replay and parallel.

Replay attacks are conducted in two phases: information recording and information replay. The objective of the attack is to examine existing processes, typically access processes, and record both the input information and sequence of entry. This provides a thief with not only critical information, but also a link with business process, which provides added insight into the inner workings of the application. The thief can then replay the information at a later date and gain access to the system. Such attacks are easily averted with encryption technology and strong authentication. However, this does not preclude attacks conducted by legitimate users of systems to gain access to regions of services that they are not permitted to enter.

Parallel attacks conduct synchronous intrusions on a given target. In conjunction with replay attacks, adversaries vary the information supplied to EC systems for the purpose of obtaining a desirable result. In the past, thieves have taken the following steps to create valid credit cards:

1. generated a series of credit card numbers using the generally available module ten generators
2. searched several Internet sites to conduct online credit card and purchase approvals
3. recorded the manner in which approval for credit cards are conducted
4. automated the purchasing process recorded in Step 3, utilizing the generated series of credit card numbers
5. all successful purchases represent valid cards, which are now in the hands of thieves

Ironically, in this scenario, an EC facility, not directly under attack, was used as a tool for fraudulent activity. Although these attacks may seem difficult to circumvent, steps can be taken to help curtail such activities.

Risk-Reduction Measures to Consider

The following are measures that the leaders in EC take to reduce risk:

- **Strong authentication:** They install the most sophisticated methods of authentication utilizing encryption suitable for their business scale, nature, and parties involved. Chapter 5 addresses the appropriateness and types of encryption.
- **Tolerances and thresholds:** They embed triggers into their applications, watching for potential malicious activity. These triggers are related to business transactions and are parameter driven—this allows for change if new problems are detected.
- **Current fraud-detection systems:** They ensure that existing fraud-detection systems (score cards, decision trees, neural nets, inference engines, and so forth) are not circumvented. Although these systems may not address all possible issues, they nonetheless limit existing and new methods of fraud.
- **Embedding fraud detection:** For those systems classified as high risk, they consider the use of embedded fraud-detection systems. These do not have to be complex. A basic decision system and neural nets can be tailored for the purpose of profiling and pattern detection. Over time, these systems can be evolved in concert with new business functionality.
- **Audit logs:** They maintain audit logs at least as low a level of detail as the individual business transaction. This provides excellent information for the purpose of data mining for fraud detection.
- **Dynamics:** Any public application (Web or otherwise) is susceptible to automated attacks that make for an effective method for compromising systems. Add a standard and reliable interface and suddenly you may have created a service for the facilitation of fraud. Consider a storefront Web site selling t-shirts, at some point a credit card will be requested and processed. Should anyone require a facility to test for valid credit cards, this would certainly be an excellent interface to exploit. If the storefront simply adds some dynamics to the site, creating an unpredictable interface, such exploitive activities can be averted. Of course, such dynamics would have to be weighed against ease of use.

- **Conceal business rules:** Concealing business process illuminates the possibility of automation. Often, encryption is only considered during the transmission of classified information. Web-based development scripting techniques, such as HTML and JavaScript, are not designed to conceal the contents of the business logic. All propriety calculations and decision processing, depending on the sophistication of the application, are revealed to the general public. Such an approach can represent a significant risk to an organization. However, consideration should be given to concealing additional portions of the business process.

No Encryption System Is Infallible

Cooperative processing is the programmatic coordination of interconnected computers working on a common task. It's core to the Internet and to large-scale EC. It's useful for crooks, too. Examples of their feats center on cracking encryption codes. Two impressive code-breaking examples conducted through cooperative Internet processing are those of the collaborative efforts known as DESCHALL and Bovine. The DESCHALL effort focused on breaking a message encoded with the Data Encryption Standard (DES), a cipher developed in the 1970s under U.S. government sponsorship. In June of 1997, they were able to break the cipher, some 2^{56} (7×10^{16}) possibilities. Additionally, the Bovine initiative tackled the RSA RC5 algorithm, in which a brute force attack on 18,446,744,073,709,551,616 cryptographic keys was conducted. The Bovine collaboration reached new levels of cooperative processing. The efforts yielded processing capabilities well beyond those of Janus-like systems, by processing an unprecedented seven billion keys per second, a rate equivalent to the work of 26,000 Pentium computers.

There are two distinct forms of encryption—symmetric and asymmetric (we will briefly address each of these in Chapter 5). For the purpose of this discussion, asymmetric keys facilitate the distribution of symmetric keys. Symmetric keys are used between a source and a destination for the purpose of encrypting information to be exchanged. To reduce the likelihood of keys being compromised, EC solutions should limit the use of a particular symmetric key to a session or business transaction. This will require that a new symmetric key be generated and exchanged for every session or business transaction. Although this may seem excessive, it limits risks to an acceptable level. At least one big problem remains: To use cryptography for authentication or other security services such as confidentiality or integrity, keys must be used. There are strong and reliable cryptographic algorithms available, but key management is still a problem. One approach for key management has actually existed for some time. This is the ISO authentication framework, also known as the X.509 protocol. The most important part of X.509 is its structure for asymmetric (also known as public-key) certificates. This means that if Alice wants to communicate with Bob, she first gets his certificate from a database. Then she verifies its authenticity.

Uneven Quality of Black Box Processes

Black box processing, facilitated through the use of commercial off-the-shelf (COTS) products, presents an interesting dilemma. While COTS offers cost effectiveness into the development of systems, they also have an impact on the overall security design of the system. The difficult question is: To what degree can COTS components be trusted? An ideal design goal would be to make the overall system security independent from the behavior of system components. However, this is difficult to accomplish in practice.

Failures and Detections

COTS-based component use is inevitable in any EC implementation. The key concerns in the use of such technology stem from elements that fall outside of the control of the implementers. These include how the component was designed, the integration issues between components, and EC challenges.

The selection of a component falls almost entirely on trust and reputation. The poorly designed component may not become apparent until well after implementation. Inadvertent or intentional flaws in the design may result in various bugs that manifest as security violations. Another common challenge in the use of components is the excessive functionality. A component may have more features than are known, which may lead to security implications.

Integration of components has always been a difficult task—the mismatch between product security level in particular. The security conflict that may arise from the use of multiple components is typically addressed by not enforcing any security. For example, the operating system can control accessibility to files, but what files a component requires to function properly is not known to the operating system, As the relationships between the components are understood, their relative security mechanisms can be invoked to a greater extent. This is often a trial and error process, despite what the manual suggests!

EC systems, by virtue of the network connectivity, add additional risks to internal transitions and information stores. External connections such as the Internet increase exposures to a larger number of potential external attacks. Imperfections (intentional or unintentional) in code and potential back doors will be amplified by this external contact. Often, documentation of commercially available components is comprehensive (strength and weaknesses) and is generally available to the public.

Legal Gray Areas

EC is where societies driven by technological progress intersect traditional commercial law. Laws responsible for traditional commerce where tangible goods are physically transported, through custom gates and across national borders, no longer apply to EC. Laws, through social contexts, build regulations between people and actions—conventional commerce defines the context for these regulations in terms of physical environment, surroundings, circumstances, connections, and relationships. The digital society of EC creates distinct new properties that are very unlike those of the physical realm, rendering existing laws useless for the purpose of regulating human action.

EC managers should consider the involvement of legal counsel in each of the following legal contexts:

Marketing and communications is the distribution or promotion of certain information through Web pages, alternative messaging systems (such as e-mail) or referenced hypertext links. Misrepresentations of ideas or concepts that may lead to litigation or a damaged reputation are of primary concern in this implementation.

Advisory services involve the use of third-party information sources for the purpose of disclosure, guidance, analysis, and advice. The right to disclose or the misrepresentation of information either in accuracy and consistency are areas that may lead to legal concerns.

Transactional services are those involving the full spectrum of goods and/or service trades both involving and not involving (C.O.D.) financial transactions. Areas of particular interest include consumer-oriented transactions, anonymous transactions ones made without prior agreements, and transactions involving the disclosure of private or confidential information and financial transactions.

Although we don't suggest that EC managers take it upon themselves to judge the possible legal obligation, risks, and liabilities of the EC solution but rather acknowledge that they exist. The importance of audit and legal counsel grows as EC solutions move from marketing to advertising, and then to transactional levels of trading partner interactions.

Many of the issues surrounding EC focus on the anonymity of individuals in the digital domain. Digital certificates or signatures aid in resolving this issue, but much work must still be conducted to establish the appropriate legal framework to support the technology. The United Nations Commission on International Trade Law (UNCITRAL) adopted in June 1996 a Model Law on EC, intended to give a legislative framework to remove legal barriers to EC. The Model Law, broad in nature, attempts to address instances, where the law requires a signature, that requirements could be met electronically if the electronic signature provided both a link between the signer and the record (data) and evidence of the intent to be associated with the record. Each of the foregoing must be conducted with sufficient reliability.

The reality is that the advancement, acceptance and utilization of technology outpace that of the necessary legal frameworks. The brutal reality of this condition is not that there is a grace period of freedom from governmental legal constraints, but rather a period where the early adopters are subjected to undue risks. Despite the lack of established and effective legal framework, the information provided in this section will, however, help bring the EC manager closer to doing what is humanly possible to minimize risks for all involved.

WHAT CONTROL PROFESSIONALS AND AUDITORS SAY

Get the Big Picture

A control review or audit of an EC process, application, interface, or module is always risk driven: the higher the risk, the sharper the focus. The results of a risk assessment to a large extent determine the nature, scope, and extent of the audit. Of course, there are other situations where audits are performed, even if the risk ranking of a particular auditable entity is not as high as others. When this happens, it usually has something to do with changes in regulatory compliance, emerging technology, consumer concern, new policy initiatives, or special requests from management. Understanding the business risks of EC is a prerequisite to performing audit work. When an auditor is auditing a technical aspect of, say, the MVS or Unix operating system, because the topic is relatively self-contained, the risk assessment will center around the known security weaknesses, performance, support, change management, backup, recovery, and utilities associated with the product. This focus is quite narrow and specific. But the same approach does not seem to be effective when auditing EC.

Let's take the audit of SET as an example. Auditing SET is not the same as auditing MVS or Unix. Although there are the technical areas of public key infrastructure (PKI) that must be reviewed, by focusing on just the technical robustness of SET, the risks surrounding this product will not be apparent. Failure of SET to authenticate is only one of the key risks. The very goal of the credit card companies to set an a priori standard for payment over the Internet carries risks in having a single standard. If there is one bug or an error in implementing SET, *all* credit card payments using SET protocol are affected, with no exceptions. This type of risk can be systemic in proportions due to interconnectivity of networks. So let's first ask the fundamental questions associated with the risks of a single standard and the contingencies that must be in place to cope with the worst case scenarios.

The above risk-driven mindset works well with IT managers as well as with the auditors.

Put Risk in the Right Context

From time to time, we come across people from all walks of life who talk about risks and conveniently catalog them in neat compartments. Whatever risks that we have identified for EC—competitive, technology, reputation, or regulatory—these risks by themselves are meaningless if they are not placed in the right business context. We can't start assessing the risks of a particular EC application without a broad-based understanding of the relationships and interactions between local risks of an EC product or service, and the EC world at large.

Regulatory Risks

IT auditors in general are not compliance oriented. But things may change when regulators issue new policies on EC. It is likely that existing regulation on the collection, protection, and retention of records, and the location, processing, and use of information will take on a new significance and interpretation. Be familiar with the regulators' topical pronouncements. They are easily obtained from their Web sites. Prior to an audit of a particular EC product or service, get the big picture first, then do some research in this area, and challenge the provider of the EC solution to suitably address the regulators' concerns. We provide details in Chapter 9.

Outsourcing Risks

Outsourcing risk is not new. What's new is the heavy reliance on almost every EC product or service of third parties to provide part of the total solution. It's not all in-house or IBM as it used to be; you have to trust Microsoft or Netscape browser or Verisign's SET software, for instance. The related risk extends to include any outsourcing vendors' inability to comply with your organization's information security policies and the dependence of the vendor to process or manage some of your core businesses. It helps to ask the fundamental "risk-seeking" questions:

1. How many EC components are outsourced?
2. Of the outsourced components, how many are core or critical?
3. What is the capability/expertise of the outsourcing vendors?
4. Are these vendors regulated, unregulated, or ISO compliant?

5. Is there oversight by senior management on critical and core functions?
6. Is there a dedicated group to work with management on a contingency plan in case of vendor default?
7. Is there due diligence review of the outsourcer?
8. What are the contract terms, especially with an outsourcer outside your country of residence?

Risk of Reduced Segregation of Duties

The cornerstone of control is the segregation of duties: Checks are cosigned, keys are under dual custody, payments are entered, verified, and released by different individuals. These classic controls can be compromised by collusion, the risk of which is people initiated.

Traditional forms of segregation will not be functional in the EC world. Checks are replaced by electronic debits, keys by digital signatures, and funds transfer include a "do it yourself" option. What happens if a transaction fails to properly authenticate? What are the consequences of an error in the implementation of a new version of universal standard encryption software? Needless to say, the consequences are more far-reaching. But this is not so much a reduction in segregation as a substitution of manual control by electronic means. What is lost is human/manual intervention. Let's then start with an evaluation of the electronic form of segregation; for example, the role of the Certificate Authority, the electronic audit trail, and a properly controlled technical environment in place to protect the EC relationships, systems, and applications. These topics are discussed in detail in later chapters.

THE ROLE OF THE IT MANAGER IN RISK MANAGEMENT

Beyond Technology Risk

Building a real electronic nation involves a lot more than laying down the cable. There are hard problems and there are soft issues. So far in this chapter, we have presented some major hard issues. But this is not the total risk profile for EC. There are always the soft issues we have to grapple with. These are not technology dependent, but rather, management related.

People and Reputation

We know that risks can never be 100% contained. No one security solution is all encompassing and 100% foolproof. If it were, someone sooner or later would be tempted to find a way to break it. We all know that insider-assisted attacks or fraudulent activities are the hardest to control. Employee education, marriage of responsibility and authority, and the hiring of ethical, qualified staff are just as important as finding the most optimal technical EC solution. Risk is a dynamic phenomenon that must be revisited as the business environment changes. Reputation risks may arise from the inappropriate handling or use of EC information, all of which would impair the image of the organization, resulting in the loss of business or threat of legal action. Even though technical controls are often discussed in the context EC, they are not a substitute for management oversight.

Sharedness and Competition

EC is characterized by programmed coordination of interconnected computers working on a common task. It implies cooperative processing as a norm rather than an exception. Because networks now enable countless computer systems to exchange information, the information will be more widely distributed than it used to be. On the one hand, the sharing of information on Web sites is encouraged and promoted for good business reasons (presence, visibility, and advertising to name a few), but equally there is the need to protect confidential and competitive information within their domain. Management carries out a continuous balancing act between costs/degree of protection versus the value and sensitivity of the information. As access increases, integrity decreases. Security runs counter to maximum openness and ease of use; therefore, increasing access potentially decreases integrity. Where do we draw the line? This is a management issue, not a technology issue.

Balancing the sharing of business information and protection of competitive information begin with an appreciation of the "temptation value" of the information, its location, and the knowledge of the people who would be most tempted. If there is no temptation value, there is little motivation to do something to get the competitive information, so we can say that the risk is low.

Risk management is most usefully thought of—usefully in management terms—as a professional discipline that is part of the responsibility of everyone in the organization concerned in any area of EC. Managers need to make sure that (1) the professional skills are available, either in-house or through external professional advisers and technical experts; and (2) the responsibility is recognized at all levels, and meeting it is monitored appropriately. The questions for managers to ask and to require answers are straightforward, whether in the planning stage for a new EC system or application, implementation, testing, training, or operations:

1. Who is responsible for what area of risk management? (e.g., IT is responsible for network and software risk management but not for fraud or reputation risk management.)
2. What professional skills are required and how are they being obtained?
3. What monitoring and reporting measures will link performance to responsibilities?

Answers are provided in the remaining chapters, particularly Chapters 8 and 9.

3

Gaining Control of Electronic Commerce

CONTROL IS MORE THAN SECURITY

It is dangerous to single out security as the number-one concern in EC. Although it is a major concern, the exclusive treatment of the same subject over and over again can be misleading. Companies tend to easily focus on it as the central issue, and lose sight of some other equally significant concerns. The broader agenda has to be ensuring that EC is quite literally under control in every area of transaction, relationship, and support. The purpose of this chapter is to show that gaining control of EC on behalf of the customers can create a service advantage.

It appears that the general public has a good grasp of the meaning of security. Not so with *controls*. If they do, they probably associate it with everything that is restrictive and counterproductive. Recall our reminder in this book that the fundamental conflict in telecommunications is between access and control. Very roughly, the customer wants more freedom to choose, whereas the seller wants more control to exercise. As long as this is the popular thinking, there will always be two opposing camps in an organization: those who want less control and those who want to act as watchdogs.

Broadly speaking, controls are simply what make an organization *reliable* in achieving its objectives. When controls are intelligently applied, they are an enhancement to business, not just a cost. This shift in thinking is the subject of Chapter 7.

Benefits and Importance of Control

One of the barriers to companies implementing successful EC-based programs is that they fail to see audit and control processes as part of the mainstream of business as much as customer relationship and product quality. It is not uncommon for senior management in many organizations to consider the control and audit functions as "necessary evils," leading to a generally negative disposition toward these processes. Few, if any, individuals within a company see the prospect of a control review or an audit as anything but an unnecessary intrusion into what they consider a well-thought-out and business-driven initiative, as they themselves provide the company with "value added" through products or services. Truly successful organizations have been able to recognize that ensuring the implementation of a well-managed and well-controlled (and well-audited) process will generate long-term value for their firm.

The creation of the project office (PO) to manage a company's IT resources is a prime example. The PO provides consulting services, tools, support, and coaching for project managers, but it also prescribes specific disciplines and review points for a project, subject to the application of proper and reviewed results, which can stop a project from proceeding until key components or results are in place. The PO asks many audit-related questions about what was supposed to be done, what were the original goals, and are we achieving those goals? The benefits and importance of control are measured not by what happens, but how closely we steer the course towards the goals that were originally set. Such questions are control-oriented, and are as much value-added as any other element in the process, yet the PO is careful not to be seen as the police (which is considered counterproductive, and very quickly the "value-adding" component disappears). This aspect was succinctly reported by Kathleen Melymuka in an article entitled "The Project Office: A path to better performance" that appeared in the August 2, 1999 issue of *Computerworld.*

Building Customer Confidence

Even though establishing trust is critical in developing customer relationships, maintaining and growing this trust comes from ensuring that there is a consistent and reliable environment that continues to warrant this confidence. Providing evidence of a well-controlled and well-managed environment requires constant review of the process and the creation of a customer perception that the organization is vigilant in maintaining its control processes. We see this everyday in the annual reports of organizations, providing audited financial statements: The reputation and objectivity of the auditor is as much a factor of the company's confidence as are controls. As EC becomes a part of *every* organization's business process, the organization is obligated to update and review the relevance of its processes using relevant tools and recognized processes. Confidence is based on the belief that the organization is both committed and capable of maintaining the reliability and integrity of its information and the IT structure that supports it.

Financial institutions and public sector organizations that manage trust need to continually reassure their clients that they are ensuring that their IT structure and their control processes have the level of service (reliability, robustness, effectiveness, and so on) that is commensurate with the value of that trust. When introducing EC processes, whether for access to information (like products and services over the Web) or for transactional process such as EDI ordering or electronic funds transfer, not only are adequate security measures needed, but there must also be an investment in the public disclosure of issues and responses that are in place. Control processes are part of the marketing and public relations content that a firm uses to establish and maintain its brand and customer satisfaction as much as product/service quality or price is.

Business Enhancement

Beyond the concept of building confidence, a well-controlled business can be seen as a marketable commodity—especially in the current environment of concern over the intangibility of EC. How many businesses have you seen that now fly the flag of "ISO 9002-Certified"? How many are advertising the fact that they have survived the Y2K problem unscathed? How many have put the Privacy Seal on their Web sites? These are clear uses of the well-controlled and well-managed IT infrastructure playing a major part in enhancing the perceived value and confidence that the business presents. Even those businesses who are investing heavily in the use of enterprise resource planning (ERP) systems such as Baan, SAP, and PeopleSoft are marketing the fact that once they have implemented a new, integrated and strong IT application infrastructure, they will perform better and will be a higher quality and better managed business. This equates, if not in reality then certainly in the perception, that the business that focuses on controls and managed EC is a better provider of service, product, or information. As the information flows continue to move toward the EC platform, this type of assurance will undoubtedly become a major marketing factor.

CONTROL OBJECTIVES OF A TRUSTED COMMERCIAL SYSTEM . . . .

To establish an effective EC environment that will support the business goals of a firm, the first thing that needs to be established is the goal or objective for that environment. Sometimes, the components are within the company's own technology base—establishing the need for internal levels of control to ensure quality and trust is created or maintained toward these goals. This thought can be summed up in the old adage, "If you don't know where you are going, how do you know when you get there?"

Beyond this internalized view, EC drives "extended enterprise": electronically linking your firm with your suppliers and customers. This means, in essence, that your customers can directly input data and requirements into systems that have been traditionally isolated from external access through input forms or trained internal staff.

Whether or not this relates to an EDI ordering process or Web-based purchases, the effect is the same—you can no longer ensure the absolute sanctity of your data input through managed procedures. How then can you maintain adequate control? Developing a methodology for customers to use your EC offerings needs to rely on a number of traditional elements, but it also creates the need for two new components: an external review capability and an internal process review for EC.

The external review asks the questions about who can gain access to the environment, under what authority or level of access, and how can you ensure that these accesses do not compromise the business goals and control objectives of the firm? Similarly, the internal process review relies on the concept that the velocity and impact of EC require continuous verification that all systems are meeting their performance goals and maintaining their controls processes continuously while operating. How can a client be sure that their important data is well protected and not being shared with a competitor? How can a supplier be assured that orders it receives are legitimate and will not be disputed? For a company to trust its systems, and more importantly, for clients and suppliers to trust in the EC relationships, controls form the basis for dialog and proof. Firewalls have been penetrated, data has been misplaced or not acted on, and production lines have been silenced due to various breakdowns in communications or logistics. Tools to deal with these issues are part of the ongoing evolution of what can be defined as a "trusted system."

Criteria of Control

Traditionally, the criteria of control are concerned with security, accountability, and levels of assurance. The same fundamental principles can all be applied to EC. Security is the subject of Chapter 5. Here in this chapter, we discuss the accountability in the context of organization and management processes and levels of assurance.

COSO, CoCo, CobiT, and IT Control Guidelines

In recent years, the concept of control takes on a new significance. Five publications have appeared since 1992 which set out to refine control concepts and to raise corporate governance awareness in varying breadth and depth. These publications include:

1. *Internal Control—Integrated Framework*—issued by the Committee of Sponsoring Organizations (COSO) of the Treadway Commission, 1994 Edition.

2. *Guidance on Control*—issued by the Criteria of Control Board (CoCo) of the Canadian Institute of Chartered Accountants (CICA) in 1995, and its sequel
3. *Criteria on Assessing Control* in 1999.
4. *Control Objectives for Information and Related Technology* (CobiT) Second Edition, 1998.
5. *Information Technology Control Guidelines* by CICA, Third Edition, 1998.

All of the above publications contributed to a heightened awareness and the promotion of good control practices in organizations. The application of these concepts in EC is found in Chapter 8.

Levels of Assurance

Auditing is about assurances. It is about independent assessment of the controls designed and operated in a particular environment and the ultimate formation of an opinion on the state of control of the auditable entity, either at one point in time or over a period of time. An audit in general involves the identification, evaluation, and verification of new risks and new controls and the adequacy of existing controls applied in the new environment. These days, there is a growing number of public companies practicing control self-assessment, where the operating unit undertakes to identify and evaluate controls. The auditor's focus accordingly shifts to attesting management's assertions. Starting from the grassroots, the work unit or project group's control self-assessment forms the base for independent reviews by internal and external auditors. This independent review process has not changed with the introduction of new forms of EC.

EC CONTROLS: THE MACRO VIEW

As with all forms of new or emerging technologies, both the IT manager's and the auditor's job usually begin with finding out the unique features that distinguish new modes of EC, such as Internet-based transactions (electronic cash), from other similar products grouped under the same generic EC label: EDI, EFT, fax, e-mail. The benefit of this exercise is obvious. Existing and proven controls, if they can be effectively applied to a new form of EC, are the best controls at the lowest development cost.

This explains why in Chapter 2 we go through in some detail what we perceive as the new risks in the EC world as a necessary first step in helping us design controls in the new environment.

Internal controls should only be implemented if they are relevant to an organization's business objectives. Whereas the definition of internal control varies in different contexts and from different perspectives, the existence of control and its relevance to organizational, management, and business objectives has never been questioned. This view is reconfirmed in COSO, CoCo, and CobiT. In Chapter 8, the current thinking on internal control will be applied in the audit of EC from a management perspective.

Controls do not exist in isolation either. There is no value in the world's most sophisticated encryption technique if there is no demand for it. Demand is created by business need. Therefore, security is the responsibility of business, not of the service provider. Until recent years, it was not uncommon for business managers to declare that controls are built into a system because "it is an audit requirement." Inherent in this comment is the misconception that control is for the auditors. It is "their" need versus "our" need attitude—a fundamental and grave misunderstanding of the role of audit.

Control Is an Evolutionary Process

The controls to be examined in this chapter are intended to address principally the new risks identified in Chapter 2.

The introduction of the Internet or other new delivery channels does not invalidate any of the business, management, or control objectives that already exist in an organization. Rather, they prompt us to look for new ways to address current concerns to satisfy these objectives.

Learn from Earlier Forms of EC: EFT, EDI, and Various Forms of Electronic Banking

Like EFT and EDI, Internet-based EC is also characterized by three factors: the disappearance of paper audit trails, high speed, and low human intervention. But the consequences of new EC are more far-reaching. Just take a few scenarios: its immediate global reach, potential high volume, and simultaneous multiple relationships between customers, merchants, financial institutions, and everything in between, from third-party vendors, and outsourcing companies to telecommunications carriers. The compounded effect of all this on one transaction has yet to be fully assessed.

We learn from our audit of EFT, EDI, and other forms of electronic banking that preventive controls rank higher than detective controls. Like these earlier forms of EC, there is little value in finding errors after the fact. If timely "event" trigger is critical in these transactions, it is super-critical in the new forms of EC. This leads us to conclude that in designing EC controls in the new environment, all validation, certification, authentication, or proof of privacy must take place in real-time, as well as the resubmission and error correction. Invite your auditors to participate in EC development projects up-front. Expect them to spend a considerable amount of time evaluating and testing controls before they are implemented. Early audit participation at every phase of EC development is highly recommended if the auditor is to make any contribution.

Reliance on Experts

There are as many approaches to designing controls as there are encryption techniques to address security. It is impossible for one single person to come up with a single opinion on the adequacy of the controls to be built into each EC application. Like any systems initiative, we urge you to carefully assess the skills inventory of the staff on the EC projects. More often than not, these individuals, including staff auditors, may not be fully conversant with many of the implications of the new commerce. Increasingly, the work of everyone will be driven by technology that is changing constantly and dramatically, and has to deal with the rapid growth in the scope and nature of the change. One area that today's auditors have to be constantly on the alert for is the continuing education requirements for their job and to see that others are also qualified to do theirs. We have to see that EC project management is sufficiently proactive in acquiring specialists in those areas where in-house expertise is lacking.

Assurances from Service Providers

One characteristic of Internet-based EC is the heavy reliance on purchased or licensed software, and the outsourcing of many of the development efforts to consultants and specialists. Unlike home-grown software, where quality control is an internal affair, we don't know the discipline applied in the development of these vendor-supplied products and services. Conventional project management wisdom, which is mostly enterprise-centered, may or may not cover many facets of inter-enterprise management issues. For instance, many components of the Mondex electronic cash, or SET applied to credit card transactions over the Internet, are developed by outside companies. It is not easy to directly find out the quality assurance applied to these products and services. To obtain an acceptable level of comfort, we may need an independent opinion on the control environment of these companies.

Another issue that is a hot topic for current debate is the role of the certification authority (CA) in the production of the authentication certificates. What type of cross-verification will be performed on these CAs? Assuming that a hierarchy of CAs will evolve, that some are more authoritative than others, a hierarchy of independent control reviews based on business and technology risk profile, will also make sense.

The independent reviews of the external vendors or CAs will likely be in the form of an SAS 70 Report (United States) or Section 5900 Report (Canada) generally known as "opinions on the control procedures at a service organization." They cover matters that an external auditor would consider when engaged to express an opinion on the design and existence of control procedures or the design and effective operation and continuity of control procedures at service organizations. The authors expect that many EC vendors will be subject of a SAS 70 or Section 5900 type of review as one way to inspire public confidence.

The latest development in this area includes joint efforts by the CICA Task Force on Assurance Services (TFAS) and the AICPA Cohen Committee in the establishment of EC principles as a means to build trust brand. Their publication—*WebTrust*^{sm} *Principles and Criteria for Business-to-Consumer Electronic Commerce Version 1.1* (July 1999)—lays down the three principles that an entity must meet to obtain a seal of approval: (1) business practices disclosure; (2) transaction integrity, and (3) information protection. The last two principles are also the focus of this book.

It is likely that some of the EC service providers are too small to warrant a formal SAS 70 or Section 5900 type of external review. The responsibility of communicating your organization's control practices to the service providers rests within. Negotiate a "right to audit" clause to allow yourself an opportunity to independently assess the adequacy of the service provider's control environment firsthand. But there is a catch to the "right to audit" clause, as these service providers may demand similar reciprocal arrangements. If they all want to exercise the same rights, it could be very impractical. Again expertise and resources may not be available within the organization to undertake the review. There is also another catch: If something goes awry and the organization does not conduct its audit, the firm may have very little recourse in the event of loss. Our past experience suggests that the service acquirers normally would band together and hire one external reviewer to undertake the engagement on behalf of all the interested parties. Of course if all your EC partners are regularly audited, and their audit reports are available on request, there is no issue. Regardless of the situation, such arrangements need to be well thought out, and legal advice is indispensable.

Controls for Payment Exchange

Even though various forms of EC have been around for several decades, it wasn't until the application of the principles in finance and processing of sensitive business transactions that there arose a heightened interest in security and control issues. Obviously, much of this interest had to do with the issues related to the movement of funds and the natural concern that it generates for both customers and banks. There was also a realization that the changing face of control within banks, particularly from the ATM network and electronic banking issues of the past, necessitated a change in the fundamental approach to the managing of security and control in the general business marketplace.

With new commerce, the old practice of "data dumping" and "after the fact" review by auditors is no longer a reasonable—or effective—methodology for the electronic age. Things move too fast and have further-reaching implications to rely on the old processes; therefore, a rethinking of how and what the auditor/control process is there to do is required. A "snapshot" view of a company does not allow for a change in methodology within the organization, as it relates to ensuring that proper controls and long-term management issues are being dealt with. We have to "anticipate" the financial risks associated with the EC processes, be involved in all phases of EC development, and focus on preventive controls prior to payment release, rather than the expensive investigation or damage control of financial errors and loss.

Paperless Audit Evidence

A traditional form of evidence is paper documentation, which often comes from third parties. EDI and EC eliminate paper and thus could pose problems in satisfying auditors as to the soundness of the evidence. Because the auditor previously relied on paper source documents, generated both within the audit client's organization and from outside to support balances in financial statements, with these documents now electronic, auditors are now faced with new challenges:

1. *How can the auditor be satisfied that a document is authentic?* The issue here is not paper versus electronic medium, but whether the information is retrievable and certifiable to be a true copy of the records kept. Other issues to consider include how the origin of a document can be verified. Without appropriate controls, the document could have been changed, either accidentally or intentionally. EC audit trails are more difficult to manage, because there are more parties involved in a transaction: from customer to merchant to financial institution and every service provider in between. But typical information kept of an audit trail—paper-based or electronic—remains the same. They pertain to details used to prove the existence and evidence of an obligation by each party to the transaction. These include, whether it is paper-based or electronic, information pertaining to date/time stamp, access information, operator-ID, terminal-ID, identifier of the sender and receiver—all of which must be machine-readable, authentic, and can be produced on demand.
2. *How does the auditor know what the complete population of documents is?* The auditor must find new ways to examine and verify EC source documents that are mostly electronic. Computer-assisted audit techniques

(programs that reperform processing and sample data and report on unusual conditions) can, and should, continue to be used. The auditor must also look at the quality of evidence that is obtained from both internal and external sources and the ease of obtaining this evidence.

The auditor will also need more certainty about controls over the transmission, recording, and retention of electronic data. Whereas traditional completeness checks such as control totals, hash totals, batch header, and trailer are still applicable, the vulnerable areas seem to lie in the interfaces between systems and when control (or lack of control) is passed from one party to the next. Because auditors are familiar with completeness checks within and between applications, the new focus appears to be the reciprocity of controls passed from one external EC party to the next. Remember the practical wisdom: You are only as good as your weakest link.

3. *How can the auditor be satisfied that the control environment where the records being transmitted and retained is adequately protected?* The key issue here is not on stored information at destination points. There is nothing new with the introduction of EC into the equation. In a computer environment, the security of stored information is covered by existing policies and procedures and the application of proven commercial security software. In the EC context, we focus on the new ways and means to protect data in transition. This hinges on the new delivery mechanisms, their performance, robustness, and security features or options available. Also, remote access, dial-up, and others introduce a new exposure right away before data is sent over the line. Details on protection of data in transit are covered in Chapters 4 and 5.

Another issue that has emerged in EC is the question of what data to store, in what manner, and for what period. The fact that the data is originated in electronic format does not change some of the fundamental philosophies for data retention. In many jurisdictions, the view is that electronic data, reconstituted from reliable and well-managed systems, is only as valid as the original paper documents.

To date, there has been no successful recorded litigation between trading partners related to EC or EDI disputes. In other words, even after decades of use, there has not been a challenge to the application of doing business through forms of structured EC; again, this suggests that there is general acceptance of electronic methods and process in business practice—if well managed and controlled.

EC processes are related to ensuring that the proper controls and limits are in line with not only the auditor's goals, but management's as well. The realization that these objectives are the same provides the basis for an overall improved business process and changes the view of the control and audit function from being simply overhead to more of a value-added component of the entire process.

STEPS TO CREATE A SAFE EC ENVIRONMENT

Identification of "Crown Jewels"

Before we can decide on what controls are appropriate for EC, we have to know what the potential risks facing a particular EC system or application, product, or service are. Risk assessment starts with the identification of the most-valued assets that must be protected first. Controls that are appropriate in one environment may be too lax or stringent in another. Undercontrol may expose the EC organization to undue risk; overcontrol is not cost-effective either. In any event, the focus is to protect those components that are most business critical.

Traditionally, IT managers tended to concentrate on implementing systems that were on time and within budget. If risks were considered, it was done within the confines of not meeting the time/cost target or missing the market. They were limited to project controls. In general, the integrity and even accuracy of data is less than satisfactory. Indeed, one survey claimed that over one half of the data in a typical corporation are incomplete, missing, or inconsistent. The conception of data as an enterprise resource, and hence business responsibility, is very recent. EC raises the vital importance of data quality, because it can't be kept isolated within the company but is used by parties outside the firm, including customers, suppliers, distributors, and insurers. The old IT view of individual applications focused only on the internal system needs for controls.

We are more concerned with the overall risks surrounding the EC product or service and the related controls beyond project management. A framework for assessing EC risks and controls is presented in Chapter 8. The following sections deal with good control practices when EC is added to the scope of IT management.

Management Controls: People and Process

There are basic control objectives that can be universally applied to all types of electronic transactions: accuracy, completeness, authenticity, security, auditability, timeliness, and recoverability. Because these attributes are also actively pursued by business and operations managers in their day-to-today activities, the equation that control objectives = business objectives = management objectives will logically follow. Unfortunately, in reality, the yardstick used to measure these control attributes varies from manager to manager, from auditors to marketing staff, and to security experts. To obtain a clear understanding of overall control requirements, we have to manage the expectation gaps among different EC parties.

Management has the overall responsibility to ensure that the business runs smoothly and makes a profit, both short- and long-term. As computer technology and telecommunications become more critical to achieving these objectives, it is important that management provide more direction for new technology development. To make sure that EC implementation is properly managed, management must play a pivotal role in the implementation process. Top management must be committed to the technology for it to be accepted. Key people must have a proper understanding of the technology and its application. The objectives and scope of the project need to be documented and articulated to avoid misinterpretation and false starts.

To achieve the benefits of EC, management needs to assess what specific changes it needs to make both to systems and to management and staff structures. How many staff are now required, and what new or different skills do they need? Which staff can be retrained to work in other areas? What training is required? These issues are critical to ensuring that management achieves a payback from its investment. The final word for EC success, however, will be the extent to which top management is prepared to commit its time and resources to the project from start to finish.

Both users and technical developers must work together to ensure that the systems meet their needs and operate as designed. The role of the user (i.e., the owner of the business application, such as the accounts payable or accounts receivable manager) is critical as technology takes over more of the day-to-day operational decision making. The user must understand how the business works and work closely with the technical people. That is, of course, easier said than done. Companies routinely talk about cross-functional team work, but there are many barriers to collaboration. Most organizational processes are built to run fairly independent of one another, but in EC, they have to work as an integrated whole. The CEO of Marshall Industries, one of the most outstanding exemplars in business-to-business EC, wrote in his 1999 book, "Free, Perfect, Now," that the single key and most controversial move he had to make to transform the business was to end the commission system and reward everyone on the same basis. He tells of how the sales force would "game play" production to make sure they got their own orders filled, even hiding inventory. Production in turn focused on its own priorities, misleading sales and marketing if need be. Finance was rewarded for keeping balances low and that meant it turned down good business for Marshall in order to meet its own interests first. Cisco, another giant in EC who makes 70% of its total sales online, also reports that the sales force is always reluctant to lose contact with the customer and account control and is slower to respond to new EC opportunities than customers are. American Airlines found initially that the individual business units did not see the firm's ambitious and effective Web site for EC as relevant to their own work.

It's outside the scope of our book to examine how to build cross-functional collaboration, but it's a must for EC—not a maybe.

Technology Dependent Controls (Tools)

EC has accelerated all events related to traditional commerce to a point where they can no longer be controlled by conventional means. Print, telegraphy, telephone, radio, and television have each accelerated the pace of previous technologies. Computers are specifically associated with speed—accelerating the disintegration and reintegration of information at rates that approach the speed of light. Transactions embodying complex processes are being executed at unheard-of rates. We are all becoming very familiar with the million of "hits" that Web servers must contend with on a daily and sometimes even hourly basis. Each of these "hits" represents a function or business process that is in an execution stage. Even though no one can reliably predict the rates of growth of EC and forecasts vary widely, one thing is for sure: volumes can only grow—and grow rapidly at that.

For leading companies, transactions are already in the billions of dollars and are over one half of the firm's business. Dell, General Electronic, Cisco, Marshall, and others reached this point in 3–6 years, from a zero base. That shows just how rapid the acceleration can be. Once a firm reaches critical mass, growth rates of 40–100% are not unusual. Business has never encountered such a volatile and unpredictable pace of transaction growth. Additionally, the flexibility of EC has allowed for far more-complex business transactions to be automated—involving multiple independent players. Bear in mind, too, that whereas previous transaction processing systems were handled within the corporation, EC can involve many parties interacting simultaneously. To take a simplified example, consider a purchase of a personal computer from Dell by someone within a large company. The purchaser interacts with Dell through its Premier Page feature, which customizes the EC Web site to the company and includes all its own controls over authorization, configuration, spending limits, and other "business rules." Dell's own systems interact with shippers and insurers, parts suppliers, and credit providers. In addition, the network communication links include Dell's own extranets, the company's intranet, and public Internet links (which are in themselves very complex; there is no "the" Internet, but rather networks of networks that comprise it).

The paramount question is: Can conventional methods in managing control and trust support these staggering demands?

The reality is simply that EC solutions must constantly be complemented with a suite of software tools to aid in managing conditions such as environment and business controls. As transaction rates and their complexity grow, the ability to observe conditions becomes more distant. Increased transaction rates also increase the amount of information that needs to be analyzed for anomalies or compliance to policy. Manual methods can never achieve the necessary granule level of observation. Just as the old expression suggests: If a tree falls in a forest and it is not observed, does it make a sound? Tools automate processes to effectively manage the conditions of EC solutions—tools observe each tree within the forest. This requires a heavy and continuing investment, but there's no choice. Control is not an optional add-on but is an integral trust design requirement.

Tools can be embedded in any or all regions of the EC transaction life cycle and spanning all levels of technology (network, transport, and application layers). Chapter 5 will distinguish these various layers of technology. Although tools have been commonplace in systems implementation, EC differs somewhat in the application of tools. Traditional tools have typically focused on operational management of distinct system components. Networks, computer systems, and applications are measures against availability, performance, and accepted accountabilities. Although the foregoing elements are important, EC is more than the sum of its components. As indicated in Chapter 2, EC solutions are complex arrangements of relationships between independent business process. As such, the conditions brought about by these relationships must be addressed with appropriate measures.

Tools are nothing more than electronic controls. Prior to considering the use of tools, EC managers must first understand the context in which they must be applied. The starting point is the accountability controls that require some level of enforcement. These include:

- **Source and destination identifiers** create a means of definitively associating a transaction with a source and a destination partner.
- **Access control** ensures the governance over the ability or right of a source or destination to enter, interact, or access a zone, service, or transaction.
- **Distinct accountabilities** address the need for establishing methods for binding a person or automated process to an action.
- **Discrete accountabilities** help to distinguish relative authorities in the collaborative management of a transaction by independent partners or groups through its life cycle. This division of authority establishes a common relationship management forum for the purpose of evaluating potential breaches in trust. For instance, custodial responsibility for assets is normally segregated from the record-keeping activity.
- **Transaction state tracking** helps verify the compliance of the progress, sequence, integrity, location, and state of a transaction to defined business processes. In addition, such compliance can be tied to terms and conditions of electronic contracts.
- **Audit logs** represent the repository of recorded transaction and processing events that are tracked in an automated fashion. All events relating to distinct and discrete accountabilities, transaction state, source and destination identifiers, and access control are recorded, retrieved, analyzed, and presented based on defined criteria relevant to establishing some form of control.

Each of the foregoing controls can be automated using tools to increase the level of trust in an EC solution. Tools aid in mitigating the risk of managing the complex relationships formed as well as coping with events at a rate no longer discernible by humankind. Tools can be classified into the following categories: credential-based authentication, policy based on access control lists and credentials, and hardened audit repositories.

Credential-based authentication tools employ cryptography as a means of establishing strong credentials. Credentials are derived by utilizing a public and private key pair representing the unique identifier (discussed in greater detail in Chapter 5). Public key cryptography tool kits aid in establishing standard-based authentication mechanisms in an effective and timely manner. These tool kits help to insulate the complexity of managing the creation, issuance, and revoking of certificate credentials that are tied to EC systems. Such authentication tool kits represent an opportunity for organizations to establish a common model for authentication, leading to a single sign-on model. Inherent in these tool kits are "hooks" that allow for interfacing to other tool sets, thus not limiting its functionality.

Policy-based access-control tools enforce the integrity of business policy within EC solutions. Business policies include but are not limited to access control lists rules. Examples of such tools include real-time virus detection (removal, rejection, warning, and so on), message management (filtering), and intrusion management. Policy-based access-control tools bundle to form flexible enforcement engines that centralize the management of EC systems. The policy-based control tools are a natural extension of the credential-based authentication by tying business policies to credentials.

Hardened audit repositories record the vital signs of the EC system. Information regarding all aspects of the operations of the system is recorded for post facto reviews. The hardening process of the logs guarantees that audit logs cannot be tampered with and controlled by appropriate policy-based access-control mechanisms. Logging can occur at both a systems (network, hardware, operating systems, and so on) operations level as well as a business operations level (business rules).

Not long ago, only people were clever. But the computer-assisted world is becoming very clever and faster than people are. Ultra-fast processors, networks, and high-speed integration in standards will soon create a collective technological intelligence that will outperform people both in speed and integration. And just as the complex human societies require monitoring, so will those of the technological society.

Role of the IT Manager: Point–Counterpoint

Point 1: Many of the risks and controls identified in the EC process are not new. However, the quality of management controls over computer systems have traditionally not been adequate. Much of this comes from a reluctance of user management to get involved in the development process.

Counterpoint 1: Just as we encourage auditors to get involved up-front, we also urge that business/user management do the same. IT managers can be pivotal in ensuring that the representation in the EC project is proper. Representation depends on the type of EC application. When selecting the business representative, be up-front about time commitments. Many IT projects go awry, because the business representative is not actively coheading the project with the IT manager. Experience has shown that one of the success factors in any development project is the business manager's "technical champion" mentality and the willingness to commit the time to the project. This is no different for EC projects.

Point 2: Over the years, there has also been a gradual change in the nature of controls—shifting from a heavily clerical orientation to a progressively automated one. The speed at which the transactions occur in EC tends to preclude the ability to stop and consider the implications of a problem.

Counterpoint 2: Design preventive controls (i.e., controls that prevent errors) into EC systems. "After-the-fact" detective controls (i.e., controls that detect errors) are too late to help critical processes unless timely feedback is provided via context-sensitive help or "triggers" are built into the system to stop normal processing until further action is taken. Controls in the EC application, the user and technical environment, must be mapped out in advance.

Point 3: As automated systems put control into fewer and fewer hands, the risk of fraud or error not being detected increases. This puts reliance on sound, automated controls. The inherent nature of EC is so structured that it's more difficult to intrude on the process.

Counterpoint 3: The key caution is that it is often the original application and not the new EC application that carries the inherent risk. We are accustomed to focusing on the front-end (transaction origination) and the back-end (settlement) systems where the exposures are high, but tend not to pay enough attention to the arguably insignificant interfaces that may turn out to be the most vulnerable. So it does not relieve the EC application of the responsibility to obtain assurances that the upstream and downstream systems are working properly. The control gaps are likely to occur at the system interface level. Don't overlook the importance of assessing the new EC interfaces to determine where the controls are to be designed or housed. In EC, it is the front-end where the relationship dialog with the Internet user begins. It is at this interface that new safety opportunities lie. This is discussed further in Chapter 7.

Point 4: The meaning of control to consumers, merchants, financial intermediaries, and product/service providers may not be the same. It is dangerous to assume that each party is looking for the same level of assurance. How do you know that your organization's "level of comfort" is the same as your customer's? How do we define "public confidence?"

Counterpoint 4: Before we attempt to answer any question on the state of control in EC, ask two more questions: (1) What is the risk? and (2) Whose risk is it anyway? As the management of the organization offering the EC product or service, it is not enough to look at risk and controls from your own point of view. Take time to find out what the consumer's real concerns are. Do a customer reality check. Find out what your key customers and business partners are doing. EC management have the dual responsibility to report truthfully and regularly on the health of their control environment to the public and to promote good control practices to the recipient of those products and services. It is through this two-way process (both business-to-business and business-to-consumer) with you that "public confidence" can be earned. In recent business reports about EC, the concern of consumer has shifted from security to usability, as the result of their dissatisfaction with ease of use when ordering even from brand-name online stores.

The above is only a sample of the control-related management issues that must be resolved. We promise the answers throughout this book.

4

Maintaining the Trust Bond: Certainty, Confidentiality, and Privacy

INTRODUCTION

It can take many years to build a trust bond, whether in personal or business life. It can take a mere second to destroy it. It's tragic if it is destroyed by an event that could easily have been anticipated and avoided. In EC, the risks of such events occurring are highest in the areas of information and operational reliability. The trust side of information rests on the protection of privacy and confidentiality—"You did not tell me you were selling data about me to others. You don't respect my privacy, and I can't be sure anymore that you'll protect the confidentiality of our business together." In the same way, failures in operations as trivial as miscoding of a payment transaction for overnight computer processing can lead to disaster, and the consequence—"You didn't keep your promise—I need to be able to count on you. I can't be sure of you any more." When the money doesn't arrive, neither does the trust.

Trust is about feeling sure, confident, comfortable. Our previous chapters have been about building the trust relationship; this one is about maintaining it. Here, trust is in the details, and this chapter is about the details, most of which are well known to auditors, and the managers responsible for the information and operational side of EC. They are less familiar to the managers at the "front end" of the trust relationship, such as marketing, sales, and contracting. The customer service department doesn't know the details, but finds out that they are very important: that is called an "angry customer."

Much of the "being sure" side of EC centers around transactions. There is a whole technology discipline for ensuring that data is kept secure and accurate, that unauthorized access to data is prevented, that transactions are completed as intended. But these tools far too often don't look at the trust relationship in the context of the party who is damaged by a failure. For instance, when an error occurs, customer service may say, "It will be corrected next month," but that may be too late to prevent damage. Even more severe is when the mistake can't be removed from, say, your own credit history. Then customer service keeps apologizing and saying they have done all they can, and maybe you should contact the president.

This is a routine aspect of all commerce—why should EC make it any different? Because, like ATMs, telephones, and using your credit card, EC systems are designed to be transaction factories: convenient, fast, and able to handle very high volumes. The system is built to handle the routine superbly and is not designed to handle the exceptions. So, in the credit history example, the customer may have interacted with the company a thousand times, but the thousand and first—the exception—is the one that destroyed the trust. And the thousand previous perfect performances don't count.

Definitions and Implications for EC

Integrity is a process that ensures that information delivered is unbroken; and that, where applicable, the information is the same as agreed on by all parties—in other words, integrity implies certainty. Integrity in EC solutions insures that information, such as payments, agreed-on goods and services can only be changed in a specified and authorized manner. Integrity issues arise from traditional errors and omissions as well as the possibility of unscrupulous activity. Integrity is addressed through the use of technology and, more importantly, policy. Policies, agreed on by all parties, spell out the acceptable thresholds on accuracy.

EC solutions require integrity to ensure transaction consistency: All relevant parties agree on critical facts of the exchange. If a customer makes a purchase of X dollars, then the merchant, the customer, and the bank all agree that the customer has X fewer dollars and the merchant gained X dollars. Integrity also contributes to the durability of information; any transaction can be recovered from its last consistent state. For example, if a dollar is physically dropped, the dollar does not disappear. When retrieved, the dollar's last consistent state is restored. The same should apply during a compromised network, system crash, and so forth.

Confidentiality helps insure that sensitive information is not disclosed to parties other than those on an approved access control list. Confidentiality is closely related to the relationships forged through EC business transactions. Information exchanged between parties must be classified to prevent inadvertent release of private information.

The implications of confidentiality on EC can be any one of national security, legal considerations, competitive advantage, or simply personal privacy. EC solutions span all industry verticals, including government, healthcare, insurance, financial, natural resources, and international trade. As such, the implication of breaching individuals' health records, undercover agents, nuclear weapons, or marketing and research data can be devastating. *Not only can the repercussions be financially damaging, but they can also be permanent, as with a human life.*

Privacy means that the subject (individual or entity) of information can participate in controlling the information. One can look at the subject as the originator of information: rentals, credit card purchases, airline reservations, and other such electronic transactions that define or represent the habits of individuals. Therefore, privacy requires security mechanisms, policy, and technology to provide control over information. However, such security mechanisms may not be sufficient for privacy, because the owner and the subject of the information could have different interests in and uses for the information. The irony with security mechanisms is their ability to preclude privacy by ensuring that the subjects of the information have neither control nor knowledge of the uses of that information. Activities such as gathering statistics and using the information for reasons other than improving the subjects' experience are prime examples of the foregoing conclusion (e.g., sites leaving cookies to be retrieved later or by other sites). Privacy risks stem from the association of information to a person. If, for instance, a medical record indicated disturbing information, in itself it would not be harmful unless associated with an individual. Thus, anonymity ensures privacy. Of course, anonymity can also enable misconduct. A growing problem in the United States has been individuals creating newsletters or discussion groups to bid up the price of a small company stock that they hold, dump it, and then disappear. Anonymity and integrity here can be in conflict.

The very nature of EC is the movement of information that can at some point be associated with a person or party—"commerce" is an exchange relationship. Structured information affords the capability of segregating the subject from the information. In health care, transmitted information can be divided into three components: patient information (name, address, etc.), medical information (medical history), and the relationship information between patient and medical information. The relationship information can be encrypted and managed by the patient. However, when unstructured information, such e-mail, is used, the possibility of maintaining information anonymity becomes a greater challenge. Amazon.com's 1999 venture into selling pharmaceuticals online has been widely discussed in this regard. There are very few privacy concerns about buying books online, but medications? That said, there are very few concerns about standing in line in a pharmacy to buy aspirin, but who wants others to overhear a discussion with the pharmacist about some embarrassing ailment? As we stated at the start, there is no one cookbook answer for identifying and meeting the specific needs for integrity, privacy, and confidentiality. The design choices may, as in the case of Amazon, determine the success or failure of the EC venture.

Protection

Items of perceived value are typically subjected to some measure of protection. The value associated with EC is the information that drives the processes that make up the business transactions. Value in the digital world of EC can be enhanced with the reliable controls for protecting information. Information as a medium of exchange requires reliability in transactions, and providing transactional reliability in EC is the focus of this section. As EC moves from being predominantly handled over well-protected private and value-added networks to being even more predominantly based on the Internet, new challenges have emerged here by the very fact that the original design and intent of the Internet were based on an entirely different conception of information and its value. One of the epigrams of the Net community is that information wants to be free. They (the creators of the Internet) were in many cases against any business use of the Net, and wanted it to provide for the full and open flow of information. That and the technical limitations of telecommunications and software meant that many of the security and control requirements for EC were omitted. The operating system, Unix, the base of Internet computing, had only primitive security and authentication facilities and the Internet Protocol (IP), the telecommunications base, equally focused on the practicalities of communicating and sharing information, not on protecting it. There are several wry jokes about this. One summarizes the Net's original error-handling as, "If you don't get this message, let me know." Another states, "On error, drop message. If anyone cares, you'll find out."

There have been many improvements in all areas of Internet control and security, but it's important to keep in mind that they are not integral to its design, so no EC service can assume they'll be provided for.

Integrity

The integrity of EC data begins with a definition of the business transaction that is agreed on by all parties—the rules of commerce. The business transaction may involve multiple parties and may also be transformed or modified by each of these parties. Therefore, it is imperative that all parties agree on the original, final, and all intermediate states of the information. All transformation and modifications should correspond to a legitimate agreed-on business function. Essentially, the community/participants are establishing a standard method of interacting. This is not entirely unlike the establishment of an EDI standard, with the exception of the embedding of the business transformation and modification rules into the standard.

EC also includes the added dimension of networked-based interaction, often over public networks. Now that we understand the various states of the information, mechanisms can be devised to verify its correct exchange over networks. One such mechanism involves the use of common cryptographic algorithms known as hash algorithms. The function of hash algorithms is to take message inputs and create data outputs, known as a message digest, that are mathematically related to the inputted messages. Hash algorithms are agreed-on standards for validating the consistency of information from an origin to a destination. By calculating the hash at the origin and supplying the result message digest with the transmitted information, the destination is then capable of recalculating and comparing the resulting message digest to the delivered digest for consistency. If the results are identical, the information can be said to be consistent; otherwise, the information has been affected in some respect. Furthermore, message digests exhibit the properties of being one-way (it cannot determine the source information from the message digest) and unique. (It is sufficiently unique that it is a low probability to find two messages with the same message digest.) When the hash is combined with encryption, information can effectively be exchanged between a source and a destination with integrity. The generalized process is as follows: First, a source creates a message and generates an associated message digest. Second, the message and message digest are encrypted and delivered to a destination. Third, the destination retries the encrypted information and hash. Fourth, the destination generates yet another hash from the source message and compares it to the delivered hash; if they are equal, the information was unaltered during transmission.

At this point, we have all the necessary elements to ensure integrity for commercial EC transactions. What remains is the enforcing of hash and encryption algorithms, and defined business transactions through technology. The defined business transaction should provide the necessary information for when to apply hash algorithms. The degree in which hash algorithms are utilized will vary based on the perceived risks. The following list describes moments in which hashing can be used, increasing in sophistication and integrity:

1. *Any information that moves over a public network.* This is classified as the most basic form of integrity for an EC solution. Even though the integrity of information between a source and a destination is upheld, integrity cannot be guaranteed beyond the perimeters of the source and destination. Such implementation must rely heavily on internalized operational procedures to ensure that internalized networks and systems do not compromise data.
2. *Any information that moves over a private network.* This approach does not assume that corporate networks are free from integrity issues. Rather, the model described in item 1 is extended to internal networks.
3. *Any information that moves between systems on a localized network (Local Area Network, serial networks, etc.).* Localized networks are the lowest level of networking between computers. Although the risks are localized, the strength of any process is only as good as its weakest link.

4. *Any information that moves between independent computing processes within a computer*. It is commonplace to find computer systems executing independent applications, each contributing to a common goal. For instance, a single computer system could be operating a database, Web, and mail server all at once. The exchange of information between applications can be complex, and often designers of these systems defer to more rudimentary methods, methods that lack the necessary control. Unfortunately, this can lead to unanticipated data-integrity conditions. EC systems with critically important data would consider such an implementation.
5. *Any information that is stored on a system*. The final approach is simply concerned with the management of stored information (data or application) on computer systems. Inevitably, information will have to be stored on a computer. Transactions moving between parties will eventually reside in a file system or in a database. Often, the information is stored temporarily, only to move on to the next party involved in the business process. Again, information at this state is susceptible to potential compromise of integrity (system crash, tampering, etc.). However, if a message digest, prior to storage, was generated and maintained on an independent system, the integrity of the information can be validated. If it were discovered that the information was compromised, the transaction could be aborted, or the data could be retrieved from the off-line or near-online backups.

Prior to determining to what degree your system warrants such methods of data integrity management, some detailed risk analysis should be conducted to consider the impacts and related costs of protection. In this way, you can avoid the mistake of spending more to protect something than its worth. We talk more about this in Chapter 5.

Confidentiality

Information is the medium through which concepts and ideas are exchanged. The embodiment of information by human beings creates knowledge from which actions may result. A relatively simple process that has transcended the agrarian age, industrial age, and now the information age. The Internet has melted and evaporated the tangible information artifacts of the agrarian and industrial age into airwaves of the information highway accessible to all who wish to breathe it in. Recall that in Chapter 2, we illustrated that convenient access to information represents a direct conflict to maintaining the value of the information. Essentially, the Internet is a medium and is not concerned with the affairs of the relative importance of information between individuals or entities.

EC is a different matter in this respect; it does not propose to solve the simple exchange of information but rather to exploit such facilities to improve, extend, and offer new opportunities for collaboration. As such, mechanisms to guarantee the confidentiality of such transactions must be established for fruitful business transactions to occur. Collaboration, as described in Chapter 2, is the formation of dynamic relationships through the embodiment of player interaction through technologies, policies, and methodologies. A key condition in the formation of such relationships is that information exchanged between players remains confidential.

Protecting the confidentiality of information is often achieved through controlled access and redefining the rules of representing information itself. Protecting the confidentiality of information for EC requires encryption, a language system that comprises these three basic criteria:

1. A unique language system that consistently represents information in an unambiguous manner.
2. A sufficiently complex language system that cannot easily be interpreted and therefore cannot divulge the content of information, other than by those who are deemed with such access privileges. Furthermore, the level of complexity should not be limited in degree.
3. A language system that can easily change its rules based on a commonly understood algorithm. In time, all language systems based on a rule set can be deciphered. Therefore, a language system that is not bound to any one rule set is a requirement.

Encryption provides a mechanism to meet the aforementioned requirements. Encryption can be thought of as a dynamic language system for representing information in a confidential manner. Encryption allows for the creation of a new and unique language, and can be utilized for every level of information exchange between parties. Technologies facilitating encryption processes convert information from the native language (commonly known as human or system language) to the newly created–shared (between designated parties) language. The encryption process consists of an algorithm and a key. The algorithm produces a different output (referred to as ciphertext), depending on the specific key being used at the time. As such, the use of a different and unique key allows for the language specified (and in turn the content) by the algorithm to be unique to those who possess (designated parties) a copy of the key. The security of the encryption system depends on the secrecy of the unique key, not on the secrecy of the algorithm. The strength of the encryption system is dependent on the algorithm. Although encryption systems will be covered in greater detail in Chapter 5, suffice it to say that systems that offer flexibility, such as variable key lengths to increase the complexity of the ciphertext, are among the most successful and useful algorithms currently being adopted in EC solutions.

Encryption systems, through their algorithms and keys, truly deliver a unique (unique keys and publicly available algorithms), complex (variable algorithms and key lengths), and dynamic (changeable key system) language system that meets the requirements of EC.

Privacy

Privacy is primarily a human condition. Often confused with confidentiality, privacy is concerned with maintaining the confidentiality of the association of information to a person. The virtues of an electronic/digital society are clearly evident, but with all good comes a little bad. Enabling a business process through EC creates two risks that stand to compromise the privacy of individuals. First, information once thought to be inaccessible (information on paper in an unstructured manner locked in filing cabinets) has been standardized (electronic data interchange standards) and made accessible through open networks (Internet, intranets, and extranets). A medical record indicating an HIV-positive lab test is completely harmless, but when associated to an individual, the information can be very damaging. Second, EC-enabled processes are creating new information association sources that are revealing the habits and individuals. Web sites are now becoming the medium of choice for travel, take-out, insurance, financial services (securities, mortgages, banking, and so on), literature, and other high-transaction commerce. Each of these facilities represents a profile-generating information repository that is intended to better service the consumer. This activity is particularly evident with Web sites that require registration prior to accessing the site's services. However, the jury is still out on whether the public is prepared or willing to participate in such activity. The discomfort stems from the area of control. This is the dilemma we highlighted at the beginning of Chapter 3.

Privacy issues are certainly not novel, but in the context of EC, they are greatly exacerbated. As suggested earlier in this chapter, the solution to achieving privacy is through anonymity—disassociation of an individual to the content of information. Achieving such a configuration is not an easy exercise and contradicts traditional practices. Consider, for example, the two systems for conducting payments on the Internet: credit card encryption (Secure Electronic Transaction) and electronic cash systems. Both systems have their advantages and disadvantages. Credit card encryption schemes are convenient and don't ask customers to change their usual purchasing methods. Transactions are charged to the credit card and appear on the customer's credit card statement, as does any other purchase. Electronic cash is a little less convenient because customers have to buy electronic currency before they can use it. However, electronic currency also brings a certain amount of privacy to electronic purchases.

Anonymity of information within repositories can also be achieved with a combination of encryption and configuration of database structures. For instance, within healthcare, the foreseeable reality is that patient information will reside in anonymous database structures. Such databases segregate the patient record from the health records with the association between the two encrypted with the patients' personal key. In such an implementation, only the patient can make the association between the two—in extreme circumstances (the patient is unconsciousness, etc.), an escrowed copy of the patient's key could be retrieved by approved staff for access to vital information (e.g., the patient is allergic to penicillin). Such implementations are not technically impossible but do require substantial planning and heavily depend on a suitable policy.

EC INFORMATION FLOW . . . .

In the digital world of the Internet and EC, the notion of neutral space does not exist. That is, space is a continuous flow, alive with interactions and ruled by a precise sense of timing and pacing. The Japanese refer to this phenomena as *ma*. Ma is the Japanese word for space or "space-time," but it does not correspond to traditional ideas of space. The main difference is that, when we say space, we imply room or empty areas. To the Japanese, ma connotes the complex network of relationships between people and entities. This seems to be a fitting representation of EC information flows.

CORPORATE DATA FLOW AND INTERACTIONS . . . . . .

Corporations are quickly adopting Internet technology to create private networks called intranets that will replace local area networks, and will be the prime computing resources of corporations. Intranets are set up for a wide variety of purposes, including e-mail, group services (scheduling, project management, and so on), access to corporate data sources, as well as buying and selling goods and services.

Intranets employ Internet-based technologies such as TCP/IP as the protocol, the browser as the client access point, and others. The distinction between the corporate intranet and the Internet is simply that intranets are segregated networks only accessible to the people within the company. Perimeters between these two regions are imposed and controlled by firewalls—a hardware and software combination that prohibits unauthorized access to the intranet.

The intranet is an effective means of providing to the corporate community cost-effective and easy access to information and applications. However, the intranet does tend to loosen controls on information—compromises are made for the sake of convenience and expense control. The structure of the intranet implies that highly distributed information may reside in multiple locations at any given time. Caching of information on Web servers, client browsers, GroupWare servers, proxy servers, and mail servers may act as points of convenient access to information that might otherwise be considered private. The growth of information repositories for the purpose of data mining and the creation of Web-based corporate applications increase the risks with regard to maintaining corporate information integrity, confidentiality, and privacy.

The corporate intranet represents a learning process for organizations endeavoring to enter into the EC fray. Therefore, if lessons are to be learned, this had better be the place where the access is limited and is an appropriately controlled environment. Table 4.1 represents areas EC managers should focus their attention on to establish necessary controls for a secure implementation. Included are potential areas of compromise and solutions.

Table 4.1 Application Control Measures for EC Managers

Intranet Service	General Operation	Risks related to Integrity, Confidentiality, Privacy	Protection Considerations
Web server and data	The Web operates in a client/server model. You run Web client browser software such as Netscape Navigator or Microsoft's Internet Explorer on your computer. The client contacts a Web server and requests information or resources. The Web server locates and then sends the information to the Web browser, which displays the result.	The Web server sits in a region that is accessible to the public (typically outside of the firewall) and as such puts data at risk.	The employment of Secure Socket Layer (SSL) and Secure Electronic Transaction (SET). All sensitive information should be placed behind firewalls and only accessed through carefully crafted Common Gateway Interfaces (CGIs) (includes intelligent middle-tier technologies).
Mail Server	Mail servers act as excellent facilities to manage the distribution of unstructured information. Binary files, such as executable programs, video, and sound can be attached to the e-mail message. These files are typically encoded using the popular schemes known as MIME and uuencode.	Access to the information is generally only protected by a basic user-id and password system. Information is easily accessible by administrative staff and clever hackers. Thus, information can not only be read, but also changed and destroyed.	Distribution of digital certificates employ Secure/ Multipurpose Internet Mail Extension (S/MIME) and Pretty Good Privacy (PGP) to source distributing sensitive mail.

(continued)

Table 4.1 (continued)

Intranet Service	General Operation	Risks related to Integrity, Confidentiality, Privacy	Protection Considerations
Telnet	Telnet follows a client/server model, which means that you run a piece of software on your PC to use the resources of a distant server computer (host).	May pass highly confidential information such as user-ids and password to other internal systems. The execution of native commands can cause substantial damage to internal data and systems.	Secure Telnet implementation utilizing digital certificates. Alternatively, the use of Telnet within a virtual private network with known participants can also substantially reduce risks.
File Transfer Protocol (FTP)	FTP works in a client/server model. You run FTP client software on your computer to connect to an FTP daemon, allowing you to download and upload files. FTP allows users to browse through available files by changing directories, and you can see a listing of all the files available in each directory.	FTP services are excellent avenues to data rich systems. Although commands are restricted to those offered by the protocol, the protocol does offer the ability to create, transmit, receive, and destroy information.	Secure FTP implementation utilizing digital certificates. Alternatively, the use of FTP within a virtual private network with known participants can also substantially reduce risks.
Internet relay chat and instant messaging	Internet chat refers to conducting live keyboard/mouse "conversations" with other individuals on the Internet. Also possible is the use of white board applications.	Interactive information sources provide an extra-dimension of information. Not only does the content provide insight, but also the interaction with the other party. All actions can be recorded and later reviewed for deeper analysis. Privacy is key with this application.	Should be conducted over virtual private network connections or, at the minimum, passed through an SSL channel.

(continued)

Table 4.1 (continued)

Intranet Service	General Operation	Risks related to Integrity, Confidentiality, Privacy	Protection Considerations
Video	The exchange of video over the Internet. The process involves a technology referred to as streaming video, breaking up video into manageable chunks for transmission and reassembled and viewed on receipt.	A rich source of visual and auditory information. The greatest risk would be that of privacy.	Should be conducted over virtual private network connections or at minimum passed through an SSL channel. Due to the sheer amount of information passed in these sessions, this may not be an effective service once encryption is used.
Common Gateway Interface (CGI)	These are communication protocols by which a Web server can communicate with other applications. For example, CGI application if often used for accessing information resident in databases.	Compromise of these processes essentially provides access to services in which they have been bestowed. The greatest risk is that of replacing or modifying the processes to allow for further access or manipulation of information.	All back-end processes including applications should be hardened. Processes responsible for hashing, maintaining in a secure repository, and verifying the integrity (hash compares) of CGIs and agents should be conducted in an automated and frequent manner. Penetration tests by independent third parties should be conducted to validate the integrity of the implementation.
Java and ActiveX	The ability to run applications that reside on the Internet rather than on a computer.	The processing of information at the client subject the client information to potential risk.	Java applets and ActiveX controls should be accompanied by digital certificates or be distributed by servers with reputable digital certificates. For example, when you accept the use of a signed Java applet, you collect a certificate from the applet requesting access.

DATA FLOWS BETWEEN TRADING PARTNERS . . . .

As corporate data stores and automation of business processes grow within an organization, the opportunity for interorganizational automation becomes a natural next step. The exchange of information between trading partners has existed for some time through private networks known as value-added networks (VANs). As the automation of business process extends beyond the boarders of the corporation, EC is stepping up to the plate and solving the issues that have existed with traditional value-added networks. Open networks, rich industry standards, and huge market acceptance of Internet-based technologies have allowed organizations to construct inexpensive and highly flexible mechanisms for process automation and information exchange.

With this new found power to manage the flow of information, organizations are faced with a new challenge that if not addressed can stand to compromise the success of EC between trading partners. With flexibility comes choice, and choice can be a subjective matter. As organizations begin to create their EC infrastructures, they will be faced with multiple dilemmas that will require compromising on their processing standards and degree of security versus cost, risk, and time. For example, as will be discussed in Chapter 5, each organization will have to devise a practical security design that will take into consideration such constraints as perimeters, user and system authentication, access control and authorization, cryptography, and process controls. And, though Internet technologies are maturing at an alarming rate, little exists in the way of what constitutes as a correct EC implementation.

As organizations build tighter relationships through technology—moving from pure batch-oriented data exchange to real-time interdata processing mechanisms—their mutual dependency on one another for success also grows. Given the present lack of information and subjectivity for evaluating inter-organizational processing and information, management standards, organizations endeavoring to exchange electronic information open themselves to new risks of process, access, integrity, confidentiality, and privacy compromise. Organizations must not only concern themselves with fostering and not compromising EC best practices, but also employ methods that will allow for appropriate synchronization of best practices between trading partners.

Synchronizing best practices is not a simple endeavor. As suggested earlier, what constitutes best practices is highly debatable. The challenges are not simply solving the differences between two organizations but those of each of the organizations among themselves. Consider Table 4.2, which indicates the potential number of policies required for trading partner communities.

Table 4.2 Number of Policies per Trading Partner Groups

Number of Trading Partners (n)	Number of policies that may be required: $n(n - 1)/2$
5	10
10	45
100	4,950
1,000	499,500
5,000	12,497,500

Obviously, building policies for every relationship is simply not feasible. Therefore, some normalizing of processes must be introduced to increase the level of trust and reduce the risks between trading partners. EC managers must look to independent and trusted models and third parties to help in evaluating and establishing levels of mutually acceptable trust. Third parties help to establish a normalized representation of the level of trust for an EC system. The following is a list of methods in which EC managers can raise and represent, in a normalized fashion, the level of trust of their EC solutions.

- *Audit and penetration tests.* All EC implementation should involve an audit review, from start to end, as well as a penetration test to ensure that the system cannot be compromised. Presently, most if not all of the large accounting firms are offering such services and will certify the implementation as trusted and secure.
- *White box.* Organizations wishing to conduct EC who require a high level of trust and integrity of transaction processing can employ a white box approach. The white box involves commissioning a reputable and trusted third party who is tasked to audit all trading partner systems to a mutually agreed on "high-level" standard. The objective of the approach is to allow normalization of trust standards while maintaining secrecy between each of the trading partners.
- *Intermediaries.* This may seem counterintuitive to EC but is becoming more prevalent as a viable option. Third-party EC service providers are offering mechanisms to help resolve trust issues between trading partners. Electronic notaries are a case in point: information that is exchanged between trading partners can be notarized by a trusted third party. Certificate authorities are another example, conducting due diligence and issuing certificates to individuals, WWW servers, and software for download.

- *Accredited certification.* Finally, more and more organizations are becoming ISO 9000 certified, which defines a commitment to quality. Although not a definitive indicator, ISO and such accredited certifications will lend a measure of credibility and organization ability to conduct business with utmost quality in mind.
- *Standards bodies.* Adopting well established and in some cases emerging standards will also help normalize expectations between organizations. Bodies such as the Internet Engineering Task Force (IETF) www.ietf.org, Object Management Group (OMG) www.omg.org, and World Wide Web Consortium (W3C) www.w3.org are among those that contribute substantially to Internet transaction interoperability.

Even though these methods are by no means absolute, they represent a means in which organizations can gain some level of trust in the exchange of information between their borders.

Data-in-Transit

As corporeal beings, we have designed our environment accordingly to allow for effective transport of our bodies. Our society consists of sidewalks for walking; highways and stoplights for motor vehicles; tracks, signals, and stations for trains; airways, air traffic controllers, and airports for airplanes; seaways and ports for boats; all of which contribute to human transit. The transport of data follows an analog approach to that of human transit.

The data transit system is composed of a complex network of transportation options varying in performance, cost, and quality. The transportation systems are composed of various components including:

- *Regional networks.* The networks in a particular geographic area are connected into a large regional network. Routers pass information within that area from network to network.
- *Internet service provider (ISP) and online services.* You get onto the Internet through a LAN at your home or place of business in one of two ways. You can dial into a large computer connected to the Internet via online services or a dial-in ISP. Ethernet and token–ring networks are two kinds of networks that can be connected to the Internet.

- *Telecommunications*. The methods that are most prevalent include dedicated telephone lines, T1 and T3 leased lines, OC-12 links (622 Mbps)—the fastest speeds available today—as well as Asymmetric Digital Subscriber Lines (ADSL). Furthermore, satellites can also link networks, as can fiber optic cables, or special Integrated Service Digital Network (ISDN) telephone lines.
- *Network access points (NAP) and very high-speed backbone networks (vBNS)*. Regional networks are connected to one another via high-speed backbone connections that can send data at extremely high speeds. When data is sent from one regional network to another, it is first sent to a NAP. The NAP then routes the data to high-speed backbones, such as vBNS. The data is then sent along the backbone to another regional network. Finally, it is passed to a specific network and computer within that regional network.
- *Routers*. Routers, which connect networks, perform most of the work of directing traffic on networks. Routers examine the packets of the data that travels across the network to see where the data is headed. Based on the data's destination, the packet is routed in the most efficient way—generally to another router, which in turn sends the packet to the next router, and so on.

When information is sent across the Internet, the Transmission Control Protocol (TCP) first breaks it up into packets. Your computer sends those packets to your local network, Internet service provider (ISP), or online service. From there, the packets travel through many levels of networks, computers, and communications lines before they reach their final destination, which may be across town or around the world.

Although the architecture of Internet-based networks are extremely adaptive and flexible, the infrastructure is highly decentralized and has no single point of ownership. Data in transit traverses multiple network domains of ownership (see Figure 4.1).

Figure 4.1 is a fictional representation of the relationships between the network components comprising the Internet, intranets, and so on. The diagram demonstrates that information in transit can follow a multitude of paths from source to destination. Obvious is the fact that issues relating to data integrity, confidentiality, and privacy must be considered for information traversing such a complex and distributed transport mechanism. Chapter 5 will delve into solutions for these issues. However, more fundamental to these issues are arrangements of networks and relationships they share. The relations these networks share define the level of bandwidth (the capacity in which information can be managed through the network, start to end), redundancy (reliability of the network, start to end), and performance (data-only networks).

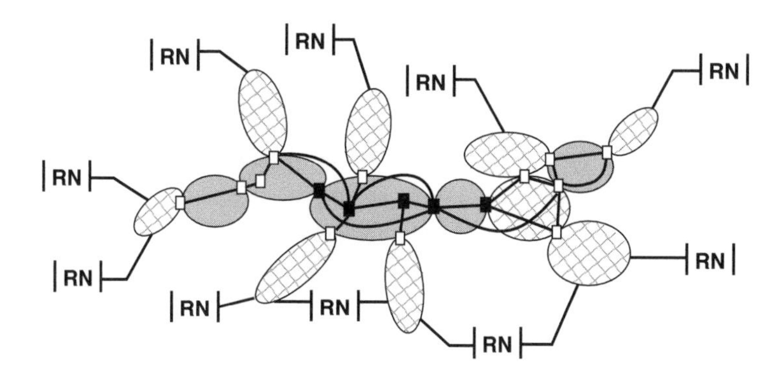

| | Regional Network (RN) (LANs/personal computers)

Independent ISPs

Telephone Network (Plain Old Telephone (POT), digital network, etc.)

Points of presence/routing

Network access points (NAP)

Internet Telecommunications Bandwidth

Figure 4.1

Hypothetical structure of the Internet.

EC managers must evaluate the above three conditions relative to the network traffic associated with their EC solution while considering the source and destination of the data and quantity of data including sustained averages and peaks.

Bandwidth is the telecommunications capacity that exists between the source of data and intended destination. Bandwidth analysis begins with the ISP and telecommunications service provider. Each would share the relationships shared between the routing points, including how and which NAPs are accessed. Furthermore, EC managers must also remember the importance of local points of presence (POPs). Selecting a local POP that is directly connected to a NAP or is affiliated with an ISP that owns and manages NAPs would be an excellent starting point for EC managers.

Adequate redundancy. As suggested in Figure 4.1, the flow of information can have one or more paths of flow. The objective for EC managers is to determine first that more than one path of information flow exits from start to end (if this is a requirement). This entails that every routing point will have had an alternative path at the prior routing point. This may seem more like an exception than a rule, but that is not the case. It is not unusual for a good ISP to consist of what is referred to as multiple hub locations, where a large number of links destined to the same routing point and others exist.

Performance. Although both bandwidth and reliability contribute to network performance, it has been separated to describe the condition of voice and data-blended networks. EC managers must be aware that some telecommunications organizations leverage their legacy voice networks for the transportation of data. This blending of voice and data results in unpredictable service, such as increased line errors, resulting in multiple sends and receives before a successful delivery is accomplished.

Data with ISP

To understand the implications of the data with ISPs, one must first understand what ISPs do and how they operate. The rudimentary services offered by ISPs fall into the three main categories: intermediate bandwidth provider to dial-up users and small businesses, sustained bandwidth providers to large organizations, and national and international bandwidth providers. ISPs may participate in many of these service areas but typically specialize in one or two. ISPs support the underlying Internet architecture (TCP/IP, routing, domain name services, and so on) that facilitates the flow of information. Information flowing from a source to a destination follows a path of interlinked ISP networks, which demands that careful attention be given to the features of these networks (see Table 4.3).

Table 4.3 Network Features and Evaluation Points

Issues	Safety features to look for	
Orientation	Many Internet providers target their services toward consumers and individual users rather than toward commercial use. Be sure to seek out a provider that focuses on the needs of business.	
Quality of service	Reliability	Look for a provider with **redundant equipment** at all major switching hubs and **redundant backbone links**, so that any single failure will be isolated to that part of the network. Because the Network Operation Center (NOC) is such a critical element in any provider's network reliability, it should be backed up with an **uninterruptible power supply (UPS)**, including a self-contained (gas or diesel) generator.

(continued)

Table 4.3 (continued)

Issues	Safety features to look for	
	Availability	This is a measure of the percentage of time you can actually get to the network and get your information through. Getting to the network is easy if you have a **dedicated connection**, such as a **leased line** or a **Frame Relay link**. But if you were dialing in, you wouldn't want to get a busy signal very often. There is an actual measurement that describes this phenomenon; it is called the **p-grade of service**. In general, one should only consider networks with a p-grade of no more than 05, meaning that no more than 5 out of 100 calls result in a busy signal. The lower the figure, the better. Be sure to ask about it.
	Performance	The last thing your customers want is a service fraught with delays and slow throughput. You can ascertain the degree of performance a given network will deliver by examining a network diagram. Things to look for include the **speed of the backbone** and **the speed at which large nodes connect to the backbone** (T-1, 1.5 Mbps, is far better than 56 Kbps). A high-speed, high-capacity backbone ensures a service with minimal delays and the ability to transmit bandwidth-hungry multimedia information with ease.
Points of Presence (POP)	The closer a network's POP is to your site, the less expensive it will be to connect to the network from your site. Thus, **it is advantageous to use a provider with a large national, even international, base of POPs, if you have national presence yourself.**	
Products/Services	It is important to choose a provider with a broad range of services to meet your various needs. Access servers generally fall into two areas.	
	Dial-Up	A provider should offer dial connectivity for individual users as well as for LANs. For higher-speed needs, ISDN delivers 64 Kbps at a cost close to regular (56 Kbps) dial service, so it is highly desirable.

(continued)

Table 4.3 (continued)

Issues	Safety features to look for	
	Dedicated	A **dedicated high-speed service** will provide your site with a full-time link to the Internet. The main criteria here are a range of speeds. A good Internet provider will offer dedicated access at speeds from 56 Kbps, through to T-1, T-3 (45 Mbps), and up to OC-12 links (622 Mbps). The opportunity to upgrade while remaining with the same service.
Support	Your provider of choice should operate a Network Operation Center (NOC), which is staffed 24 hours a day, every day of the year. A courteous and responsive customer service and support staff must be available. If you are a business user, you'll want to make sure those representatives aren't the same ones tending to the high-volume, time-intensive needs of consumer users too. Training and/or specialized consulting services should be available as well.	
Experience	How long has the provider you are considering been in the service provider business? Is it their main business or a side element? How large is their customer base, and are those customers happy?	
Cost	This criterion is listed last, not because it is the least important, but rather to illustrate that cost, while significant, is only one of many factors that should be weighed with equal value.	

Data at Client Sites, Server Site, and Outsourced Vendors

As described in Chapter 2, EC is in effect collaboration—defined by relationships—between organizations that contribute to a common process. As such, information relating to these processes may reside with independent organizations. These organizations will contribute in the origination, transformation, distribution, and management of the information. The objective for EC managers is to understand the implication these conditions will have on data integrity, confidentiality, and privacy. The above section addresses many of these issues; however, the client, server, and outsource relationship is of particular interest in maintaining the trust bond. These three parties are prevalent in most EC relationships.

Consider, for example, a secure electronic transaction (SET) implementation where the outsourced vendor represents the certificate authority, the client is the consumer with a wallet containing a SET certificate, and the server is the merchant server holding a digital certificate. In this EC implementation, special conditions apply to the management of data (specifically the digital certificate) by each party. Each of the clients, servers, and outsourced vendors will, based on their roles, have associated data management practices. These practices, driven by risk management processes, are typically formed with relation to data integrity, confidentiality, and privacy issues.

The managing digital certificates can be characterized as composing the practices of community and applicability, identification and authentication, key management, local security, technical security, and operations policy. These will be discussed in greater length in Chapter 5; however, suffice it to say that each of these practices will vary in degree and implementation across each of the parties.

The objective of the EC manager is to establish a framework for building confidence in the EC implementation. This is achieved by effective method of evaluating risks and establishing cost-effective measures to protect the integrity of the EC process. The intent of Chapter 5 is to provide such a framework.

Trans-Border Information Flow

It is fair to say that the Internet knows no borders. Information on the Internet is not bound by or referred to in a geographical sense but in an addressing sense. It is as though all the information on the Internet is everywhere at all times. The difficulty with this reality is that there exists a legacy of controls that describes the management of information across borders. Depending on what information is being managed by the EC implementation, a set of controls may exist that requires special treatment of information relative to geography.

The issues in this respect are not necessarily technological in nature but rather are policy based. The Internet has created a condition in which information can no longer be controlled by traditional methods. The controls we are speaking of are both the distribution and export/import of information—the former of the two representing the greatest challenge. One jurisdiction's content law may prohibit what another's jurisdiction's content laws promote. The press has been littered with some of the controversies associated with the distribution of pornography and hate literature. Also under siege are the well-established laws of advertising, political content, consumer protection, health protection, defamation, misappropriation of personality, and intellectual property. These are not easy issues to solve, and we certainly do not profess to have the answers. However, even though the Internet and EC have a lot to offer, implementers of EC solutions must bear in mind some of the outstanding issues that have yet to be resolved. As the Internet matures, so will the laws and with that comes controls. EC managers must be conscious of some of these outstanding issues and how they may impact EC implementation when legislation is enacted within their region.

THE AUDITOR'S PERSPECTIVE . . . .

Maintaining the trust bond is the mutual responsibility of the financial institution, the network carrier, and the merchant. All parties to the transaction have to prove not only the identity at the sender, receiver, or network level, but also the completeness and accuracy of the content. From a consumer's viewpoint, it makes sense to demand public statements from these parties on *how* they can live up to their assertions.

Authorization

There are many ways IT auditors attest to the integrity of electronic transactions and the integrity of files. One basic principle works in both paper-based and electronic environments. Transactions must be authorized. Unauthorized access could result in authorized messages being altered or falsified. As far as warehoused EC data is concerned, the protection, usage, distribution, and retention aspects can be dealt with in the same way as with other stored data files. This usually begins with a data classification, followed by assessing the value of corporate information to be protected. Existing security policies and authorization procedures for EC and non-EC transactions are quite similar.

Incoming Transactions

There are many elements that the auditor must verify to attest to the authenticity of incoming EC transactions. Classical items of an audit trail, such as the identity of the sender, date and time stamp, operator and terminal ID, and access information will help prove the existence and evidence of an obligation, but they cannot solely be used to prove that the transaction has not been altered in transit. This is where the risks of EC become bigger than traditional funds transfer or EDI, where the parties are dealing in a closed community. An in-transit EC transaction is traveling in the world at large, players are potentially everyone with a modem and a PC, the probability of a transaction being intercepted, falsified, misdirected, or lost will depend on the sophistication of telecommunication lines and protocols and transmission security features available. This is the topic for Chapter 5. An auditor will have to be satisfied with the level of protection accorded to each type of in-transit EC transaction, the means of protection, and the cost-effectiveness that goes with the protection.

Outgoing Transactions

As for outgoing EC transactions, the results of a risk assessment of the content of the transaction are most useful in determining the type of transmission controls to be applied. Where controls for messages with no financial impact could be satisfied with encryption alone, financial messages may require various types of authentication and digital signatures to preserve message integrity. This is discussed in Chapter 5.

We believe that in the next few years, there will be a rise of EC professionals, who will certify Web sites, and issue independent control reviews, and security professionals who will be asked to publish third-party "lab" reports on the currency and effectiveness of security as a means of attaining integrity for their products and services. It should be noted that even such independent reviews are only good for a short period of time, by virtue of the fact that any security devices that stay in the market too long will be vulnerable to penetration and compromise. Anyone (the consumer included) who has an interest in EC will want to be assured that the certificates are renewed, control reviews are only "period" reviews, just like the financial statements of public companies, and security "lab" reports have an expiration date. When EC has matured and become a way of life of every cyber-citizen, the reference to the "freshness" of these assertions will be as automatic as looking for the "best before" date on a loaf of bread. A case in point: To continue to display AICPA/CICA's *WebTrust* Seal of Assurance or SETCo's SET Mark on its Web site (after obtaining it), the service provider will be subject to regular audits. The frequency of these audits will depend on the conditions set by the assurance practitioner.

Confidentiality/Privacy Regulations: An International Sample

The increasing risks of disclosure of information have been covered in Chapter 2. Auditors, like the compliance officers within an organization, are expected to know the new guidelines and the position of the regulators on this subject in the global context. It does not matter where the information travels, confidentiality and privacy must be observed. Financial institutions have long-established policies and principles governing these topics. The reigning principle has always been that customer information cannot be disclosed without explicit client consent, with, of course, the usual exceptions that are clearly spelled out. Auditors should assure that the organization in fact follows what it promises its customers. The following are samples of new developments that are relevant to our discussions in this chapter.

Privacy Bills in the Senate and the House of Representatives of the U.S. 106th Congress 1999–2000

At the time of the publication of this book, there are 17 privacy-related bills being read in the House of Representatives and 9 in the Senate of the U.S. 106th Congress (http://thomas.loc.gov). Of these privacy bills, the following are relevant to EC. The first 3 are now in the Senate, and the last one in the House of Representatives:

S798	*Promote Reliable Online Transactions to Encourage Commerce and Trade (PROTECT)*: A bill to promote EC by encouraging and facilitating the use of encryption in interstate commerce consistent with the protection of national security.
S809	*Online Privacy Protection Act of 1999*: A bill to require the Federal Trade Commission to prescribe regulations to protect the privacy of personal information collected from and about private individuals who are not covered by the Children's Online Privacy Protection Act of 1998 on the Internet, and to provide greater individual control over the collection and use of that information.
S854	*Electronic Rights for the 21st Century Act*: A bill to protect the privacy and constitutional rights of Americans; to establish standards and procedures regarding law enforcement access to location of information, decryption assistance for encrypted communications and stored electronic information and other private information; to affirm the rights of Americans to use and sell encryption products as a tool for protecting their online privacy.
H.R.313	*Consumer Internet Privacy Protection Act of 1999*: A bill to regulate the use by interactive computer services of personally identifiable information provided by subscribers to such services.

Privacy is a significant issue and concern to all cyber-citizens. For a detailed treatment of this subject, readers can refer to Albert Marcella Jr.'s upcoming book, *www.StopThief.net-Protecting Your Identity on the Web*, published by the Institute of Internal Auditors in October 1999.

Licensing of Trusted Third Parties (U.K.)

In March 1997, the United Kingdom's Department of Trade and Industry produced a public consultation paper containing detailed proposals for legislation of the role of trusted third parties (TTPs) in the provision of encryption services over the public telecommunications network. The bottom line is that any TTP offering encryption services to the U.K. public must be licensed. Of particular interest to auditors and control consultants are the criteria of the licensing authority: competence or trustworthiness of information security personnel, information security management and directors; technical assurances of the IT security equipment used; quality standards and procedures in place; level of liability cover; ability to meet access conditions; business plan, evidence of commitment to the market, structure and ownership; procedures for interface with TTPs; and the level of isolation of TTP operations from other nonoperations of the same company.

The criteria exhibits many of the principles of good control practices discussed throughout this book: control is everyone's business; the need for independent assurances from experts in the field; standards and procedures; relationship of EC as part of the overall business plan; and the need for segregation of incompatible duties. These criteria are excellent reference points in reviewing the role of the TTPs. These may be licensing criteria, but every one of them is relevant in determining the trustworthiness of the TTP or any security vendor.

Office of the Superintendent of Financial Institutions (OSFI)—Canada—Interim Policy on Outsourcing of Business Functions (1997) and Replacement Guideline (1999)

In August 1997, OSFI released an interim outsourcing policy statement that affects all Canadian Federally Regulated Financial Institutions (FRFIs). Further to the policy statement, OSFI is now preparing an outsourcing guideline that will replace the policy statement, which is expected to be finalized in October 1999. The guideline expands upon the nine guiding principles set out in the policy statement: Oversight by Board of Directors; Retention of Management Control; Capability/Expertise of Service Provider; Acceptable Contract for Services; Confidentiality and Security; Records and Examinations; Location of Service Provider; Commingled Assets; and Agreement with Non-Arms-Length Parties. Readers will notice that some of the principles echo U.K.'s licensing criteria of TTPs! Obviously, there are common good EC practices to be gleaned from these recent developments.

In the *Confidentiality and Security* principle, OSFI is firm on its stand regarding security of information provided by the service provider: "Security of information must be taken into account of an outsourcing decision and addressed in the contractual relations between the parties." It goes on to say, "As a minimum, FRFIs should identify the business requirements for security."

No organization engaging in EC builds all the EC components from scratch. As a matter of fact, there are more components being serviced or supplied by vendors than those of their own making. This means that the Confidentiality and Security principle will always be high on the regulators' agenda and must be fully addressed in the contracts. Organizations should be prepared to clearly communicate their privacy, confidentiality, and security expectations to their vendors. These expectations should be verified by the vendor's external auditors; especially those that relate to the vendor's ability to ensure the privacy and confidential company data being disclosed to the vendor's electronic files; and that the company's privacy and security policy is not breached.

The Personal Data (Privacy) Ordinance (Hong Kong)—Revised 1997

The Personal Data (Privacy) Ordinance (PDO) requires that companies doing business in Hong Kong comply with data privacy practices when collecting, holding, processing, or using personal data. Personal data can be anything from employee files, customer details to financial information, and credit histories. It will affect almost every business, not just EC. PDO sets out to protect the privacy of individuals and demands the compliance with the PDO from the data users. The office of the Privacy Commissioner has extensive powers to enforce this legislation.

The PDO is based on six personal data protection principles relating to Collection, Accuracy, Use, Security, Openness, and Access.

Of particular relevance to the EC in this legislation is the subject of transborder flow of information. Many countries that have established data protection legislation often include provisions restricting the transfer of data to anywhere that does not have similar laws. So EC service providers, regardless of the location of their business, should have in place a confidentiality and privacy policy, taking into consideration the six principles of the PDO. As the PDO principles were designed to bring Hong Kong data protection in line with similar legislation in other countries, the PDO to some degree reflects current data protection worldwide trends and expectations.

Total Quality in the EC Transaction Factory

In EC, trust rests on the whole relationship. The transaction is just part of that relationship, not the relationship itself. By definition, a relationship has continuity—repeat business. Many studies show that it costs around $250 to initially acquire a customer. That figure applies to online trading and book sales. Here, you need a lot of transactions to recover that investment. In mid-1999, Amazon.com was spending over 20% of its revenue on marketing; more than it spent on technology. Obviously, if a customer can set his or her browser to find just the lowest price, i.e., the "best" transaction, then Amazon's strategy is likely to fail. If it can turn those transactions into a long-term trusted relationship, then it has a strong chance of success.

That said, obviously, if a company is very poor at transactions and the processes that support them, they can forget about relationships.

The transaction factory has to work, just like any other factory that produces "real" goods. It took 20 years to recover trust in North American manufactured products. Today's high level of expectation of quality in physical products coming out of factories was built on a new management commitment to quality management and quality assurance processes. This chapter has really been about quality assurance in the EC factory. Managers should keep in mind when addressing EC that it was only when business management had to take the lead to make "Quality Is Job One" (Ford) and Six Sigma (Motorola) that North American manufacturing began its comeback. Business managers must make trust at the operational level of the transaction their own "Job One" as they do at the strategic level of services and relationship.

5

Security: What Are You Protecting . . . and Why?

Unless commercial transactions are secure from intrusion, misuse, sabotage, and theft, they cannot generate trust-based relationships. There's a long list of cliches and aphorisms that capture this reality: "In God we trust—all others pay cash." "Trust but verify." "Even paranoids have enemies." "It's no use bolting the stable doors after the horse is out." "I don't trust him further than I can see him."

EC has to be secure, but its very nature gets in the way of what these phrases imply. First, you can't pay cash. You don't have time to verify. If you're paranoid, the customer is already accessing some other provider. You can't bolt the doors—your Web site is an invitation to come into the stable. With EC, you don't see the other party face-to-face.

We can expect growing volumes of attacks on the security of EC and growing sophistication of attackers. So far, our book has been about the Good Guys: businesses and their customers, suppliers and partners collaborating to make their EC relationships smooth, convenient, and reliable. Alas, there are plenty of Bad Guys out there, and the nature of EC attracts far too many of them. Along with trust goes prudence: It's prudent to add security to the relationship—just in case.

There's nothing new here, of course. Every new form of commerce has brought with it some formidable threat for which new safeguards had to be built. In the sixteenth century, the rich new shipping of gold and silver from the Americas by the galleons of Spain helped turn England from a minor offshoot of Europe into its most powerful navy through what was very much like today's hackers: The pirates and privateers who hovered along the trade routes and attacked quickly and left quickly, avoiding the centers of the fleet and capturing the stragglers. The U.S. rail network in the eighteenth century was nearly undermined by gangs—Jesse Woodson, more commonly known as Jesse James, Bill Doolin, and the Dalton Brothers—by their simple exploitation of the weaknesses in the railway system. Today, there's a whole industry of credit card and cellular phone fraud that, again, looks for the weaknesses in the complex set of trading links. Advances in technology in themselves open up new avenues for attackers. A recent example is the very high quality of desktop computer software and printers that enable forgers to produce superb copies of banknotes. One German villain complained at his trial that his professional pride was offended by the inferior quality of the government's printing office workmanship compared with his own far superior copies.

By their very design and intent, today's electronic networks are hard to protect. They offer access—access to the world in the case of the Web and to trading partners in more tightly controlled electronic data interchange networks. The fundamental problem for security is then the trade-off between access and control; one largely comes at the risk of the other. By offering access to all, you offer access to malicious pranksters, amateur hackers, professional conmen and thieves, and even hardened terrorists. The threats are very real but they can be protected against. The art form for EC is to achieve this while maintaining freedom of access.

Trust by design—secure by design.

The digital world of telecommunications networks, software, and information assets is obviously very different from that of physical commerce networks, such as railroads, shipping, and by air. There, the product is physical, and there are well-defined control points and well-established regulations and codes of good practice. While smuggling is a worldwide problem, whether of drugs or fake Rolex watches, the system knows where, why, how, and what to monitor. Few of these conditions for control apply to the networks of EC.

Perhaps the most disconcerting aspect of the digital network EC world, specifically the Internet, is its lack of central governance and a manner in which it can regulate those using it. Essentially, the Internet is an international collection of independent networks owned and operated by many organizations. There are no uniform culture, legal, or legislative committees for addressing misconduct. We don't even know in most instances what laws apply, let alone how they can be enforced. For example, a hacker in East Germany made many successful and far-reaching attacks on U.S. Defense Department and university networks—supposedly secure—in the late 1980s. (He was uncovered by a self-admittedly compulsive university network administrator who observed small discrepancies in transaction records.) Although the hacker and his accomplices were prosecuted, they were tried in German court under German laws. As it turns out, the individuals were convicted, but with no more than a slap on the hand receiving only probation sentences with minor fines. Had the individuals been tried under United States espionage laws, the punishment would have certainly been more severe. Of course, had they not been able to get into the system, the issue of law would have been irrelevant.

LOOK AFTER THE INFORMATION FIRST: LINKING SECURITY WITH DATA PROTECTION . . . .

That leads to the first key component of a company's efforts to handle security: *Look after your own information assets first and foremost.* If information can't be stolen, it can't be used or misused. Regardless of the level and nature of service, and hence access, a fundamental principle of security is the "encryption" of data so that no outside party can hijack it. Encryption is a very complex discipline and area of technical specialization, but its principles are as simple as its mathematics are complex. Basically, it involves using an algorithm, a formula, to convert data into what looks like a random stream of bits—0s and 1s gibberish. It uses a "key" to do so and either the same or another key to decode the bit stream back to the original information. Even though business managers don't need to know much about how this is done, it's worth their having insight into the basic issues, because they are so critical to both security and customer sense of safety and because they can be expensive. Just as there's an access/control tradeoff, there's a security/cost one too.

You see encryption in action if you carry out a transaction with any of the leading EC Web sites, such as Amazon.com. Amazon.com, when greater security is required, seamlessly moves from an unencrypted to an encrypted secure socket layer (SSL) link; SSL encryption means the link between your PC and their service will be secured and that sending your credit card number to them over the Net remains private. Similarly, whenever you use your ATM card, the bank's network will use the venerable data encryption standard (DES) scheme. DES has worked well for around two decades, but the algorithm and keys it uses are not fully secure; someone with a powerful enough computer could try out trial-and-error calculations—referred to as a brute force attack—to deduce the key and thus break the code. Regularly, the press reports that an expert or amateur had done this; their computers may have had to compute nonstop for days or even weeks, but that's merely a matter of running up their electricity bill a mere few more dollars. One of the realities of encryption is that, as the tools that enable ever-more-complex algorithms and keys to be used to encode and decode data become more and more powerful, that very same power can be used in attempts to break the code. Encryption rests on the use of keys. These are actually prime numbers—ones that cannot be divided by any combination of other numbers except itself and 1. Examples are 3, 5, 7, and 47. If you knew that the key used to convert a data item was 15, it would take you only a few seconds to see that this is 3 x 5. But how about a number:

1259832720019282847466328291828289192999011929292010101872168736
2524517

Well, that would take a computer a few milliseconds—thousandths of a second—to check that out. The larger the number of bits an encryption key uses to store and apply its calculations, the more time a computer would need. Bear in mind that the binary (0/1) coding scheme of digital technology represents numbers in powers of 2, so that 1111 equals 2 cubed plus 2 squared plus 2 to the power of one plus 2 to the power of zero or 15. A 128-bit key can represent more than all the grains of sand on the planet Earth. Use them in mathematical algorithms that are about a million times more complex than anything you learn in high school math, and you have a system for making data appear incomprehensible to any intruder. But, alas, the new intruders have computers that can put their power to work to attempt a reverse calculation. It's for this reason that many experts argue that the keys and calculations used in the DES system that is the core of ATM transaction handling is just not adequate for the next generation of EC. The counter-argument is that it's good enough and the cost of adding processing power and delay time to encrypt and decrypt data is not justified in most instances. That argument will go on for decades. It may appear esoteric and technical, but it's at the core of every security issue—technical and nontechnical: How good is good enough?

Value and Approach for Public Key Versus Private Key

Contemporary encryption systems fall into two main categories: symmetric and asymmetric encryption. Symmetric encryption is based on a model that requires that a common key (shared secret) exist between every trusted relationship. An example of such a model is the retail store debit terminal, in which every terminal's PIN (personal identification number) pad device (the device where your PIN number is entered) is loaded with a secret key, generally by the issuing bank of the terminal. The bank has the key and so does the device. That makes it easy and fast for the pad device to encrypt the data and the bank to decrypt it. Levels of trust and authentication of parties is primarily a function of the symmetric key distribution process; that is, only the bank and the device can issue and use the key.

The integrity of such a trusted relationship is heavily dependent on the control mechanisms for dispensing and managing the keys. Symmetric key systems cater well to highly defined transaction sets, established many-to-one relationships managed by the central organization, and with small key numbers of parties. These constitute established networks of trust that are closed (well-bounded) and ongoing, rather than new or occasional. Think of your personal relationship with your bank: You have your account and ATM card. You expect the bank to provide security; indeed, you take it for granted, in that very few people have even thought about data encryption at the cash machine.

In contrast, EC solutions are not networks of established trust but rather consist of a large number of decentralized interactions with no central coordinator. They are sometimes ad hoc and often between parties with no previous history of working together. For each of these parties to have encryption keys already in place would be impossible. Whereas your bank handles this when it issues you an ATM card, the new online customer needs to be able to carry out secure transactions at once. Customers can't each be given a symmetric, that is, shared, key on demand. For a symmetric model, 1,000 users require 1 million distinct keys to be managed, while 10,000 users require 100 million keys. All of these must be distributed in advance, just as your ATM card is sent to you before you can use it.

Asymmetric encryption systems (often referred to as public key systems) resolve the key distribution issue by removing the need to distribute a shared secret. Here the math and technology get really complicated. They utilize two keys rather than one: a public and a private key. Information encrypted with the freely distributed public key can only be decrypted with the complementary private key. Private keys are never distributed, remaining unique to each party.

Symmetric key encryption, by contrast, requires the secret key systems be transmitted, introducing the possibility of an adversary discovering the secret key. Think of this as rather like using a dictionary. (The example also helps illustrate the general approach of crypto systems, which is to make it easy to send information and hard to work out what's been sent without knowing the key.) Assume I send a message to you that uses a German dictionary as the encoding key instead of a complex number. My message begins "Heilig," which means holy. I used an English-to-German dictionary to encode it. Anyone can pick up my message, but unless they have a German-to-English dictionary, they can't easily decode it; they'd have to comb through the English-to-German one—the public key—to work out what I've sent. You, who have the private key, the German-to-English dictionary, can do so immediately. Symmetric key systems in effect tell you what dictionary to use, but it's a secret and could be Serbo-Croat, Erse, Xhosa, or Shaangan (yes, we the authors know what that is because we have the secret key to translate "Nygana" into . . .—but that's *our* secret). If you know the language and have the dictionary, decoding information is just a simple exercise of looking the word up in the index. If you don't, then expect to spend a lot of time in the library. Unless you have a computer hacker who looks at this and says, "Ah, looks like non-European. Could be African. Let's do a shortcut."

So think of symmetric key systems as shared dictionaries and asymmetric ones as private and personal dictionary services. Symmetric key systems manage relationships through rigorous policies in their key distribution processes. Asymmetric encryption systems, through digital signatures and certificate authorities (to be discussed later in this chapter), produce highly flexible trusted relationships capable of meeting the demands of EC, because they are personal and private.

One disadvantage of asymmetric key systems is their distinct lack of performance. Using the dictionary analogy, they require a multitude of dictionaries and a new one for every transaction. Commonly available symmetric encryption systems are substantially faster than present-day asymmetric encryption systems (100 times as fast as in software and between 1,000 and 10,000 times as fast in hardware). Symmetric systems are most efficient, including cost-efficient, whereas asymmetric ones are most effective—including being cost-inefficient. However, by combining symmetric with asymmetric encryption systems, a best-of-breed approach can be achieved. An example of this best-of-breed implementation can be found in MasterCard and Visa's secure electronic transaction (SET)—a secure protocol to protect credit card transactions on the Internet. The active participants in every SET transaction include a cardholder, merchant, and issuer. In the world of credit card transactions, it is not uncommon for issuers to manage many hundreds of transactions a second (airline reservation systems process thousands per second). Therefore, it is imperative that the process not only be effective but also efficient. It can be done. The following steps describe a basic interaction between a Web browser and a server (steps have been simplified to clearly depict symmetric and asymmetric interactions):

1. The browser and server exchange public keys.
2. The browser creates a symmetric key (session key) and encrypts it with the server public key and submits a message package to the server.
3. The server decrypts the package and obtains the symmetric key.
4. A trusted session is established and subsequent information is exchanged, utilizing the symmetric key for the duration of the session.

All encryption systems are susceptible to attacks, a practice referred to as cryptoanalysis. These attacks, inevitably, hinge on the type of algorithm and the length of secret key utilized. As key lengths grow, the time required to decipher/break the code grows as well. The commonly available symmetric and asymmetric encryption algorithms are formidable. However, asymmetric encryption algorithms allow (unlike symmetric algorithms) for dynamic key lengths. This added flexibility inherent in asymmetric encryption systems strengthens the system well beyond that of symmetric key systems.

Table 5.1 indicates the distinguishing properties for symmetric and asymmetric key systems based on encryption strength (probability of compromise), performance (time and computational expense), functionality (fundamental services), and distribution (keys and other cryptographic materials).

Table 5.1 Symmetric Key vs. Asymmetrical Key Systems and Their Implications

	Symmetric (Private Key)	Asymmetric (Public Key)	EC Perspective
Strengths/ Versatility	- Well-understood flaws. - Structure of encryption techniques suited to efficient implementation in hardware. - Fast to encrypt and decrypt messages. - Robust tool kits from a variety of vendors. - Relatively small key sizes for the level of security afforded.	- Secret information does not need to be exchanged. - Versatile algorithm makes it suitable for a variety of security related functions. - Strong suite of tools from RSA.	- A blend of symmetric and asymmetric key systems will be required.
Protection afforded – resistance to attack	*Key Length* 56 64 80 112 128 On July 17, 1998, the Electronic Frontier Foundation cracked 56-bit DES encryption in 56 hours.	*Key Length* 384 512 768 (personal) 1792 (corporate – executive) 2304 (Certificate Authority) A 512-bit RSA encrypted data item may be decrypted, in 1997, for a cost of less than $1,000,000 and in less than 8 months.	- Asymmetric keys a must for authentication, integrity, nonrepudiation, and symmetric key distribution. - Symmetric key should be used on a session or transaction basis. - Symmetric key length is a function of performance vs. risk of compromise.
Performance – time required to encrypt/decrypt data	- In software, the symmetric algorithm is at least one hundred times as fast as a public key system. - In hardware, the symmetric algorithm's from 1,000 to 10,000 times as fast.		- A blend of symmetric and asymmetric key systems will be required. - Hardware encryption will aid in establishing virtual networks (authentication between corporate intranets based on mutually agreed on policies).

(continued)

Table 5.1 (continued)

	Symmetric (Private Key)	Asymmetric (Public Key)	EC Perspective
Functionality – digital signatures	Cannot be conducted without a public and private key pair.	Encryption with a sender's unique private key. Successful decryption with the sender's public key confirms the origin of the data/message.	- Only true universally accepted unique identifier in existence. - Necessary for establishing trusted relationships.
Functionality – nonrepudiation (the act of binding parties to a transaction)	Rigorous symmetric key distribution process. It is possible to repudiate a transmission by claiming that the secret was compromised.	Applying a digital signature. Because only one copy of a sender's private key exists, the transaction cannot be repudiated.	- Digital signatures limit liabilities for all parties. - Digital signatures are a fundamental part of SET (credit card transaction over the Internet).
Functionality – integrity	If the decrypted data is not discernible, then the assumption can be made that either the data was compromised after encryption or that the private key being used is incorrect. In either case, the sending party should be notified that a problem occurred. Should this problem persist, the corporate security group should be notified of a possible hacking.	If a check on the digital signature fails, then either the encrypting key was incorrect or the data was altered after the signature was created (e.g., during transmission). In either case, the sending party should be notified that a problem occurred. Should this problem persist, the corporate security group should be notified of a possible hacking.	Critical function for the transportation of information over public or low trusted networks.
Functionality – private key escrow	Although the key sizes are small, symmetric systems are ill suited to large-scale escrow techniques as the number of keys grows when quadratic functions of the number of users. One thousand users requires 1 million distinct keys to be managed, whereas 10 thousand users requires 100 million.	Even though the keys are larger (generally more than ten times the size) than those of symmetric systems, the number of keys required grows linearly as a function of the number of users. As such, the complexity and space requirements are considerably less in large-scale operations.	- Means of recovering encrypted information (e.g., corporate employees private key kept in escrow). - For asymmetric systems, private key is no longer unique and open issues of nonrepudiation disputes.

(continued)

Table 5.1 (continued)

	Symmetric (Private Key)	Asymmetric (Public Key)	EC Perspective
Key distribution/ publication	Keys are usually generated on the server and distributed via a secure channel to the user. Asymmetric encryption techniques are often used to encrypt symmetric keys for distribution.	Public keys can be posted in a public directory system. The keys are usually generated locally and the public keys are then registered with a central directory or certificate authority (CA).	Asymmetric keys are fundamental to EC.

Security techniques have matured to include both symmetric and asymmetric encryption. Each contributes a distinct functionality that has aided in the proliferation of EC. Both symmetric and asymmetric encryption schemes must be considered for appropriately securing EC solutions.

From the business manager's perspective, encryption is far away from the commerce side of EC, but it's very close to the customer, even if the customer doesn't know about it. It's the customer who initiates the information flow and sends and receives data of value: credit card information, orders, and personal identification. That data triggers software accessing of the company's own private information, its databases, processing systems, and operations. It may also initiate online links to other companies: credit card processors, supply chain partners, service providers, retailers, shippers, and others. Every party in the EC chain relies on security of information. If one of them lacks adequate encryption capabilities, it's almost sure to be dropped as a partner. It's just not worth the risk. That makes security very much a business consideration. The chain is only as strong as its weakest link and that link mustn't be your firm.

The Economics of Security (Risk Analysis Versus Cost)

Investments in security technology seem almost a necessary evil. However, in the case of EC, investments in security can make the difference between success and failure. Furthermore, EC systems differ from traditional systems in that they are in a state of constant flux. This dynamic nature of EC is symptomatic of the rapid evolution of technology that underpins these solutions and of a consumer culture that expects constant product and service innovation. EC managers must reflect these expectations in their risk-avoidance investments. The question that remains is, How and when should one invest in EC security technology? Historically, organizations have largely deployed security software and processes as an afterthought to system implementation.

The difficulty with such an approach is that the outcome often involves sacrifice in service functionality or added expense in retrofitting security measures. Such tactics may have fared well in closed implementations, but they are impractical for EC. The very nature of EC is provision of services everywhere, anytime, on any device. EC extends beyond organization boundaries, opening up corporate system and information sources (static and dynamic data repositories), which in turn extend organizational risks. As such, EC solutions have a lower tolerance for afterthought security, so much so that it can undermine the success of an implementation. Our experience has shown that implementations with an integrated security component rather than retrofitted can substantially reduce the security investment, protect the functional integrity of the solution and maintain the level of trust.

The objective, therefore, is to conduct the risk analysis in conjunction with the system design. Once the system services have been defined, potential threats can be inferred and appropriate countermeasures can be included into the design. Traditional risk analyses are generalized approaches employing probability and brute force methods. These methods are methodical and cost intensive, which resolves security issues by scaling back or masking functionality. Alternatively, threat analysis during the design phase allows security to be applied relative to discrete business functions. Consider an organization faced with implementing a simple new EC application, such as adding an online catalog for customers to make orders via the Web instead of only through the firm's call center. Having implemented previous EC solutions, the firm decides to leverage existing facilities and services—reduce the expense through the reuse of existing technology, policy, and processes—as part of the design of the solution. It already has a comprehensive inventory management system that can be linked to the catalog service. During the implementation of the solution an audit was conducted to determine if the existing systems' security would be compromised by the new implementation. The audit concluded that the functionality of the new system did introduce new risks that needed to be mitigated. The inventory management system was a closed system; it could be accessed only through the company's in-house network, which used basic protections, such as passwords. The internal network was protected by a firewall—the equally standard method of placing a combination of hardware and software tools that screen traffic to and from the process system and monitor any problems or attempts to gain unauthorized access. The call center agents placed orders from their workstations, which were part of the closed company network and thus did not need extra protection. The network used a 128-bit symmetric key, fully adequate for the closed system but not for one that is literally wide open to the world. It would be easy to break into by any skilled hacker (the long-established term for people who like to play around with computers to see what they can do and/or show off) or crackers (hackers who like to mess up computers and/or steal from them).

There were only two practical solutions to resolve the issue: Remove the risky new functionality or spend substantial funds to protect the assets, the value being the combined assets of both solutions. The investment exceeded the value of the opportunity but not that of the combined assets. Therefore, in this instance, the funds required rendered the initiative entirely unprofitable. Had the threat analysis been conducted at the onset, this issue would have been averted with a cost-effective alternative that caters to the discrete EC solution. The system design would have included a new firewall built to handle the public flow of traffic with its own encryption capabilities plus with a new firewall link into the private network system.

The lesson to be learned from this typical example is that the esoteric technical issues of security are easily left out of the EC business dialog. In this case, the business opportunity was clear and simple: Let customers access a multimedia catalog. The business justification assumed the use of the public Internet for customer access and the internal system for the ordering. Why should the business planners, the software company providing the catalog software package, and the small team building the system think about the security issue? They knew the internal network was secure and assumed that was all that was needed. They looked at security as a utility, not as a response to risk and as a risk/cost tradeoff. The new functionality added a new risk that they were unaware of. And their decision generated a much bigger risk/cost dilemma than they intended.

It's for this reason that we have described encryption at a greater level of detail than many of our readers will ever need in their own EC planning and implementation: Business choices generate technology consequences, and vice versa. Managers will achieve effective and economical security EC solutions through synchronization of risk analysis with business objectives. Traditional analysis of physical and environmental, hardware, software, operations, and communications security are still required but should be driven by business and management issues *from the inception of planning*. This builds safety into the design of EC solutions rather than disjointed defenses requiring the complexities of coordination and retrofitting.

FRAMEWORK FOR BUILDING CONFIDENCE . . . .

The continuing growth of networks and dependence of organizations on them attract adversaries to exploit their vulnerabilities. To conceive the possible threats, we must first establish a context from which to discuss these matters. Figure 5.1 is a simple model identifying the key elements that are susceptible to threats from adversaries.

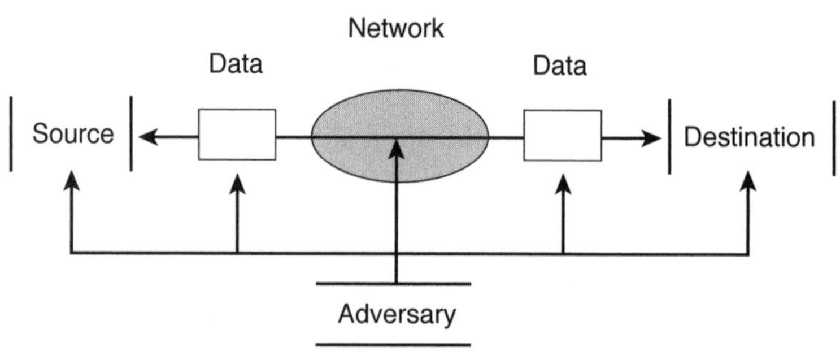

Figure 5.1
Generalized model for EC transactions.

Although a simplification that hides the complexity of the many details and intermediate steps, the depiction in Figure 5.1 describes three key components that can be compromised by adversaries: source, destination, and network. The two parties cooperate to exchange data/information. A logical channel (relationship) is created on the network/Internet by identifying the source and destination addresses, a complex process managed and carefully masked by communication protocols (e.g., TCP/IP for the Internet). Securing an EC system requires putting in place the necessary precautions to avert threats. In doing so, EC managers must focus their attentions on elements which they can directly affect or control. The most nebulous element in our context diagram is the network. The anonymity of networks provides perfect conditions for adversaries to thrive. Areas that touch the network should be of particular concern to EC managers.

Understanding the Risks of Distributed Systems

Perhaps the greatest threat to the success of EC is ignorance. Often, organizations fail to understand the potential threats that come with the implementation of an EC system. According to industry experts, more than 50% of attacks succeed. Threats are subtle and not easily discernable. To exemplify this issue, the following scenario is offered: An adversary intent on conducting malicious activity decides to obtain IDs and password from an online banking service. The adversary understands that transmissions between the browser and server are protected by encryption (SSL). Therefore, he or she elects to obtain a password by placing pamphlets at the bank's ATMs, urging customers to try a new and improved version of the service at www.new_service_site.com. Unbeknown to these customers, the adversary has simply replicated the front page and sign-on process of the original online banking service. When the consumer attempts to sign on, the adversary simply captures the IDs and passwords and indicates the service is not presently available and reroutes the user to the original site. Later the adversary can tamper with customer accounts with antics such as draining customer accounts by conducting legitimate bill payments on their behalf. Although, in this example, the customers' net worth was not compromised, the possibility of humiliation associated with accessibility to funds or potential bounced checks would certainly negatively affect the relationship with the financial institution. The reputations of the customer and the bank have been damaged by this compromise that represents a far more damaging effect than a simple one-time loss of funds.

The motives behind adversaries' attacks can be any one or combination of the following: theft of documents or other valuable data, destruction of data, corruption of data, destruction of network integrity, denial of services, and tarnishing of reputation.

Before discussing Figure 5.2, we move the topic from hypothetical to real by summarizing an article in *U.S. News and World Report* (June 14, 1999), which provides statistics and examples of deliberate attacks on networks. We could have picked one example from almost any comparable magazine and found comparable figures. They show that in the struggle to protect EC assets, no matter how skilled your company is in this regard and no matter how much you have available to spend, there are so many equally skilled people spending a great deal of time trying to beat you. That said, keep in mind that the same issue of the magazine also discusses the $8 billion a year trade in stealing and exporting cars. The EC challenge is very serious but doesn't—so far at least—impede the overall growth and operation of EC.

Here are some of the reported adversary attacks:

1. Within the past 12 months of this book being published, hackers successfully broke into the Web sites of eBay, The White House, Ameritech, and Bell South.
2. A survey of large organizations by the FBI found that 30% admitted that their systems had been broken into in 1998, and 55% reported intrusions by inside staff.
3. Combined losses of $124 million from business disruptions caused by intrusions were reported by 163 organizations.
4. A teenager knocked out the entire phone service and airport operations of a town in Massachusetts by "poking" around the system of NYNEX, the regional phone company (now part of Bell Atlantic).
5. Two members of a group calling itself Hacking for Girlies were arrested after they had made off with 1,749 credit card numbers.

6. Another group, Back Orifice, offers free downloading software that enables its user to take over any unprotected PC running Microsoft Windows 95 or 98, the operating system of choice for most consumers and hence most EC customers.
7. A senior adviser to the U.S. National Security Council commented that "the real threat is from foreign countries . . . We know there are foreign governments interested in our critical infrastructure, and they are developing plans to go after it."
8. Crackers are themselves using "nearly unbeatable" encryption.

So that's the scale of the problem. It's obviously one that no organization can ignore in its EC business planning. Before assets can be protected, one must first understand how attacks are conducted. Figure 5.2 categorizes the forms of attack that can be conducted on distributed systems.

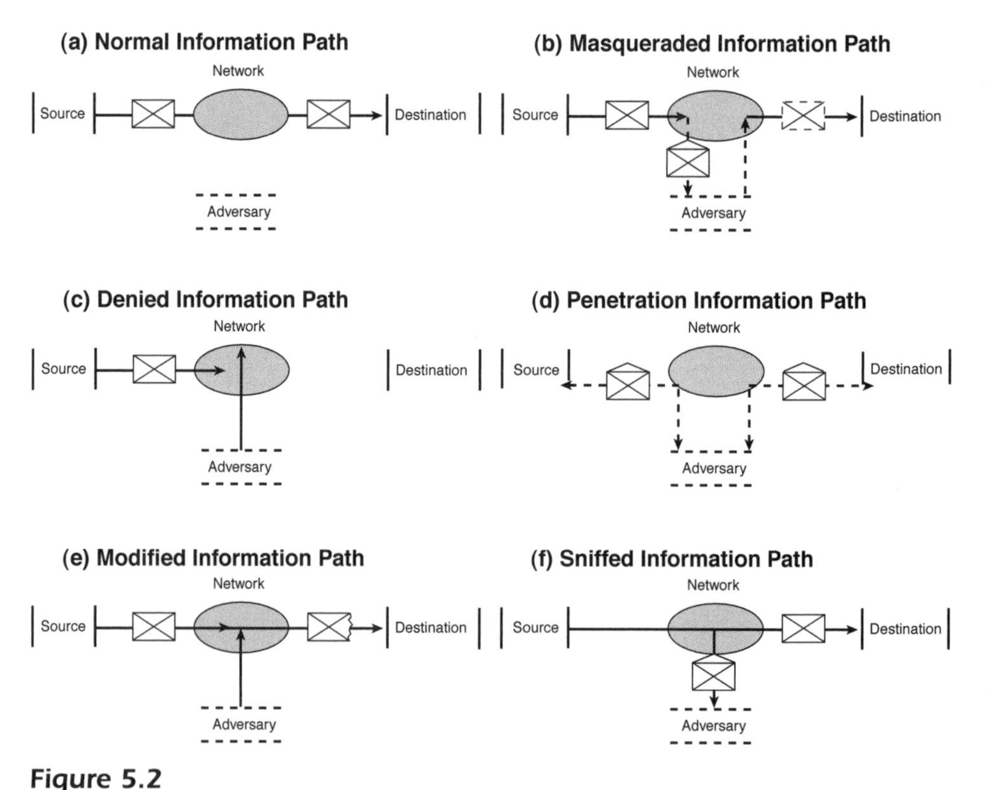

Figure 5.2

Common modes of EC attacks portrayed on generalized EC transaction model.

A **masqueraded information path** (Fig. 5.2b) is one in which the destination is deceived into believing that information sent by an adversary originated from the source. Masquerade attacks typically include one or more of the other forms of attack. During a masquerade attack, a source or destination may be affected. Information sent from a source is intercepted and potentially modified. This modified or alternate message is then delivered to the destination under the name of the source. Not only has information now been disclosed, such as source and destination authentication sequences, but the collaboration may also have been undermined as a result of the tampering.

The **denied information path** (Fig. 5.2c) is a focused attack. The sole intention of this attack is to shut down, degrade performance, or consume resources during the normal flow of information. Typical denial of service attacks involve bombarding the source or destination with requests or introducing a virus in the source or destination systems, among others.

The **penetration information path** (Fig. 5.2d) is usually the result of unauthorized logins. Penetration into either a source or a destination can occur by misuse in stealing, guessing passwords, applying social engineering tactics, or lacking appropriate authentication. A compromise occurs when an adversary illegitimately obtains a password and uses it to intrude into systems. Typical targets for theft of passwords are systems administrators, who have administrative privileges over systems and other user accounts. If an adversary succeeds in compromising a systems administrator's account, that adversary may assume any identity he or she wishes. Diligent adversaries will also create backdoors—obscure identities to be used at a later date—in the event they are caught and passwords are changed.

The **modified information path** (Fig. 5.2e) is the malicious behavior of modifying or destroying files as they pass through the network. Although files can be encrypted during transmission, these files can also be damaged in transit. The resulting files, after arrival at a destination would be useless, for decryption would not be possible.

The **sniffed information path** (Fig. 5.2f) involves an adversary passively accumulating information that is exchanged between a source and a destination. Sniffing is typically a covert activity that occurs without the knowledge of the source or destination. Organizations using Internet e-mail that have neglected to protect critical business matters through encryption are ripe targets for a sniffing adversary.

EC systems are vulnerable to each of these forms of attack. Furthermore, the traditional threats (physical and procedural) are still a very important part of EC implementation and must be dealt with accordingly. What form of attack is of greatest concern will depend on the type of EC application implemented. Adversaries range from pranksters, proving their abilities among their peers, to serious thieves. Pranksters act overtly and simplistically with actions such as modification and denial of service, whereas serious adversaries prefer being unnoticed by using such tactics as masquerading, sniffing, and penetrations (unauthorized use of IDs and passwords). Table 5.2 summarizes the previously mentioned threats with proposed preventative measures.

Table 5.2 EC Threat Analysis

Vulnerabilities	Threats	Consequences	Preventative Measures	EC Consequences
Modification	- Manipulation of source data. - Manipulation of message traffic in transit.	- Loss of information. - Compromise of business transaction.	- Digital signatures	- Misrepresentation of information. - Reduced legitimization of information. - Potential dispute issues.
Masquerading and sniffing	- Eavesdropping on the network. - Theft of information from source and destination. - Information about network configuration. - Information about which source talks to destination.	- Loss of information - Loss of privacy	- Authentication - Encryption	- Violation of customer privacy resulting in legal repercussions. - Compromise of relationship trust.
Denial of Service	- Killing source or destination requests or processes. - Flooding machine with bogus requests or processes. - Filling up disk or memory. - Isolating machine by DNS attacks.	- Disruptive - Annoying - Degradation of service levels.	- Firewalls	- Customer dissatisfaction. - Violation of service-level agreements. - Reputation for poor quality service.
Penetration	- Impersonation of legitimate users. - Data forgery.	- Misrepresentation of user. - Belief that false information is valid.	- Authentication - Encryption	- All of the above.

Cost of Risk Protection

As in all system implementations, some costs must be allocated to security enhancements. The costs of risk avoidance fall in two broad categories of technical and nontechnical expenses. Technical costs can include hardware, software, maintenance, training, upgrades, supplies, physical space requirements, and power. Nontechnical costs can consist of staff, training, installing, managing, upgrading, and monitoring the solution. And, finally, the time and convenience factors for making these decisions should not be ignored.

Securing EC systems is more of an art than a science. Protection against threats inevitably results in an exercise in economic risk analysis. Because there are no unconditional security mechanisms, the risk to the business must be weighed against the cost of avoiding adversary threats. Unfortunately, assessing information security risks is not as precise as one would like to believe. Security is a continuum. Perfect security is impossible, but a machine that is turned off and embedded in concrete comes the closest. For networked computers, cutting the network connection is the next best thing. Unfortunately, none of these options is practical for EC facilities. Instead, tradeoffs must be made between security, functionality, reliability, and cost. The issue is one of risk management. As indicated in Figure 5.3, investments in EC security are meant to offset the investment (rendering the compromising activity useless) required to penetrate the system (security leverage).

The key to choosing the right combination is to consider the value of what is being protected and the cost to protect it (asset). There are no $10,000 bike locks, because there are no bikes worth that much. In opposition, there are no bank vaults with cardboard doors because the value of what is being protected makes it worth an investment in a steel vault several feet thick. For your product, consider the potential for loss and the potential value to your company of that loss. What is the cost to decrease that risk potential (security implementation)? Are there solutions that reduce the risk to several aspects of the system? Could multiple layers of less-expensive solutions provide a better solution?

EC managers must also bear in mind the cost incurred from cross-impacts brought on by the securing of systems. Technical or nontechnical solutions may adversely affect the performance and quality of the service. Such situations may require bolstering of systems (capacity and facilities) and or processes (more staff) to compensate.

As indicated earlier in this chapter, risk analysis should be conducted during the design phase of a new EC system. And so EC managers, for greater accuracy and security effectiveness, should conduct these steps during system functionality definition.

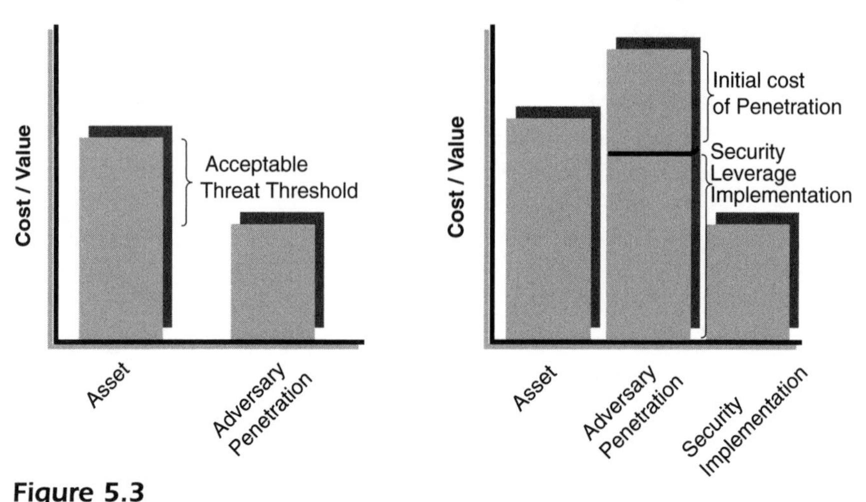

Figure 5.3
Security coverage.

Risk Management

Throughout this chapter, sets of activities and mechanisms for understanding, evaluating, and managing information–security threats have been outlined. Armed with this information, the EC manager must now decide what is the right security configuration for his or her EC solution. As such, tradeoffs between security, functionality, reliability, and cost will have to be conducted. The issue is one of risk management.

The method by which this is accomplished is to employ a process that best meets the needs of the organization and EC solution. The process, based on the previously mentioned practices in this chapter, should be flexible and serve the specific needs of the endeavor. There is no one standard process for EC solutions. However, we can offer a framework from which your organization can devise its risk management process. There are five elemental measures that must be considered for an effective risk management process: identification, classification, planning, tracking, and execution. Often the maturity of an organization's risk management capability is a function of its ability to effectively invoke these measures.

Identifying risks and the source of risks is conducted by creating a pool of risk information. This activity is typically conducted by soliciting information through question and answer sessions. EC managers are encouraged to ask questions such as, Are there any risks or problems? What uncertainty surrounds this issue? What are the assumptions? Critical to this process is to ensure that risk is discussed intelligently and in-depth. Risk must be distinguished from opportunities, issues, and problems. The cause of the risk must be made explicit in terms of uncertainty in time, control, or information.

The traditional methods of risk determination still apply and should be conducted within the context of this framework. Methods such as exposure-based risk determination—overlaying a taxonomy of known threats to the environment being analyzed, revealing areas of potential attack by adversaries—can limit the risk analysis to known quantities and allows for a rapid classification of risks. And, quantitative risk determination, which employs a theoretical approach, involving mathematical methods for identifying and classifying risks.

Classification of risks is a process of normalization to known quantities. Normalization reduces the level of ambiguity among all concerned with appropriately managing risk. Risks should be defined in terms of:

- *Impact.* The nature (cost, schedule, customer satisfaction, etc.) and magnitude of a risk's consequence.
- *Probability.* The likelihood that a risk's consequence will be realized if the current design is to be implemented (proactive) or current situation to continue (reactive).
- *Time frame.* The time during which the team can exercise proactive choices associated with a risk. Past this point, choices will be eliminated because it will be too late to make them.
- *Coupling.* The effect a risk's occurrence would have on risks and opportunities. When the risk becomes a problem, it may increase the probability of other risks, increasing their effect, limit the choices for dealing with them, or reduce the time frame for making choices about them.
- *Uncertainty.* Lack of understanding about the nature of a risk's probability or how it may vary over time.

Managers employing these terms will have greater success in understanding the nature of the risk and hence establish effective preventative measures.

Planning is the process whereby strategies for dealing with the risks are conceived. Classified risks must not be ignored; conscious steps must be spelled out to contribute to the overall definition of risk for the EC system. Managers should consider the following four risk strategies:

- *Mitigate.* Reduce the probability and/or impact of the risk through system enhancements.
- *Avoid.* Eliminate the possibility of a specific risk by choosing an alternative path. This often means trading one risk for others that are acceptable or easier to deal with.

- *Transfer.* Get someone else to share or assume the consequence of the risk. Insurance is a form of risk transfer.
- *Accept.* Plan a contingency, track the risk, and enact the plan if it becomes a problem. Managers should view these strategy tasks as action items to be executed.

Tracking provides an effective method for managers to guarantee that risk strategies are acted on. The risk classification acts as a trigger signaling the need to execute a risk strategy plan. Additionally, managers can conduct accurate and effective reviews, through tracking, as a means to establish predictability and accuracy in their risk management process.

Execution is exactly what it means, the execution of risk strategy plans once driven by the tracking mechanism.

Managers, auditors, coworkers, consultants, or those contributing actual money should embrace this framework as a means to understand risks associated with EC projects, the value of what could be lost, and the cost of solutions and decisions.

LAYERS OF RISK PROTECTION . . . .

In all likeliness, some number of technical solutions will be needed to secure your EC solution. At the heart of any EC endeavor is a complex set of systems driving out new relationships. There are several reasons for implementing security in layers rather than all at one level. The two keys are effectiveness and price. No software or hardware device is perfect, so it would be foolish to depend on one piece of software or hardware to be the sole protector of your facility. By layering solutions, a bug in one layer may be inconsequential because another layer affords protection against that problem. Simple solutions tend to be less costly than complex ones, another benefit of the layered approach.

For example, a machine may be secured by installing an all-encompassing security, which handles authentication, vulnerability detection, break-in monitoring, and network protection. Alternately, a firewall can provide network protection for all machines, and individual machines are secured by patch installation, unnecessary-facility removal, and a break-in monitoring package. The best solutions for a facility will depend on the security needs, staff expertise, and, of course, the assessed risks.

Perimeter

Perimeter security is essential, but generally not sufficient. A facility with perimeter defense only can be likened to an M&M candy. It's got a hard shell, but once the shell is cracked, it has a soft, chewy center. An M&M facility can lead to a false sense of security. The knowledge that a firewall is in place is frequently enough of a placebo that internal security is decreased or sometimes completely ignored. A full understanding of the vulnerabilities of such a facility is necessary to counter this feeling of well being.

Perimeters are broad security controls that control traffic between independent regions of transaction interactions. The premise is that there are distinguishable individuals or systems (networks, computers, and so on) that can be grouped together, based on varying levels of trust. Perimeters can be limited to two separated regions, such as an outside and an inside, or more sophisticated models can be created that may include perimeters within perimeters. The degree in which one would create new perimeters is entirely a function of a risk analysis and the derived benefits relative to the value of the asset. For instance, an obvious perimeter would be the separation of a corporate intranet from the Internet. Furthermore, an organization may elect to establish additional parameter within their intranet to protect human resource information systems from the general corporate information sources (intranet Web sites, and so on).

The first step in establishing a perimeter is to understand what requires fortification. Previously, Figure 5.2 depicted in-transit information threats. Figure 5.4 depicts information flows that represent potential points of access into source and destination internal information systems. This figure, a generalized model, reveals source and destination details that need to be considered in the perimeter model. The net result is the need for both a network information and access security perimeter model. Key areas of concern include network access points (public and private dial-in facilities) as well as alternative information flows that do not fall within the technical domain. An EC example is a credit card purchase from the Web site: how the information travels and is protected and how the merchant can ensure the consumer that it is safe to buy from his/her online store (the intent being to let prospective buyers see the value of security as an inducement to actual purchase; the merchant thus sees security as a business enhancement). Consider Figure 5.4 to be your roadmap highlighting major touchpoints that require protection in typical EC systems.

Firewalls are effective devices for establishing EC solution perimeters: boundaries between networks. Firewalls establish perimeters by building barriers between two or more connected networks with the intent of creating a private network and foreign network (public or other private). Firewalls are intended to control all pass-through traffic, to allow only authorized traffic to pass between regions, and to withstand any form of penetration. The common types of firewalls that exist include network layer packet-filtering, application layer gateways, and circuit layer gateways. All forms are important in the context of EC and in our experience rarely are any of these forms neglected in an implementation. Firewall security can range from lax (no security) to extremely sophisticated security schemas preventing all access if required. Effective as firewalls may be, they are not impervious to the transfer of viruses or other such volatile files. Furthermore, firewalls cannot prevent insider intrusion. Firewalls are gateways between networks and therefore do not add value within a contained network. The magazine article quoted earlier summarized firewalls as "practically useless *as stand-alone defenses*" (our emphasis added).

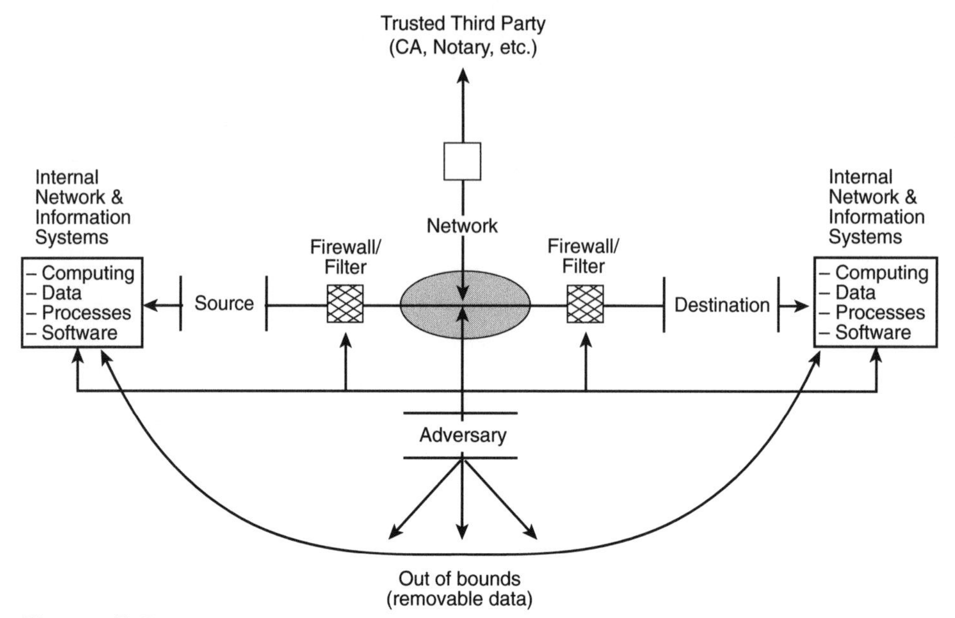

Figure 5.4
Possible points of attack/compromise.

Thus far, we have described the perimeter in terms of "outside" and "inside." When firewalls are combined with screening routers, sophisticated configurations can be created with varying levels of security. One such configuration not only establishes an internal and external region but also an intermediary region in between. This area is often referred to as the demilitarized zone (DMZ). Managers of EC solutions employing Internet Web services, which tie back to corporate data, would be remiss not to establish a DMZ. A DMZ can be thought of as a network structure that through configuration and policy establishes regions of security (low to high) where network devices can be physically connected. A typical DMZ is divided into three zones: Red, Yellow, and Green Zones (Figure 5.5). Red, being the riskiest zone, would be in the public domain where perhaps a corporate router may be located. The Yellow Zone would house services, such as the corporate Web and FTP sites. And finally, the Green Zone would be the tightly controlled corporate intranet.

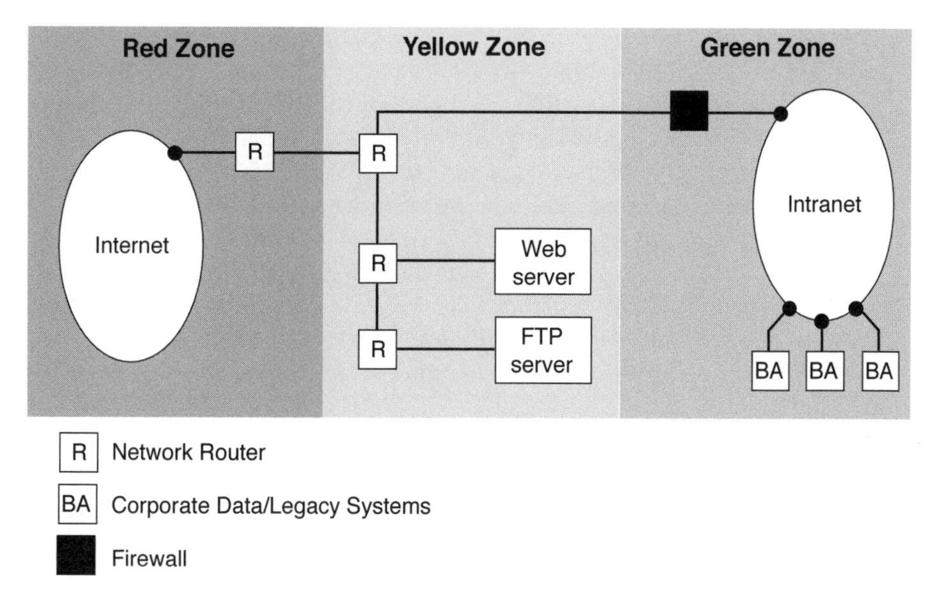

Figure 5.5
DMZ network security model.

User Authentication

Authentication validates that information is received from a desired source or is granted to a desired destination. Additionally, digital signatures (also referred to as digital certificates or digital IDs) extend the authentication process to include nonrepudiation (irrefutable proof) by either source of destination. The level of security that authentication provides establishes preventive measures for the following threats: sniffing, masquerading, modification, and some measure of protection for penetration. A process is known to be authenticating if it requests something that is either known, composed of, or possessed. An everyday example is when a retailer asks you for your driving license to authenticate your check payment.

What drives the simplest form of authentication is based on what is known, such as passwords. Access to data or systems can be granted to those who possess a recognized identification and associated password. Passwords do not provide any additional value beyond basic authentication. They are also easy targets for adversaries and act as a base level of security.

A more sophisticated form of authentication is based on a possession, such as an encryption algorithm with a unique key or tokens. The level of trust of an authentication process is enhanced through the use of centrally administered unique devices. Furthermore, depending on the type of devices used, the added value of data confidentiality and integrity may be realized. Tokens are physical devices injected with a shared symmetric key and algorithm. The authentication process for tokens is straightforward, beginning with the user authenticating into a system with an ID along with a number generated by token (utilizing the shared symmetric key). The system calculates a number from the source ID and shared asymmetric key and then compares it with the source's generated number. If the values are the same, the user is authenticated. Many companies use security cards for this purpose; the card contains information that is processed before one is allowed entry.

An important development from the work of asymmetric key cryptography is the digital signature. It is not, of course, a real signature, but a series of digital bits that serves the same purpose and is far harder to forge. They associate a message with a unique source, which may be a device or a person, depending on the EC function. Digital signatures provide a unique set of security features that are unlike any other implementation; they include confidentiality, data integrity, and nonrepudiation. Nonrepudiation occurs when the destination has trust in the legitimacy of the source's public key. Authentication with digital signatures is conducted through the exchange of messages encrypted by the source's private key and decrypted by the destination utilizing the source's complementary public key. Authentication occurs if the message is successfully decrypted. An important application of this model is that of mutual authentication protocols. The mutual authentication protocol enables parties to mutually authenticate one another and to exchange a one-time symmetric session key. One-time session keys extend the level of trust in the security system by limiting the key's usefulness to the current session.

Digital signatures are only effective if a trust relationship between sources and destinations exists. They are expensive to set up and implement and thus are not practical for one-time or occasional interactions. It means that this sophisticated approach to security works well for small interacting pockets of sources and destinations but breaks down for larger groups and relationships that lack the necessary trust. A typical application would be that of the exchange of e-mail between two trusted parties. John and Mary work together and have a need to exchange sensitive corporate information via e-mail over the Internet. At the office, John and Mary each create a public–private key pair (through a commercially available off-the-shelf piece of software) and exchange public keys. John encrypts all messages destined for Mary with Mary's public key as well as his own private key. When Mary receives any messages from John, she can validate him as the source by simply decrypting his message with his public key. If successful, Mary would feel confident that the message originated from John and would continue to decrypt the e-mail with her private key to gain access to its contents.

Public Key Infrastructure (PKI)

A more ubiquitous trust model is required for the broader use of digital signatures. Certificate authorities (CAs) provide this. CAs are in effect online notarized signatures. Broad-based public key technology for security purposes requires a public-key infrastructure (PKI) to securely manage public keys for widely distributed users or systems. The Internet Engineering Task Force (IETF) X.509 standard constitutes a widely accepted basis for such an infrastructure, defining data formats and procedures related to distribution of public keys via certificates digitally signed by CAs. A certificate can be thought of as an electronic passport containing standardized information for properly identifying an individual, system or software. The contents of a certificate includes: name, organization, address, issuing authority's (certification authority) digital signature and identification information, public key of the person who will be issued the digital certificate, dates of validity of the digital certificate, class of certificate (further subdivision based on privilege), and digital identification certificate number.

The certificate authority is a third party, trusted in its ability to register, certify, issue, expire, and revoke digital certificates on behalf of the general public or community of interest. The question of whether a CA can provide the level of assurance required for EC solutions depends on the CA capability and credibility to operate—typically measured relative to the standards of the institution requiring the service. Analyses of CA tend to focus on community and applicability, identification and authentication, key management, local security, technical security, and operations policy. Banks and legal organizations are obvious candidates for CAs, but they may have a conflict of interest in their role in EC. The authorities must obviously be highly trusted for them to play a central role in trust relationships. The promises of PKI are substantial, but the development of such an infrastructure is by no means a simple task. PKI services have evolved by way of the outsourcing model and cater well to the medium to small sized business that simply cannot afford to establish a PKI. However, larger organizations such as banks and governments will need to determine whether or not they will act as a certificate authority themselves or outsource to the likes of IBM, Equifax, or VeriSign.

One thing is for sure, the confidence in the industry with PKI is very high. PKI-enabled technologies are being developed at a phenomenal rate and are only expected to grow. For instance, most if not all Web browsers and e-mail systems support digital certificates and most even have many of the prominent PKI's digital certificate (VeriSign, Microsoft, GTE CyberTrust, KeyWitness, and others) shipped with the product. Analysts such as the Global Research Unit of the Union Bank of Switzerland, DataMonitor, and others predict the market for PKI will be worth near or more than $1 billion in 2001. The inevitability of PKI is written on the wall. All that remains for the organizations wishing to use PKI is to understand its implications and implement it in a way that won't circumvent its benefits—hence our purpose in this book.

Other Authentication Techniques

For transactions, information exchange requiring the utmost security, the highest form of individual authentication is one involving physiological (fingerprints, handprints, and retinal scans) or behavioral (vocal patterns, signature, and keystroke patterns) characteristics. The accuracy of these authentication mechanisms is very high and although not commonly used, are becoming more mainstream. Such techniques are not uncommon to governments, particularly the defense department involved in the exchange of top secret information related to matters of national security.

As such authentication technologies become more prevalent, the use of any of these mechanisms very often runs counter to laws, practices, or consumer consent in such areas as privacy, discrimination, and civil liberties. Here again, this is a risk/cost tradeoff between business risk and social cost.

Access Control and Authorization

The burgeoning of EC over public networks has introduced interesting access control and authorization complexities. Access control is concerned with governance over a party's ability or right to enter or access a zone or service, whereas authorizations grant permission or power to functions or services within a given zone of access. Appropriate access control is crucial to the success of any service intending to leverage public networks. The basic elements of access control policy include an object (system, program, database, and so on), a subject (external entities accessing objects) and access rights (the way in which subjects access objects). These three elements are typically organized in access matrixes, control lists, and capability lists. These elements form the basis for effective access control management. Diligence is of utmost importance when constructing these devices, for they must withstand the transgressions of adversaries. Given the dynamic nature of EC, the need for diligent access control is only amplified.

The access matrix is a representation of both access control and capability lists. The matrix can be decomposed into distinct access control lists (ACL). For each object, there is an ACL with a list of subjects who are permitted access rights. The matrix is further decomposed into distinct capability lists. For each subject, there is a capability list with a list of authorized objects and operations for a subject. Figure 5.6 is a representation of a generic access control structure.

Whereas access control policies are crucial in any strong authentication scheme, enforcement is where the rubber hits the road. Traditional access control enforcement has and continues to be primarily managed by the discrete business applications, each with its own version of an ACL function. An organization faced with four business applications and a network operating system can expect its staff to have up to as many as five unique user IDs and passwords. As messy as this sounds, it gets worse. EC exacerbates the issue by providing broader access to many applications.

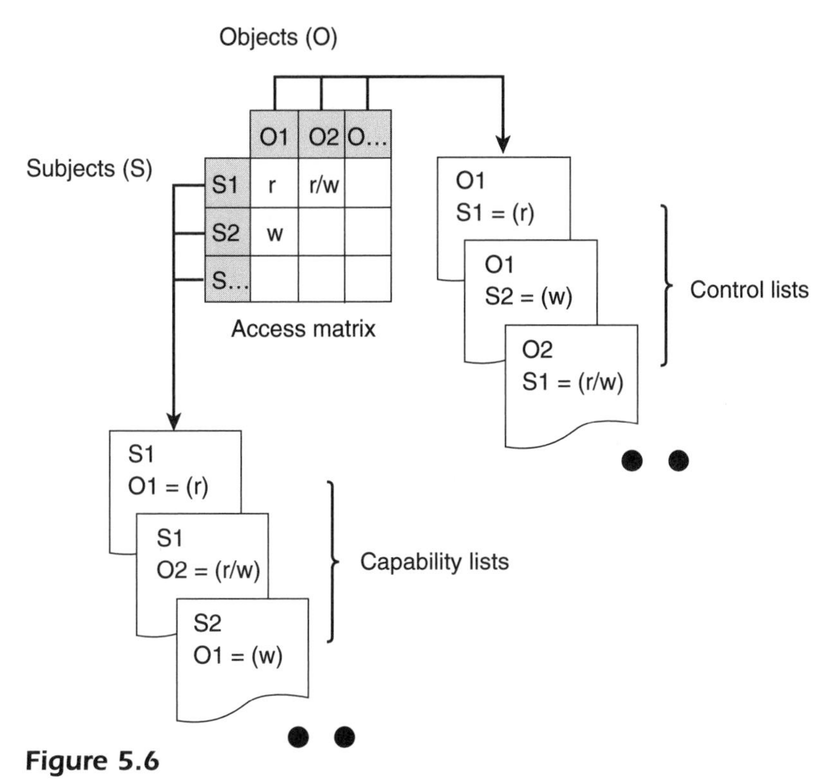

Figure 5.6
Composition and interrelation of access control elements.

Ironically, centralized access control mechanisms have existed for some time, but not until the Internet have they begun to reveal themselves. Directory services, typically X.500 databases, in conjunction with the Light Weight Directory Access Protocol (LDAP) authentication protocol, create the foundation for a centralized authentication mechanism. LDAP was originally based on the IETF's Directory Access Protocol (DAP). DAP supported a broader set of functionality, whereas LDAP supports only authentication (both plain text and Kerberos), allowing users authenticated access to sensitive information in corporate directories. LDAP provides secure access to "passwords" in a central directory/repository. This repository can then be used by independent corporate applications as a means of user authentication.

LDAP was initially designed for IP networks and is very easy to implement. Today, most business applications offer the ability to utilize an external access control mechanism—LDAP more often then not. Vendors such as Netware, Lotus, and Microsoft have given users LDAP interfaces on their proprietary directories in an attempt to woo organizational dependency to their products. This may prove to be a viable approach for some organizations; however, these directories tend not to offer the flexibility and performance required for EC applications. Additionally, network operating systems are not, strictly speaking, designed purely for access control and tend not to be as secure as dedicated solutions.

The Kerberos protocol extends the LDAP authentication model to provide access control privileges to systems–applications offering one of the highest levels of user and system access control presently available. Kerberos uses secret-key ciphers for authentication and encryption and is becoming a de facto standard for remote authentication in client–server environments. Kerberos' client–server design centralizes the authentication process for multiple systems in a secure way, an important consideration in networked environments.

Kerberos provides single-sign-on (SSO) services: the ability to access multiple computer systems or networks after logging in once with a single user ID and password. This setup resolves the common situation in which separate passwords and user IDs are required for each application. SSO has three major advantages for organizations:

- user convenience
- administrative convenience
- improved security

The benefits of SSO have been widely demonstrated. Having only one sign-on per user instead of ten makes administration easier. It also eliminates the possibility that users will write down their ten passwords in order to remember them all, thereby compromising security. Finally, SSO enhances productivity by reducing the amount of time that users spend gaining system access.

Information Transformation Layers and Associated Security Schemes

Information destined for network travel must traverse several layers: the application layer, the transport layer, and the network layer. Not only do these layers offer flexibility in the management of network messages but also introduce areas of security compromise. As a result, various security mechanisms have been designed and implemented for each of the application, transport, and network layers. Each of these layers is distinct and requires independent skill sets. EC managers must make it a priority that their hardware, network and communications, and applications specialists address all levels in the design phase of the solution. Neglecting to do so could result in compromising the effectiveness of the risk analysis and management processes. Figure 5.7 is an illustration of the aforementioned layers and their relative security implementations (shaded areas represent security implementations). It is conceivable that combinations of network, transport, and application

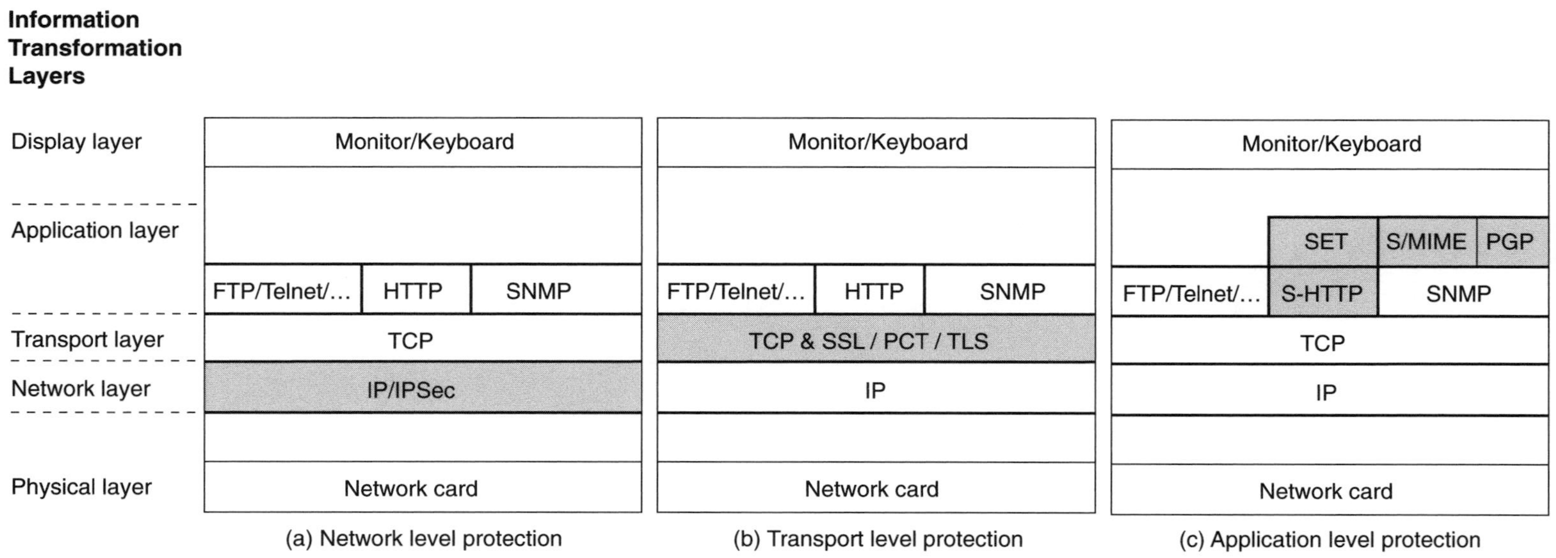

Figure 5.7
EC information transformation layers and associated security techniques.

layers could be arrived at for added security. Such implementation should be examined closely as to not add additional complexity and cost for a marginal difference in security.

The network layer (Fig. 5.7a) protection cuts across all layers and offers non-intrusive methods for secure exchange information. Internet Protocol (IP) is responsible for managing information packets on behalf of higher level applications. IP already is one of the more popular means of managing packets and has most relevance in our context of EC. It is close to certain that it will become not only the core of data communications for EC but also for phone services through what is termed Voice-over IP, a development that is gathering fast momentum.

In itself, IP does not guarantee the delivery, integrity, or origin of information packets. These functions are typically managed by higher level applications. Applying security at the IP level can secure networks for not only applications that have security mechanisms but also for security-ignorant applications. IP security (IPSec) utilizes symmetric and asymmetric key technology to facilitate the functions of authentication, confidentiality, and integrity. A common application of IPSec would be secure virtual secure private networks (SVPNs). Network layer security is typically quick, costly, and rigid—requiring expertise and associated technology for configuration and utilization. Network layer protection is an excellent means of establishing secure communications between trusted partners over public networks for EC solutions.

The transport layer (Fig. 5.7b), much like the network layer, cuts across all layers. The network layer manages information at a packet level, whereas the transport level manages information based on sessions. Secure socket layer (SSL) is one such implementation of transport layer of protection. A SSL session is defined as the secured association between a client and a server, (between the points on a network). SSL provides authentication (typically the server only) with digital certificates, confidentiality utilizing symmetric session keys, as well as message integrity and nonrepudiation with digital signatures. SSL also helps to avoid expensive negotiations of new secure sessions for each application by allowing multiple connections per session. Comparable solutions to SSL are Private Communications Technology (PCT), Microsoft's entry into the fray and Transport Layer Security (TLS), an Internet Engineering Task Force (IETF) Standard. PCT and TLS virtually mirror SSL with some minor differences. Given that PCT and TLS' are late entries as compared to SSL, and SSL's strong support in the business community, it is difficult to see either gaining much acceptance and use. The use of SSL is quite a pervasive and effective method for EC solutions for establishing secure Web-based session security.

The application layer (Fig. 5.7c) security is simply the embedding of security into business applications or programs. Unlike the network and transport layers, the application layer security mechanisms cannot be shared between applications; each application manages security independently from the other, sometimes replicating like functions. Application layer security implementations are comparable in functionality to other layer implementations. Furthermore, they are not burdened by the progression of standards and are free to explore new innovative applications of cryptography. A prime example is SET. SSL could not offer the necessary functionality required for secure credit card transactions over the Internet. As such, an applications-level implementation was undertaken to facilitate rapid solution. In all likelihood, SET, on greater adoption, will shift from the application layer to the transport layer and become a generic service for other applications. Some other notable applications include Secure Mime (S/Mime) and Pretty Good Privacy (PGP). It is our opinion that S/Mime, through the use of digital certificates issued by a trusted CA, will play a significant role in commercial EC, whereas, PGP (and like technologies) will play a role with noncommercial interactions (personal e-mail).

SOCIAL ASPECTS OF SECURITY . . . .

Information security measures are designed to prevent unauthorized individuals or systems from affecting, viewing, accessing, or preventing access to organizational systems or data. Earlier in this chapter, we addressed how proper technical solutions can thwart any technical threat posed by an adversary. Unfortunately, the noxious efficacy of adversaries is not limited to technical infiltration. Furthermore, as indicated in Chapter 2, EC has a tendency to amplify these social issues.

Social Engineering

Social engineering is the term applied to adversaries that elicit confidential security information (employee IDs, passwords, entry codes, and so on) through social interactions. Organizations with complex social structures are challenged with staff that is not fully aware of IT security policies and guidelines. Adversaries, through stochastic—apparently random, rather than predictable—methods, expose such weaknesses through planned attacks on naive staff. These attacks may range from random telephone calls asking staff for their IDs and passwords to adversaries posing as security guards or cleaners to gain access to secured areas.

Although social engineering tactics do not follow any one method (typically random attacks), some general approaches can be described. In the context of EC, attacks typically being as reconnaissance missions, pinpointing generally available resources, such as Internet databases, telephone directories, and corporate publications. Over time, adversaries, through gathering and combining information, form a comprehensive view of the organization that includes corporate structure, names of senior staff (including locations and phone numbers), key projects, and other related information. Once enough information has been gathered, an adversary may either construct a persona or assume the identity of various influential staff members. Trusting, commanding, (bribery and collusion) or intimidating relationships are formed through basic interactions with internal staff, which may be conducted in person, by telephone, or by e-mail. At this point, the adversary simply attempts to obtain critical information that may assist them in penetrating information systems. Common points of attack include mailrooms (good source of cost center numbers and employee IDs), network support (requesting resetting forgotten passwords), and receptionists and secretaries (key staff telephone numbers and scheduling).

Although these attacks seem complicated, proficient adversaries achieve success with little time and effort. Social engineering can be effectively averted with the appropriate controls. The key controls most effective at containing social engineering includes security awareness programs, security escalation systems, and institute social engineering penetration tests.

Information **security awareness programs** form an effective first level of protection. Internal staff's attention must be drawn to security-related issues and the implications they may have on them and the organization: Undermining the success of the organization effectively undermines the success of the individual. As in any effective awareness program, staff must buy into information security policy and must internalize the policies that are disseminated during education sessions.

EC solutions must also extend the awareness program to their customers. In some instances, security awareness is embedded into the technology. Digital certificates are an example of such practices that include policy and practice statements in the very standard itself.

Security escalation systems are crucial mechanisms to contain thwarted repeating attacks. Without such a mechanism, detected attackers may simply proceed or escape, knowing there is no way for staff to alter the breach of security. Furthermore, areas within organizations with weak security escalation systems represent key targets for adversaries. Consumers of EC systems also require an escalation channel. Comparable service would be those of credit card security hotlines/call centers.

Social engineering penetration tests are effective at examining instituted security policy. The process can be utilized as a baseline for the implementation of preventive measures. This can establish the organization's capability and maturity in thwarting future attacks. Once a baseline is established, new policy can be formed that best suits the characteristics and dynamics of the organization. Careful attention should be placed on such activities, ensuring that whereas reputable firms may be used, company policy may require appropriate consent from senior executives. Furthermore, such reports should be protected at all costs, for they will reveal weaknesses within the corporate social structure.

Removable Data

Data access is no longer a view from the monolithic central computing facility. Laptops, home offices, replicated databases (such as Lotus Notes, where copies of databases are maintained across the network, making them faster and easier to access and harder to protect), flex hours, hotel offices, remote mail and address books, data warehouses, knowledge–information bases, and the largest culprit of them all, EC, have created a world of removable data. Although the benefits associated with the foregoing are measurably substantial, they can be easily undermined through inappropriate access to distributed data. Such removable data, if deemed vital to the success of the organization, must be managed in a manner that addresses all potential threats. Basic measures, such as virus protection, personal encryption (system and files) and backup prove to be effective mechanisms against potential compromise. However, for these mechanisms to be effective, simple policies must be developed and strictly followed. The use of a private key escrowed PKI is the only effective manner in which removable data can be controlled. All users or systems that manage removable data would own a public and private key, along with a digital certificate, with one added twist—the PKI would not only maintain a copy of the public key but also the private key. The design of this approach is to ensure that the organization (the owner of the data) is capable of retrieving the contents of the removable repository (laptop or otherwise).

Legal Aspects

Business transactions over the information superhighway, the domain of EC, have no precedent defining potential legal obligations, risks, and liabilities. The issues of time, distance, and regional regulations associated with traditional forms of commerce do not apply to EC. Traditional commercial law must be extended to consider the unique circumstances of conducting business via EC. As a guideline, organizations planning to engage in EC must carefully consider the following key legal issues: legal provisions, regulatory restrictions, reliability of commercial records, data transmission, intellectual property protection, and segregation of privileged information.

Legal provisions, typically associated with consumer interactions, are concerned with the stipulation of notices, terms and conditions, bindings, acceptance, and warnings. Such provisions are typically overt and succinct methods of at-the-moment communication with parties engaging in EC. They are dynamic devices (dialog boxes, confirmation buttons, and so on) that can be inserted prior to actions that may result in potential risk or liability.

Regulatory restrictions are rules and regulations that describe conduct for domestic and international business transactions. Given that EC resides in a society without borders—not protected by the well-established legal controls—organizations planning to engage in international EC must replicate or maintain existing precedence for international business conduct.

Reliability of commercial records is concerned with appropriate standards for record maintenance (tax, customs, and so on). Therefore, organizations with customers in multiple jurisdictions will need to adhere to the multiple regulatory requirements.

Data transmission issues must be negotiated between all parties involved in an EC business transaction. Due to the decentralized nature of networks and the Internet, transactions through a contracted carrier may traverse multiple telecommunications carriers. This may result in less-than-desirable transaction service or flows (undesirable jurisdictions). Careful review of the chosen telecommunications carrier should be conducted, with special attention on its subcontracting and affiliate arrangements.

Intellectual property protection pertains to organizations maintaining rights of ownership to systems and services offered on the information superhighway. EC services, specifically the Web, are easily replicated. Organizations must be prepared to enforce their intellectual property rights in multiple jurisdictions.

Segregation of privileged information seeks to protect the identities and confidentiality of information associated with EC business transactions. EC services, by nature, accumulate vast amounts of information. Such information represents an excellent pool for exploitation (good and bad). Organizations are held accountable to contain such information or risk liability.

Retaining Expertise

The assumption that technology can replace human knowledge has been proven false time and time again. Knowledge is the embodiment of information in the minds of human beings. Furthermore, knowledge develops over time, through experience that includes what is absorbed from courses, books, and information learned from mentors. "Experts," Latin for "to put to the test," are people with a deep knowledge of a subject who have been tested and trained by experience.

As described earlier in this chapter, EC information security is a complex process requiring expertise and knowledge to succeed in guarding organizational assets while not compromising their net value. Organizations need to bear in mind that information relating to EC security implementation can be maintained by systems. However, knowledge of security implementations can only be maintained within the minds of those individuals involved (staff, vendors, outsource partners, and so on). The challenge for effective organizations will be how well they protect or maintain access to such information security knowledge.

Effective management of human capital for the purpose of retaining expertise is crucial in any successful information security management. Organizational human capital can include internal staff and outsource contracts with third-party organizations. Typically, organizational confidentiality, risk, and level of skill versus occurrence matters dictate the distinction between the use of either internal or external staff.

Our advice for organizations involved in EC is to consider the following:

- Choose partners with demonstrated abilities.
- Build strategic (extending the legal relationship) relationships with partners privy to sensitive security configurations.
- Reevaluate staff compensation based on currently available skills in the marketplace.
- Establish staff selection criteria based on the contents of this chapter for the purpose of consulting better experts.

EC stands at a critical juncture. After an exhilarating start-up, the issues of security and trust may stand to inhibit its continued growth. The need for security is consistent with all systems implementations. However, due to the complex relationship of EC, the associated risks are far greater than traditional systems implementations. As such, innovative and unprecedented methods are employed to contend with these challenges. A large part of the success of any EC application lies in the priority that bulletproof security has in the implementation and organization.

6

Looking After Business: The Core Components of Electronic Commerce

Electronic Commerce is about "commerce" first and "electronic" second. Within the next few years, the very term electronic commerce (EC) may become an oxymoron—just like military intelligence and airline cuisine. Today, most commerce is nonelectronic; however, that is changing very quickly, and almost every company looks at EC as integral to its future innovation. Simply put, managers think of EC in terms of possibilities, innovations, and new customer relations—that is, they focus on the *uses* of EC. They can do this without knowing much about its details: practices, procedures, and standards. Business innovation is their end, and EC is their means. Obviously, means and end have to be brought together, and in this chapter we present to business managers what has to be looked after to ensure that strategy turns into practical implementation and operations.

The questions many managers ask are:

- Is that what EC signifies?
- Did it only begin with the popularization of the Internet?
- What exactly is EC anyway?
- Does the Internet remove the need for EDI? (In other words, is EDI dead?)
- How can I gain real value from using EC?

These are the types of questions that face the business community today and, along with the introduction of these new concepts and processes, there are many fears, concerns, and issues related to the management and control of these new processes.

EC AS A CATALYST FOR CHANGE

In fact, EC is something that has been around for several decades, in forms of activity that we take for granted. The simple explanation is that EC is doing business through the use of electronic media and technologies. Using e-mail and other tools, even a fax can be considered an extension of the EC concept. Why, then, is there so much discussion about EC as a new phenomenon?

This renewed interest in the concept of EC is related more to the new activities and innovations in the business environment, at the level of the application of business processes and the very way business is conducted. The traditional forms of commerce that have been the foundation of commerce for over a century—where a paper purchase order is issued to a well-known supplier, followed by the shipment of goods, and finally an invoice and payment cycle—is changing, radically changing.

The true impact of EC is not in the fact that the paper purchase order can be sent electronically, but *whether it needs to be sent at all.* It is not that the invoice can be sent in a standardized electronic format, but whether an invoice is needed to prove the goods were received and should be paid for.

It is also becoming clear that the effective use of EC not only requires changes in traditional business process but also significantly changes the way an organization relates to its trading partners, government agencies, and other influential relationships.

- How does an organization manage itself without the use of paper documents?
- What are the concerns and issues that must be addressed to be a successful user of EC and related technologies?
- How does it relate to the traditions and expectation of its trading relationships?

An organization cannot unilaterally implement changes to its processes without the consent and participation of the important components of its relationship matrix. EC is no longer something that is occurring in specific relationships or on a "one-to-one" basis, but rather it is drawing in all relationships that organizations have, or will have, in the future.

EC means no more proprietary forms of electronic connections such as was the case with early forms of electronic order entry systems—or at least an evolution away from these highly controlled environments. The historical application of "human intervention" is no longer seen as a viable long-term approach. The use of human beings for data entry and management is costly and error prone. Only automated and integrated links from the transaction originator to the ultimate receiver will emerge as the long-term winner.

The key to EC is not simply the fact that commerce is conducted electronically, but that commerce itself requires integration and tighter links with trading partners and support organizations. All organizations are connected together in an "extended enterprise," with the success of the whole riding on the cooperation of all the individuals.

EC DEFINED

There are two general issues that emerge in defining EC: the business-to-consumer relationship and the business-to-business connection. Much of the popular view of EC, and most of the news articles, focuses on the business-to-consumer relationship. This refers to selling or promoting goods and services to individuals, taking orders and even payments, usually over the Internet. Whereas this is a new and not yet fully explored area of EC, most organizations are more concerned about the business-to-business implications of EC. What can it do to improve the operation of the business itself?

One view that aids in describing the effects of business-to-business EC suggests that it can exist in three broad states:

- person to person
- person to computer
- computer to computer

These three states form the basis for most of the technology applications that apply to the EC matrix and are critical in helping define what successful strategies and controls will evolve and thrive in the coming decades (see Table 6.1).

Person to Person

Most commonly, this covers activities in the spectrum of e-mail and fax. This is something that most individuals in the business community have been exposed to over the past several years and are able to relate to on a personal level of experience. In fact, e-mail is the fastest growing component of the EC matrix. Even though e-mail and fax use substantial amounts of technology to receive and deliver their messages and information, it is the human at either end who is able to decipher, define, and, if necessary, correct the intent of the message to ensure an appropriate action is taken. This allows for a massive amount of inference and interpretation to exist, and there can be major gaps in the information content of the message—but still a successful action or understanding may occur. Increasingly, proprietary e-mail systems have been integrated with external access facilitated by the Internet so that e-mail-based commerce is one of the fastest growing components in the EC matrix.

Person to Computer

Everything from the Automated Teller Machine (ATM) to electronic order entry to interacting with an Internet Web page involves the use of a template or preformatted computer-based activity. The result of this application of technology tools is that a computer program corrects entry errors before the information can be submitted, enforcing a message entry structure or process for the transaction to continue. This has typically been provided or operated under the auspices of a proprietary device, software program, or network environment, where the control points are provided to the data entry process in the system itself, not by the originator of the data. In the Internet world, this means that the order screen you are provided is totally constructed and controlled by the merchant, not by the customer, and formatting issues are resolved by the human who is inputting data before the data is sent.

Computer to Computer

This is where EDI and various forms of proprietary electronic data exchange (EDI) has fallen. In the case of tight relationships between a corporation and its trading partners, and where there are few companies in the relationship, then a nonstandard from of EDI has existed and has proven very effective. But with corporations globalizing and centralizing operations at the same time, there has been an increased demand for trading partners to meet recognized standards of both the message structure and the communications process. There are fewer and fewer compainies that wish to rely on the services of one supplier for their global needs, meaning that the diversity of trading relationships is increasing, and the need for standardized trading has increased accordingly.

The need for EDI as the common language and format for company-to-company transactions in the future will increase significantly rather than fade. This is even more likely as the use of the Internet widens the accessibility of electronic access and lowers the costs of data transfer and telecommunications.

Typically, EDI has been used in situations where there is a "one-to-many" or "many-to-one" business-to-business relationship, primarily because in a "one-to-one" relationship, it is easier and far more efficient for one of the parties (trading partners) to adapt to the other's message structure. This saves on the need to translate into another, intermediary structure and is often the basis of a mutually linked business process.

But when one of the trading partners is asked to connect to a large number of relationships, each of whom has a different system and message structure as well as varying accessibility times, major problems begin to emerge. Also, there are the further implications of managing separate systems in a vast network of interconnected environments, and implementing changes to these systems, all of which create an extremely complex management challenge. The application of EDI principles is often the only way that a satisfactory solution can be achieved.

Table 6.1 The EDI/e-mail/interactive Matrix

	Person to Person (e-mail, fax, etc.)	Person to Computer (e-forms, order entry)	Computer to Computer (EDI)
Speed of implementation	High	High	Low
Cost of implementation	Low	Medium	High
Accuracy	Low	Medium	High
Penetration in market	High	Medium	Low
Impact on reducing an organization's overhead costs	Low	Medium	High

EDI AS THE PRIMARY BUSINESS-TO-BUSINESS EC COMPONENT . . . .

EDI is a language and a process for EC, using standards agreed on by various groups. It allows the automation of the exchange of computerized files between different organizations that use perhaps incompatible computer systems.

Traditionally, information systems have focused on intraorganizational automation needs. Today, exchanging information between organizations is like sending goods across incompatible railway systems. Without standards, considerable efforts are required at each intersection. EDI facilitates the interorganizational information exchange from a technical perspective. Initially, like the standardization of the railway gauges, EDI simply facilitates the movement of information between organizations. Once an extensive infrastructure has been built and a critical mass of users has been reached, progressive organizations use EDI to change the way of interacting with their suppliers and customers, reach new markets, tap into new resources, and reengineer their business processes.

Real economic benefits and fundamental changes are realized when a majority of organizations start to use the system in a common business support system, reaching a critical mass within the entire trading relationship. This requires changes to the way these businesses relate to one another and how they actually do business among themselves. And once the changes have occurred, only those who are able to adapt to the effective use of the new business processes can survive.

As stated, EDI is the language and process for corporate EC. Without the conventions and structures for data exchange that have been developed over the past several decades, the concept of using EC for the business process is unimaginable. With the popularization of the Internet as a channel for EC, there have been some suggestions that it will displace, or even replace, the use of EDI.

In this context, EDI is seen as the whole system, rather than the agreements and process for business information. It is unlikely that EDI as we know it will go away in the foreseeable future; rather, it will be strengthened by the additional options of delivery and reach provided by the Internet and other channels.

EDI is the focal point for commercial EC—it is important to consider its evolution and impact on the marketplace.

THE EC VALUE PROPOSITION

The development of EC has yielded a plethora of new online tools that are beginning to have a profound effect on business in several areas, such as:

1. sales
2. customer service
3. procurement
4. information management and dissemination to internal resources

These areas are experiencing major changes in how they approach their challenges for successful business process and are looking to EC as a tool to help them achieve their goals.

Sales

This has begun to see a significant growth in the use of electronic catalogs, which initially supplemented printed catalogs and then evolved into electronic versions. For products that have either a wide consumer distribution or that are rapidly changing (price or specifications), the electronic catalog has emerged as a highly flexible and cost-effective EC tool. Also, the use of electronic forms or e-forms, which are preformatted order forms that can directly input data into a company's order entry system, can lower errors and costs for data entry. There is also the increasing use of the Internet to facilitate electronic bidding, either for auction-like situations or for submissions of quotes. In either case, the structure of the message is formatted to the receiver's specifications and allows for input of the data into an automated qualifying process, which ensures that all compulsory or critical data fields are included and speeds up the evaluation process.

Customer Service

Evolving out of the telephone approach of 1-800 numbers, the use of the Internet as a tool for customer service is now finding its way into the mainstream. Obviously, the replacement of a phone call with an e-mail is one example of how EC can be used. The more-effective EC users are finding the Internet to be a tool for collaboration between areas of expertise, different departments, or different companies. As technology has grown, so has the complexity and cost of maintaining customer service facilities. The use of EC and the Web, through Frequently Asked Questions (FAQ), chat lines, and direct interaction, has become almost commonplace. New uses of the Web for video teleconferencing and voice communications actually can increase the personal touch rather than decrease it.

Using EC effectively means developing a "pull customer in" philosophy, rather than a "push product out" approach. This involves a rethinking of how a company responds to customers' needs and, in fact, how it defines its business. Companies who have adopted EC as a platform for customer interaction do not look at EC as something to do; rather, it is inconceivable for them to do anything otherwise. Whether this involves a Web-enabled customer access channel or a full-blown electronic relationship across all functions of an organization, success is defined by the fact that EC is just there, like the telephone and fax.

Procurement

The use of EDI continues to grow for procurement activities. In fact, over the past decade, the use of procurement EDI has been increasing by an average of 20% per year. Further applications of EC are now introducing the e-form as an important new way of fulfilling ordering in lower volume situations. An e-form is simply a preformatted screen, often accessible through the Web, which requires a minimum amount of data to be entered in order to be allowed to be transmitted. Once filled in, the data is then converted into a machine-readable format (often EDI) and loaded directly into the appropriate application. This approach removes the physical effort of repeatedly key-entering data, and it lowers costs.

Another approach that is rapidly becoming a major EC force is the use of the procurement card. The procurement, or purchasing, card is a relatively recent phenomenon that applies the principle of the consumer-based credit card and its support infrastructure, but its focus is on supporting business-purchasing activities. Procurement cards work best for low-dollar, high-volume activities, such as buying office supplies.

Procurement Cards

In many organizations, low dollar buying activities account for as much as 70% of total purchasing transaction volume, yet they commonly represent less than 10% of total money spent. Often, the administration of these activities can exceed the prices of the actual purchases (as much as $130 per transaction). In these cases, conventional electronic business purchasing techniques, such as EDI, do not fit well because of the effort needed to administrate the ordering process and enroll the supplier. By charging the items to a procurement card, many costly manual procedures disappear or are streamlined.

The key values of such a card are to:

- increase efficiency by reducing the paperwork required to manage small-value transactions
- reduce inventory and space requirements by acquiring low-value commodity products as they are needed
- lower the overall cost per transaction
- exercise more control over purchasing and payables through improved tracking of the financial activity
- improve supplier relations by using a tool that has almost immediate payment (as opposed to the supplier waiting 30-plus days for an invoicing cycle)
- obtain supplier discounts, where volume can be established

Information Management and Dissemination to Internal Resources

This is an area that is often referred to as an intranet or limited-access Internet. Through this medium, employee notices, work flow changes, and even job postings can be distributed to select individuals, who must have a password and access rights to obtain the information they need. Some companies, like Silicon Graphics, have been placing their Human Resources manuals online, using the intranet as a distribution tool for information about staff requirements and to distribute corporate policies as well.

BUSINESS ISSUES . . . .

Beginning in the transportation and logistics industry as far back as the 1940s, the application of the Just-in-Time (JIT) inventory process required effective communication and management tools in order to be successful. The automotive industry began to refine these logistics processes in the late 1970s and quickly became aware that a common process and language for ordering and managing materials and inventory were critical factors of their industry's success.

For example, an automotive paint supplier in the late 1970s typically required over 750 separate interactions with its customer, from the initial color specifications to the final product shipment. In the paper-based commerce world, the cost and time to communicate the individual events took months, even years, before the paint was on the car. Now, these same processes have been refined and, supported by electronic order processes, can be accomplished in mere hours. The EC component was a key driver in this accomplishment, but it was changing the way the order process itself was designed that had the most profound effect. Rather than the car manufacturer having total and absolute control over the paint, from its color to its chemistry, the responsibility for this task was outsourced as well: a much greater impact than electronic ordering.

Studies had shown General Motors that the cost reduction from introducing EDI to the inventory management process would reduce the cost of building a car by over $200. By the late 1980s, none of the "Big Three" automobile manufacturers could operate without highly refined, EDI-based, order management and logistics processes. By the mid 1990s, none of these manufacturers generates paper orders for *any* materials to build a car—it is entirely electronic.

But it was not simply the use of electronic ordering that made the significant impacts. The introduction of Evaluated Receipt Settlement (ERS) had a profound impact on the use of EC and EDI. ERS was based on the concept that if the original order request was fulfilled, that is if all the parts arrived on time and as ordered, there was really no need for an invoice. Instead, a payment could be made based on the receipt of goods alone. A major improvement to the cost of operation, because rather than trying to refine the invoicing process, ERS eliminated the entire step. At the same time, there had to be better controls and information exchange between the receiving dock and the Accounts Payable department.

Other industries have closely followed suit. The retail industries, both food retail and general merchandise, have introduced similar forms of JIT inventory control and management to their supplier base. This has led to the application of even more-sophisticated inventory management techniques, the furthest-reaching to date being Vendor Managed Inventory (VMI). In a VMI relationship, the supplier is given total access to the inventory status of the retailer. In this way, the supplier can judge how much material is consumed and is responsible for ensuring the required inventory quotas are met on a continuous basis. Having access to the retailer's inventory position, not only for its own products, but also of all other products, even its competitors', can be seen as a risk by some retailers. This is a major component of what is the most important element in the future world of electronic business process—trust. As mentioned in Chapter 1, it is trust that is at the core of all successful application of EC.

Even though these concepts have been around for many decades, there is still a relatively small number of businesses that are using EDI and EC on a large-scale basis. The World Bank, in its Technical Paper No. 317, in November 1995, estimated that worldwide there are only about 100,000 business using EDI, over half of which are in North America. Other estimates range as high as 150,000–200,000. Even so, this is a nominal percentage of the total possible millions of businesses that could be using EC and EDI.

The key factor in the successful use of EC and EDI is the recognition that it is primarily a business, rather than a technical, issue. The use of EC must be based on the clear and established intent to accomplish a business objective, such as reducing inventory, lowering personnel costs, speeding up access to information, or reducing errors. *EDI is the key business-to-business EC tool, facilitated through technology.*

The components of EC technology have become commodity products, leaving the major factors of change to the business process as the primary force and cost. The desire to use EC can invoke a major change to the culture of any organization, often more than the impact to the organization's systems, so the factors affecting its use and implementation need to be keyed toward the minimization or control of the human impact of the process.

TECHNICAL ISSUES

There are four technical elements to any business-to-business EC system:

1. communications
2. data storage and retrieval
3. message conversion—and the related standards, if applicable
4. application interface

Communications

Communications refers to the use of telecommunications or other methods of transferral of electronic data. A key element in the EDI component of EC is the mandatory use of a positive or negative acknowledgment of the receipt of the transaction in an automated fashion. This means that for every electronic document, a corresponding response that confirms that the transaction was accepted or declined is returned to the sender. This is not necessarily the case in e-mail or interactive forms of EC, although a sender can request an acknowledgment of the message from the receiver. Very few e-mail users do this.

In the past, if two organizations wished to communicate electronically, they would have to spend a period of time resolving not only data transfer speed issues, but also data transmission protocols, timing, log-on and password IDs, and so on, as well as the data standards issues. This could be a time-consuming and frustrating experience that would have to be repeated with every trading partner.

Value-Added Networks

There are a number of companies providing facilities for the transfer and management of electronic messages between trading partners, acting as a public data network. A value-added network (VAN) provides not only the message transfer capability but also a number of services to assist the trading parties in managing their data.

Most VANs provide the communications and mail boxing facilities, as mentioned previously, as their basic services. They also may provide a form of access control security by ensuring that passwords and logon IDs are correctly used. Some networks allow the movement of encrypted or authenticated data as well. When the popularity of the Internet began to be a factor in the early 1990s, many felt that VANs would no longer be needed or certainly would not be as dominant in the intermediation business. The reality is that the major VANs have fully embraced the Internet, and most of the top commercial providers of Internet services, organizations like GE Information Systems, IBM Global Network, Sterling Commerce, Harbinger, BCE Emergis, and AT&T are all dominant VANs in their own right.

Data Storage and Retrieval

One of the main components of any EC application is the setup and use of data storage and retrieval or a mailbox. There is a slight difference in the setup and operation of an EDI mailbox from a typical e-mail mailbox or even a voice-mail system, because an EDI mailbox contains a great deal more control and intelligence than other electronic storage systems.

This difference is for several reasons:

The nature of EDI is that the exchange is of structured business data, such as purchase orders, invoices, and remittance documents. Traditional EDI using VANs, rather than the Internet, use a mailbox to check the message to ensure that it has the correct location and general quantity of data as described by the data standards. This precludes any possibility of the equivalent of electronic junk mail, as the data must first pass through a series of checks to even be recognized as valid. This is a critical control element as well, ensuring that the proper structure of data provides an assurance that data integrity can be confirmed by system processes rather than through a postreview.

Because EDI is machine-readable data, fed directly from the output of another machine, there is the additional issue of controlling accessibility to the data itself. Most EDI mailboxes have this feature whereby an identification of both sender and receiver is stringently applied. This is a critical business issue because, in fact, the data-receiving organization is facilitating the updating of its business systems by its trading partner. Controls that can assure the recipient that they are receiving data correctly, from the right party, are of significant value. With e-mail, if you acquire someone's e-mail address, you can begin sending messages, but who sees that message is a function of the physical controls around the machine, passwords (that are often taped to the front of the computer screen), and other access controls. Messages can be altered or forwarded—or even falsely originated using another's sending address—and no one knows the difference. If this is for a purchase of many hundreds of thousands of dollars of goods, better controls are needed than are typical in most e-mail systems.

In some cases, some data manipulation may occur at the store-and-retrieve level—either the insertion or deletion of certain fields or elements to allow for the data to proceed to another point. This allows for additional timestamping to be added by an independent third party for proof of validity or existence. For example, in 1996, the U.S. Postal Service introduced a service whereby it would certify the existence of any electronic transaction and add their "electronic postmark" to the transaction. Financial institutions also insert their own timestamp in an EDI payment transaction to prove receipt and correct payment date information. There are now third-party services who will validate an e-mail, using what is called an electronic watermark, to provide a third-party validation of the authenticity of the e-mail and an independent archive should there be a dispute.

In the broader context of EC, many of these issues are harder to deal with. Take the case of junk e-mail, or spam, as it is colloquially called. It is possible and easily done that someone with a grudge can send hundreds or even thousands of unwanted messages to people, filling up their mailboxes and making it difficult to discern valuable messages from the junk. In order to battle this, it is possible to set up filters, which allow messages from specific senders only and prevent unknown senders from spamming, but they can also prevent legitimate new relationships from sending messages. This is why business-critical data tend to evolve toward EDI, because the setting up and exchange of highly structured data exchanges prove more cost effective and valuable in the long run.

Timeshifting

Beyond these specific activities, a store-and-retrieve facility also provides *timeshifting,* so that the timing of data exchanges between several different trading partners and different time zones can be accommodated, minimizing conflicts between the processing time of many different organizations. For example, the purchasing system of the buyer runs at 10:00 a.m., while the order entry system of the seller runs at 4:00 p.m. In the past, either one organization would have to change its cycle time or have to default to a paper input/output mode to accommodate the other.

This approach also allows for the pickup of data and its delivery to be accomplished through different communications protocols and speeds. For example, a large company operating a mainframe system may deliver a message on a high-speed data link using a mainframe computer protocol. The receiving company may be quite small and use a PC protocol. Both sides can process the data as they wish, because all that resides in the facility is data. The communication process is a choice that is made independent of the data storage.

Point-to-Point Relationship

It is also possible for an EC relationship to be established without the use of a store-and-retrieve in what is known as a *point-to-point* or direct relationship. This means that both parties agree to send information between each other directly, without any other organization or communications provider in between. This usually is the case when there are only one or two trading partners or where there is such a large amount of data that a mailbox might slow things down. In this case, it would be possible that a proprietary link would be established, making the relationship into what is known as an *electronic order entry system*, a proprietary form of EC.

Likewise, with the growth of the use of the Internet, it is quite viable for organizations to transfer data via the TCP/IP protocol and route transactions via Internet carriers. In doing this, the organizations still need a language and structure for their data and are using the EDI standards to facilitate the exchange. There have been a number of developments where organizations have been using the Internet to transport EDI messages.

Even though the financial industry implications of the use of Internet are still not clear, there is emerging evidence that the use of EC will play a significant role in its generation of business value rather than just today's information value. The 1995 project between Lawrence Livermore National Laboratory (LLNL) and the Bank of

America (BofA), which uses the Internet to convey payment transactions, was the first all-electronic financial EDI pilot on the Internet.

Dr. Lansing "Chip" Hatfield, Program Leader of the Technology Information Systems Program (TISP) at Lawrence Livermore stated that the BofA/LLNL saved ". . . at least $60,000 per year in quantifiable administrative costs." When fully rolled out, the project will pay 1,500 vendors, making 71,000 payments worth over $300 million annually. Could this process have been facilitated without the Internet? Of course, but the fact that it can flow over this channel and can be seen as safe enough for the movement of critical payment data suggests that the Internet is a viable channel for business data.

Message Conversion

ANSI X12, EDIFACT

EDI is accomplished through the use of a common, *standardized* format. This is done through message conversion software, sometimes known as translation software. Translation software is commercially available for nearly any system, of any size. The cost can range from a few hundred dollars for a PC version to tens of thousands of dollars for a mainframe version. The function, though, is the same and is relatively straightforward in all cases: to convert data from the structure that exists within your system to a common, recognized, standard form of data. From this standard structure, a receiver of the data can pass the information through their translator and then read it into their own system without having to modify the base application.

The most prevalent cross-industry EDI standard in production use, primarily in North America, is the American National Standards Institute (ANSI) Accredited Standards Committee (ASC) X12. ANSI X12, or just X12 for short, is well known and recognized worldwide as a major standard for EDI. It has established a *data dictionary* and *syntax*, which act like the English language dictionary and grammar, and provides the structure and substance for the EDI relationship to begin.

There are other standards that are industry specific, such as UCS in the Food and Drug Industry, WINS in the warehousing industry, and others; however, the dominant standard will likely remain ANSI X12. The other relevant standard being used more frequently is EDIFACT, (EDI for Administration, Transport, and Commerce), which is administrated through the United Nations. EDIFACT is used to a greater extent in Europe than in North America, but recent developments in North America have seen some industries, like automotive, increasing their use of this standard.

In any event, either one of the formats can be used to convey messages from one application system to another, regardless of the method of communications.

XML for Internet Messages

Another emerging standard that may further the use of the Internet for business-to-business or direct computer-to-computer exchange of EC traffic is called *extensible markup language* (XML). As stated earlier, one of the greater challenges in implementing EC between organizations is achieving consensus on exactly how to communicate information directly between computers. Even with highly structured standards like ANSI or EDIFACT, the interpretation factor consistently creates problems that take much time and effort to resolve. The Internet, and more specifically the World Wide Web, has been enabled by the creation of the hypertext markup language (HTML), which gives a graphical representation to the complex and sometimes confusing machine language that is used in Internet communications. XML takes the graphical HTML interpretation one step further.

The concept behind XML is that it provides an annotation or reference guide for what is contained in the message or page of information. In other words, XML has a set of rules about how to understand what is described inside a page or document (whether it is in HTML or not) and can help a suitably equipped computer understand what the message means and how to interpret it. This would allow a message in English to be converted and understood by a Russian using Cyrillic characters. The implication of this is that it would no longer require the precise mapping and documentation steps currently needed to implement computer-to-computer data links.

If fully realized, XML would allow messages created in one standard, like ANSI, to be interpreted and applied in another standard, like EDIFACT, without any prior discussion or relationship between the trading parties. This would indeed speed up participation and facilitate more EC exchanged between companies as well as lower implementation costs. The rules should be sufficiently stable that business-to-business applications will begin to use XML in early 2000.

However, it has not yet been proven that computers can effectively apply these rules and protocols without substantial amounts of human intervention, defeating any real value to the business process. XML attempts to address the issue of "What do you mean by that?" Yet even when humans think they understand one another perfectly, there can be misunderstanding. Machines can only relate to how they have been programmed to behave, and there will be a long learning curve before we can see if machines can truly overcome what has always been the "tom*ay*to/tom*ah*to" problem using XML.

Mapping

Unfortunately, as was previously stated, even with standards, there is room for interpretation and disagreement between trading partners, which requires significant effort to resolve. The process of establishing a common understanding of the data through the translator is called *mapping*.

This is done through one of two ways:

1. Through an industry action group that establishes an implementation guide, which is the common interpretation of the standards for all participants in that industry. This is commonly done in many industries when they need a common understanding of rules and processes they all share; for instance, the adoption of the SET standard in the credit card industry has had a positive effect in speeding up the implementation of secure credit card-processing environments. This process may mean compromise by some participants but eliminates confusing and argumentative situations to the largest possible extent. This is discussed further in the Appendix.
2. Between a group of trading partners, usually initiated by the buyer or the dominant participant. In this situation, there tends to be more influence by the dominant party in setting the structure of the process than in the first example. For instance, General Motors has told its trading partners how to do business with it—there is no real negotiation or dialog between the groups. Essentially, the suppliers must comply or choose to find a new customer.

Once a data map has been established and the translator has been purchased and installed, there still remains the last and most critical step in the EDI process: integrating the data into the base application through an application interface.

Application Interface

This is the single most important, and seemingly difficult, area of the EC process. No matter whether the base application is a purchase system, order entry, accounts payable, or accounts receivable, in order to obtain benefits from the use of EC, the data must effectively flow into or out of the application. If there is rekeying of data at any point, there is an increase in the potential for error, the cost of the effort itself, and the cost of operating many other unnecessary devices, such as printers and keyboards, which using EDI standards can eliminate.

In other forms of EC, the application interface and data input process might be a human. For example, when an e-mail is sent to place an order, a human can quite easily convert this information and key it into an internal order entry system, even correcting minor formatting errors along the way. When an e-form, Web-based or not, is used, much of the formatting correctness is enforced by a software program in order to ensure correct data format is loaded in the application system; however, the data can be incorrect or miskeyed by the originator.

Although the process of the application interface may be either part of the translator or the base application, it may require a significant amount of effort to actually integrate the data into the application. In many cases, the discovery of operating problems or idiosyncrasies is flushed out when this is undertaken. This is one of the challenges that emerge when using nonstandardized message protocols for business-to-business EC and again reinforces the concept that successful EC programs will gravitate to using established—usually EDI-based—languages to integrate their relative systems with one another.

In any event, most commercial translators are able to be adapted to create suitable file output or receive input from the base application. The key to an effective EC implementation is to identify the application interface as the primary point of reference and to build controls and management processes that address the business requirements.

Trading Partner Profiling

Many EDI users of VAN services wish their VAN to provide and maintain a database of its trading partners. A primary reason for this service is to maintain integrity of trading partners to ensure that there is no EDI junk mail. Also, this database can provide a secondary check point for the hub, to ensure that all outgoing message are sent to valid and reasonable trading partners. This is particularly valuable when the accounts payable system is originating transactions, and the validity and correctness of the payment is of paramount importance.

In general EC applications, a Certificate Authority (CA) may fulfill this role; if not to the extent that the EDI application does, it certainly would help ascertain the validity and identity of relationships. We discuss the concept of CAs in greater depth in Chapter 5.

Providing for the Secure Transportation of Information

To provide for security, EDI is generally set up as a "send-only" system. In a "direct connection" relationship, after formatting the data to EDI standards, the sender transmits the data to the receiver system. If the receiver accepts the sender's password, the data is sent. But during the transmission, the receiver sends no data back to the sender, and the sender has no access to the receiver's computer except to send it information. If the receiver wants to send data back to the initial sender, a separate connection must be made, and the receiver becomes the sender.

When a third-party VAN is used as a communication intermediary, the sender can send data to the VAN and pick up information stored in an electronic mailbox during the same session. But in this case, the VAN provides a layer of security, and the sender has no direct access to the receiver's computer system.

For general EC applications, transporting information securely can mean a variety of techniques should be applied. These could involve securing the whole message through encryption techniques—ultimately scrambling the whole message into an unrecognizable mess or simply using a security method like digital signatures to ensure the message has not been altered or tampered with in any way (see Chapter 5).

EC IN THE PAYMENTS BUSINESS . . . .

So far, most banks have treated the concept of EC and EDI as simply another form of payment exchange, albeit in a new format. On a different level, many banking systems consider that EFT, with some reference information, has been part of EC for decades. This could not be further from reality; and as the process continues to evolve, demands by corporations will increasingly press banks into providing an improved—and EC-based—delivery facility.

The real concept of an EDI payment is that information, or more specifically remittance information, from a buyer to a seller, accompanies the value transfer in a concurrent manner, the idea being that the remittance detail is directly associated with the value, thereby allowing the receiving organization to apply funds against the outstanding receivable more quickly. There is the added value of the remittance data arriving in a format that is directly computer readable into the accounts-receivable database, again avoiding rekeying of data and the resulting reduction in errors and entry costs.

It has become apparent to banks that have been developing financial EDI that these remittances can be very large indeed. Some could quite easily exceed a million characters of information in a single transaction. The further issue is that this transaction may be for a relatively small value and can consume a significant amount of processing resource just to receive, store, and deliver remittance detail—and still have to deduce the value transfer and apply the necessary funds and risk controls for a relatively small fee.

Banks have begun to realize that to be successful and profitable in applying EC solutions, they will have to add greater value in supporting the payment and information flows of their customers. One of the ways they are doing this is to become a full-spectrum provider of payment solutions, where a single relationship is established from the corporate payer, and a single file containing all of the disbursements the company needs to make is sent to the bank. The bank then creates a variety of outputs, some EFT, some EDI, and even checks and faxes, to be distributed to the payees.

There is the further question of the application of hybrid (or other) solutions to the question of the "information transport" with payments. The GE worldwide COEP System, for example, provides a variety of solutions to the payment and collection process, including the transportation of information. This process has often been the basis of the concerns, which suggest that over time, banks can be easily disintermediated from the customer transaction, from an informational sense, and left to act simply as the credited or debited entity.

This implies that the banks still have a lot of the financial management risk but have little or no information about the transaction or the transactors. Furthermore, as things evolve, it is easy to extrapolate that the next step among a group of trading partners is to "net" out transactions between themselves, perhaps over a period of weeks or months, and only settle for the owed difference. GE and others have begun to exploit this opportunity with increasing success. GE alone moves billions of dollars outside the banking systems of the world, purely on information alone. There is a number of other nonbanking organizations that are following a similar path, leading to a significant diminishing of the banking industry's influence on the transactional business in the future.

FUTURE DIRECTION AND IMPLICATIONS FOR IT MANAGERS . . . .

One of the most important questions companies are asking today is whether they should regard the Internet as a new medium for transaction exchange or as an emerging market for product development and sales. Assuming the Internet is an alternative channel for exchanging transactions (at least in the short term), what are the other alternative electronic delivery channels that must be addressed, and which are the various new forms of interactive technologies that interface to these new delivery channels?

Clearly, the real market is still small. However, it is the Internet's growth rate that is really the significant factor to watch. Whereas only 10% of consumers are connected in developed countries, over 60% of the businesses are. This strongly suggests that the business-to-business aspects of the Internet are going to grow much faster than the business-to-consumer side.

This means that the traditional service providers (VANs) face a substantial customer migration away from their services unless they provide a full suite of Internet-based services as part of their overall offerings. This is now beginning to happen, with virtually all of the major VANs now offering Internet commerce as part of their suite of services.

Extended Reach

An additional factor that is influencing the move to EC on the Internet is the potential reach to trading relationships, which have been seen as beyond the reach of traditional EDI implementations. Because cost is one of the main factors influencing the move to the Internet, there is a direct correlation between the ability of larger trading organizations to bring their smaller partners via tools such as e-forms, based on a Web browser format.

The e-form is a hybrid of the EDI standard and e-mail, both facilitated through a Web browser front end, such as Netscape or Internet Explorer, or even some proprietary software products. The user can access the larger firm's Web site via this e-form, key in the necessary data elements, which may be either a purchase order or perhaps an invoice, and is formatted by the form to specific data construction protocols. The document is then transported via the Internet in true EDI format, ready to be directly entered into the larger firm's system without any further intervention. There is still the problem of incorrect or miskeyed data that is inherent in human data entry; however, this does provide a broader reach to the company determined to have electronic trading with its customers and suppliers, a solution that would not be possible without the ubiquitous Internet.

In the financial arena, there are numerous impacts that are emerging from the introduction of the Internet to the EC equation. New products and channels are both converging to support the concept of electronic trading on the Internet, although not always in a clear or useful fashion. Financial tools to help facilitate the payments and settlement cycles on the Internet are still very crude and have not yet achieved consensus on a regional, let alone a global, basis.

Micropayments

One of the more talked-about concepts emerging from the Internet milieu is the idea of the "micropayment," sometimes called millicent transactions. A micropayment is one that involves only a part of a cent for a transaction. For example, some organizations have made a practice of finding small pieces of information and recategorizing them for other uses, news articles from daily newspapers sorted by subject matter rather than by the paper's presentation. If someone wanted to find out something in a particular category, he could request one or two articles or even just the reference point to that article. For this information, the cost could be one tenth of a cent, and there is perceived to be a need to support this type of payment scheme. It is unlikely the solution will be to actually charge the one tenth cent transaction; rather, the number of accesses would likely have to accumulate to at least ten, and then the cost of a full cent would be charged. The reasons for this approach is that the cost of administrating and bookkeeping the transaction for a partial cent would likely outweigh the charge for the information itself. Chances are that the typical business will not see much benefit from this approach.

In a more practical vein, there are more interesting new applications for financial EC that are seen as Internet savvy.

Digital Cash

Digital cash refers to a "token-based" currency that translates into equivalent real currency units backed by a bank. Usually, there is a trusted authority that allows you to conduct and pay for transactions of this nature after a predetermined relationship has been established. This approach can also be called e-money or any other similar term.

You are likely familiar with this concept of token-based commerce from the use of American Express travelers checks; this approach is similar, but electronic. American Express enjoys its success as a result of not only its process but also the significant trust factor it has built up over the years. Any successful token-based approach will have to establish the same level of trust before it will succeed. Token-based trade will not likely find itself in the business-to-business settlement process in the near future and is more appropriate in the consumer-to-business realm.

Smart Cards

Smart cards can have stored value or nonstored value. They are a "smart" extension of today's debit cash cards; however, users can pay with them without having to connect to a remote system. If they have a stored value, they are what will be also known as electronic wallets (i.e., they replace actual cash). They can be connected via a remote telephone connection (through the Internet or other private network) and download money into their memory. If there is no stored value, they may contain a private encryption key or digital signature that are used to accomplish a transaction. One of the most publicized schemes for stored-value cards is Mondex.

Mondex

Mondex is the proprietary name for a particular type and brand of smart card used for holding and dispensing. Part of the concept of "stored-value" cards, initially popularized by prepaid telephone value cards, the general concept of a stored-value card is that a certain amount of money value is loaded onto the card, and this value can be sent electronically by inserting the card in a reader and having the amount decremented from the card. The recipient of the value then redeems the amount from their banker at a future date. Mondex specifically, and other similar schemes, uses extremely sophisticated cryptographic techniques to prevent forgery and fraud. It is conceptually possible that a smart card could have its code broken and then replicated; however, this is currently seen as well beyond the realm of probability.

The concept of stored-value cards has been around for a number of years, but what Mondex purports to do is allow for a more-generic, cross-service money card that can interact with a large and diverse number of vendors and individuals. Money value stored in Mondex is able to be transferred from person to person, using a special device, and even over the phone. It is intended that the Mondex approach would be used for the relatively low-value transactions that are not appropriate for credit or even debit card transactions. One might consider Mondex's ultimate goal to be seen as electronic pocket change.

Mondex's current advantage is that it is an electronic payment method that is usable both in a personal context and through other electronic means such as the Internet.

Will it succeed, let alone dominate? Only time will tell. But not so far.

Encrypted Credit Cards

This scenario allows a client to securely transmit a credit card number that has been encrypted by a variety of mechanisms. This transaction may or may not include authentication, nonrepudiation, and access control. One of the most likely scenarios for secure credit card involves the use of the SET standard, which we discuss in much more detail in our SET study at the end of this book. Developed jointly by VISA and MasterCard, the SET protocol is designed to secure credit card transactions over the Internet. Both Microsoft and Netscape have also participated in the design and development of the protocol and will enable users to use their credit card numbers while making transactions on the Internet with improved security protection.

Electronic Checks

Electronic checks are the equivalent of paper-based checks, but they are initiated during an on-screen dialog that results in the payment transaction. Authentication and verification are usually performed instantaneously by using digital signatures and timestamping controls during the transaction.

Today's reality has customers (both on the corporate side and retail consumer side) demanding alternative electronic connections based on standards. Even though customers want a range of alternate delivery systems, it is not yet clear which are the ones of greater significance or value, due to the limited experience in the real world of the Internet today. The exception is obviously the ATMs that proliferated in the 1980s and have significantly affected the behavior of individuals toward electronic transactions. The introduction of the ATM was not met with great excitement by the consumer market until five years after its introduction.

Since the mid-1980s, there is a major change in the transactional habits of consumers, both in terms of when they access their banking services and where they expect to be served. Now, in the 1990s, the concept of a paperless transaction, whether through an ATM or a debit POS terminal is not met with skepticism or concern. These are the status quo for today's society, just as EC will be for tomorrow's.

Electronic Bill Presentment

Again, the use of the Internet's growing pervasiveness can be seen in the introduction of the electronic bill presentment (EBP). EBP suggests that instead of receiving a bill from a utility company, an individual (or organization) would have access to an image or representative electronic bill, likely over an HTML Web page. In other words, no hard copy bill, just go take a look in a password-secured Web site. It is not yet clear if this is a winning strategy for a number of reasons:

1. If you are one of the many people who have already subscribed to a direct debit system with your utility provider, you are unlikely to see any real benefit in switching from receiving the paper-based notice you do today. As well, many utilities are required to notify you of your billing so they cannot enroll you without overt actions from you.
2. If you are resistance to automated debits today, EBP is unlikely a compelling argument to move you to this choice, simply because it doesn't change your concerns.
3. If you are indifferent, there has to be a willingness to change and enough of an indifferent base has to make this scheme work—from the biller's perspective.

All in all, there are some interesting technology choices here but not many that address the human issues.

IMPLICATIONS OF NEW EC DELIVERY CHANNELS . . . .

Full deployment of new delivery channels over EC networks will have many and complex implications, with various scenarios that must be taken seriously by organizations. The following trends are going to have significant impact on the organization of the creation of new products and services that will be specifically designed for EC and Internet access.

1. Reduction of the number of players with more global players and less regional organizations. Organizations become able to service customers worldwide regardless of their physical location.
2. Threat of disintermediation as more, and easier, electronic linkages allow smaller or nontraditional players to reach the organizations through the "back door," leaving the front door or traditional providers less able to defend their position from a technology or geographic position.
3. Learning how to handle new payment types over electronic networks.
4. Shifting to increased data warehousing capabilities for clients as opposed to efficient transaction engines. This enhances the customer connection online.
5. Relaxing the reliance on internal information systems platforms; beginning to take advantage of more public infrastructures to speed up the delivery cycle and wide-scale availability of information products to customers (e.g., Internet and other networks).
6. Increasing reliance on third-party partners through transparent, automated electronic connections that add value to clients.

In the long term, as the Internet evolves into a constellation of inter- and intraprivate virtual networks, "the Net" itself will become the common platform of delivery.

Key EC Issues for the IT Manager

The IT manager needs to take a pragmatic and rational approach to using EC technologies. This means a careful evaluation of the business processes that are contemplated for an EC application and then determining what EC tool should be used. There are many cases of trying to apply Web-based commerce tools when this medium is inappropriate for the task, such as in high-volume, data-critical applications for a production management system. At the same time, where costs and reach are a factor, and data reliability can be managed at a lesser level, then a Web-based tool such as an e-form would be appropriate.

The key control issue for any EC application is the recognition that in gaining true benefit from EC, companies relinquish the traditional levels of control. One of the goals of EC is to automate the input of data from outside sources into your systems, directly and without error. This means that a successful manager understands the risks and processes that are needed to mitigate that risk, without creating an overly complex environment. This takes skill, understanding, and courage. The benefits of EC are significant, if properly managed.

Factors for the IT Manager to Consider

1. **Understand the business issues underlying the problem**. Too often, technology has seemed to hold the promise of a solution without really understanding the reason the technology is to be applied. There has been a tendency for business managers to abdicate their understanding of the technical components; not in defining how they work, but in clearly appreciating the limitations of the tools and techniques. Abdicating responsibility for this definition of purpose by the business manager has commonly been the basis for mistakes and excess costs in EC projects. The responsibility of IT will be to strongly press the business owners into taking responsibility for understanding their technology choices; otherwise, they are just asking for problems.
2. **Avoid the hype**. Even though it is the business manager's responsibility to be clear about the needs and purpose of EC programs, it is just as incumbent on the IT manager to ensure the promise of EC is not overstated. In fact, one of the most common complaints over the past decade about the application of EDI has been its failure to deliver to the level of its promise. This begs the question: Was it EDI that fell short, or were the promises too great? The same can be said of the Internet, which claimed in the mid-1990s that by 1999, there would likely be virtually no other electronic channel for communication and delivery with customers. Has this been the case? Is this a reasonable expectation to set? Not really. For both EDI and the Internet, there have been great benefits received by users and many successful applications developed that prove to have real value.

   The reality is: Implementing EC is almost always hard work and, as discussed throughout this chapter, often requires both new thinking and new processes to be effective. Simply doing what was done before, only electronically, has consistently been a recipe for disaster. Promising quick fixes simply creates unreasonable expectations. Set the expectations for the value against results that are incremental improvements—small steps taken can achieve great results.
3. **Ensure you have a balanced approach**. The balance between staying the course and using the best tool can be a frustrating one. Be prepared to change direction, but don't chase every new angle either. Some EC programs have been a continual chase of the next upgrade or the neatest tool and really haven't accomplished anything. EC tools for effective business results don't always need to be the latest and greatest—just the most effective.

4. **Don't assume that the technology can single-handedly solve all problems**. For example, while using the Internet Protocol (TCP/IP) can provide relief to part of the communications challenge, you will still have to consider issues such as business criticality of the data (What happens if the order is delayed for some reason?), accountability (Who is responsible for a delay or lost transaction?), reliability (Can I really trust the network?), and security (Who can see or touch the transaction while it is in transit?) These can only be resolved through setting business policy and goals that relate to these issues and following the guidelines that emerge.

Steps for EC Success

The following steps will aid you in ensuring that maximum effectiveness can be obtained from your EC efforts:

1. **Identify and measure your current business flows.**
   - What are the volumes in your key processes?
   - What proportion of your information is already electronic?
   - What are the current cycles required to accomplish the key flows?
   - What are the current error rates experienced to accomplish the key flows?
   - What are your current transaction costs to accomplish the key flows?
2. **Determine if an improvement can be made.**
   - Identify appropriate firms who can be benchmarked to establish a "best practice."
   - Compare yourself against this best practice to see if an improvement can be made.
   - If you are already operating near the top of your industry, improvements may be marginal (in the process reviewed—this doesn't mean another process can't be improved).
   - If you are not in the top of your industry, develop an EC strategy to use to get you there.
3. **Decide on what the best EC technology is for your situation.** This will relate to the size of your firm and the volumes that you need to process. A specific process may need a specific EC solution. This means that multiple solutions will likely be involved, including:

- EDI
- Web-based solutions such as e-forms and e-mail, automated inventory access, electronic catalogs, etc.
- Autofax, Interactive Voice Response systems
- Bar coding and scanning

4. **Determine the criteria for the best solution.**
   - Responding to customer demand
   - Costs/benefit review and analysis
   - Industry leadership
   - Corporate vision

5. **Take a look at the costs that will be incurred.**
   - Hardware
   - Software
   - Personnel, operations, support, and client services
   - Initial training
   - Ongoing training
   - System maintenance and upkeep
   - Changes in financial cycles
   - Network/communications costs
   - "Build" versus "Buy"

As we've said before, and will continue to repeat, EC is about relationships and commerce. The technologies that are used are generally quite available and easily understood. Even late breaking technologies are quickly commoditized and are rendered cost-effective in no time. The successful manager will focus on the application of the technology rather than the network, software, or hardware components. Does it really matter what VAN or ISP you use? Not really. Does a certain browser affect what you want to do on the Web? Perhaps, but not that much. The fact still remains that the technology is here now, it works, and it's relatively cheap. So what are you waiting for?

7

Business First and Safety First: Protecting Electronic Commerce Relationships

This chapter shifts the focus of our discussion from the tools and techniques of EC to the management processes needed to make them effective. Our aim is not to discuss all the often-complex details of implementation and organization but to highlight a few business management principles that ensure the technical work achieves its business goals. These principles center on what we term Big Rules, a small number of policies that have the force of organizational law. The purpose of these Rules is to achieve two often-conflicting aims: service and safety. Service requires ease of access, flexibility, and local options in many areas of technology. In contrast, safety restricts access and options and requires standards and procedures. Instead of putting one of these first at the expense of the other, the challenge and opportunity is to put them *both* first.

Service first requires a focus on relationships. Safety highlights the technical and procedural. It is very easy for the safety aspects of EC to take priority in design and implementation at the expense of business management considerations. One of the demands of EC is precision and great attention to details. Companies must have absolute confidence that when they make a transaction with a trading partner, it will be accurately and completely processed. This can lead to complex and lengthy negotiations about EC standards and about implementation of hardware, software, and telecommunications. An entertaining example—though not entertaining, we can be sure, for the people involved in it—was the Great Marshmallow Debate. As *EDI Forum* describes it, this "flared up on a cold February in Atlanta [at a meeting of an ANSI X12 committee defining Warehouse Information Network Standards]. Marshmallow manufacturers, pitted against retailers . . . turned to the committee to resolve the burning question: Given that the weight of marshmallows changes as they age, should the purchase order note the weight at the time of shipment or the weight at time of receipt?" EC is very much a matter of precise details. (The committee reached a compromise.)

But EC is *primarily* about effective relationships. The purpose of security, audit, and control is to make those relationships safe for both parties. (For this reason, we use the broad term "safety" to cover the full range of security, audit and control procedures, software, standards, firewalls, audit trails, and the like in the rest of this chapter.) That shifts them from being specialized responsibilities of a technical or accounting function in the organization to their becoming an integral part of business planning and business management. That they rarely are seen in this light reflects what we will call in this chapter the *systems defense* approach to business safety in computer systems and networks. We define a *business enhancement* strategy that augments systems defense and builds safety into the design of EC relationships.

FROM SYSTEMS DEFENSE TO BUSINESS ENHANCEMENT

The defense strategy looks at how to protect the firm's systems from errors and intrusions. It starts from the systems end of EC, not the relationship end; in general, it takes the relationships as a given and examines the systems that manage the transactions in the daily activities within those relationships. It uses security and audit tools as add-ons to the business system and in effect surrounds it; the focus is on where to locate safety mechanisms in the processing chain. Generally, these mechanisms are placed at the front and back ends of the chain. The terms "security" and "control" capture the philosophy here. Obviously, the defense approach will always be required, and the traditional skills of security and audit specialists will be even more important in the era of EC than they have been to date for the simple reason that the business risks increase the more the firm opens up its systems to outside access. The Internet dramatically expands the scale and nature of such risks. EC puts more and more of the firm's cash flow online. We are seeing firms like GE, Dell, Cisco, and Sun Microsystems achieve sales over their Internet and intranet systems of over $2 billion a year. That's $2 billion of opportunity and $2 billion of risk exposure. It's not an option here to neglect any element of safety. The well-documented growth of Amazon.com mainly focuses on the new relationships and online community of book lovers, authors, and publishers that it has created and on how easy the Web site is to use. But Amazon.com's strategy also stresses how safe it is, with careful attention to informing buyers about credit card security. Other companies that have put the same effort into ease of access have neglected such issues; every survey shows that around 60% of Internet users, when asked to provide credit card or personal information, lie or log off the site.

The easiest way to ensure safety for all parties is to restrict what they can do. Obviously, that can get in the way of electronic *commerce* and reduce buyers' and sellers' range of choices and hence benefits. Historically, when EC was mostly confined to large firms who mainly made EDI transactions among one another, the parties could and did design restrictions into their systems. For instance, The S.W.I.F.T. funds transfer system remains restricted to banks; corporate treasurers can't initiate S.W.I.F.T. transactions. The very concept of Internet commerce, though, is to permit treasurers, small businesses, and consumers to handle more and more transactions, across more and more areas of everyday activities. Cisco, for instance, has made Internet EC its business model: Between 1995 and 1998, its online sales grew from zero to over $3 billion. In achieving this, it opened up access to many systems that are tightly controlled in most companies: customer shipment information, inventory data, customer self-managing of credit and access to financial data, and so forth. As we stress throughout this chapter, the EC designer has to put service first in this regard, but equally put safety first.

This balancing act is nothing new. There has *always* been a conflict in telecommunications between access and control. The relationship elements—communication, speed, convenience, variety of transactions, provision of information, and opening up the system for more and more users and uses—pushed toward open access; for a long time that's been the ethos of the Internet and a major factor in its success and diffusion. Anything that gets in the way of these elements limits the relationship. The control elements are required for reasons of safety, regulation, protection of proprietary information, privacy, and ensuring an accurate record and audit trail. The challenge is to ensure that these augment, not intrude on, the relationship.

That's why defense needs to be complemented by the business enhancement strategy we outline in this chapter. This has the following main principles:

1. **Business policy**: an explicit decision by senior management as to which elements of safety are Big Rules—policies with teeth—and which ones are matters of trade-offs versus cost, organizational flexibility, and other considerations.
2. **Relationship design**: a careful and continuous assessment of safety requirements in terms of their contribution to the EC relationship.
3. **Front-end planning**: new systems development and project management mechanisms for (1) building safety into the basic design of software, hardware, and communication systems, and (2) for making this part of the general skill base of systems development teams rather than something left to specialists.

The rest of this chapter describes the key business and management planning agenda needed to accomplish all this. The end products are the technical systems, standards, and processes described in other chapters. It's too easy and too commonplace, though, for these to dominate attention; for example, in many firms, the security, audit, and control functions have assumed that they must demand particular procedures and safeguards from business units without considering the business trade-offs and issues *beforehand.*

"Beforehand" here refers to the work that establishes the criteria for service and, hence, for systems features and procedures. We know of several firms where, for instance, the control function insisted that all electronic transactions have specific authorization documents and signatures, thereby entirely blocking the exploration and implementation of EDI. In one of the companies, the controller continued to refuse to relax the requirements, even when the head of commercial sales showed that some key customers had informed him that they would no longer accept paper invoices and had set a timetable for suppliers to link electronically to its procurement systems. This inflexibility, based on little more than traditional practice, eroded an important business relationship. In a phrase that deserves immortalization, the controller told one of the authors of this book that he was totally opposed to EC because it was inherently insecure and that "Weston [the company's main competitor] isn't the enemy; Tesco [the customer] is!" The customer as enemy is an interesting business concept. This controller is almost a parody of the systems defense approach whose rule is "safety first, service second."

Putting Both Safety and Service First

The enhancement strategy focuses on service first; this cannot, however, mean safety second; the challenge is to balance the many trade-offs involved in ensuring service and safety. That comes from dialog between people who often do not naturally, or even willingly, talk with each other, but talk at or past each other. EC systems designers are likely to place as extreme an emphasis on service, whereas the controller in the example above placed a priority on safety. That, after all, is their job: to develop a system that the parties in the firm's EC activities find convenient, helpful, fast, and responsive. In that situation, the needed safety features are too rarely built into the design; instead, they are tacked on at the end of implementation when Audit is brought in. One major bank had to write off its entire investment in an online inventory management system that allowed customers to access information on the status of their shipments. In retrospect, it's obvious that this opens up many security concerns: authorization, ensuring that only specific data in specific databases can be accessed by specific customers, providing an audit trail, and so on. The business system designers had not even thought about access logs for a system that was a read-only service. They did not realize the implications of the database being accessed and updated by transaction processing applications. They used straightforward passwords, with the data file that stored them being part of the information access software. The end result was that the entire design of the system was flawed, and it would cost more to adapt the design to meet the control needs than to scrap it and start over from scratch.

We have often heard business people dismiss financial control staff and auditors as blockages to their own work. They actively avoid bringing them in; this is what happened in the example above. By not talking with Financial Control and Audit, the team was able to move ahead quickly, but by doing so, they didn't know what they didn't know about safety needs. This is as much an error as the narrow focus on security that is reflected in the tirade about the customer as enemy. For the operations manager who expressed it, collaborating with the customer was collaborating with the enemy, and for the developers of the banking system, collaborating with financial control was also collaborating with the enemy.

EC is *fundamentally* about collaborating with business partners, colleagues, and specialist experts. When the key players collaborate, EC combines service and safety.

Key Players in EC Development

Historically, the three parties involved in the development of EC systems, business managers, information systems professionals, and the control function, work from a different base of training, professional identity, language, and focus, and with many barriers between them. Those barriers have to be removed right from the start of any EC venture. In general, the first party, the business manager, views the two others with some degree of wariness; for them, computer programmers are on a different wavelength and even on a different planet, and control staff cause them problems: they arrive to criticize and place blame not to help. In turn, IS professionals call business people "users" and auditors "the green eye shade crew." Auditors and security staff often are very detached from the business units who handle the processes and work flows, for whom the demands of security, audit, and control can be intrusions on their autonomy and responsiveness. This problem is commonplace in everyday use of PCs, where protection of passwords, backup of systems, and other elementary procedures are routinely ignored. The rapid growth of Internet and intranet applications often widens the gap between the business mindset of open access and the control mindset of systems defense.

The starting point for a business management strategy for ensuring safety in EC relationships is to change this. That's easier said than done, obviously. Appeals for cooperation between business managers and the control function and information systems professionals are no substitute for formal policies, procedures, skills, and new practices. Our strong view is that the lead must be taken by the firm's audit and control professionals and managers. The reason for this is that they have historically had, in effect, sole responsibility for policies, procedures, skills, and practices in this area. By adopting the three principles we recommend, safety policy, relationship design, and front-end planning, they send a powerful signal to the rest of the organization.

BUSINESS POLICY AS BIG RULES . . . .

Policy can be defined as "this is the way things will be done around here." Big Rules are the standards, procedures, and tools that turn policy into practice. Big Rules have the force of organizational law; there is no room for discussion. They must have the following four characteristics:

1. a compelling business justification
2. a clearly assigned responsibility for following them
3. a single point of contact for organizational support
4. a clearly defined process for dealing with exceptions

They are not the same as "standards," though they often include them. For example, a Big Rule might be that no EC system may be accessed over an outside phone line by modem. The compelling business justification here, one that many firms have adopted and some reject as overrestrictive, is that today, the tools for safety and the costs involved make it essential that the firm's internal telecommunications network be as well-guarded as is practical. This Big Rule suggests some standards but isn't a standard in itself. Generally, the standard is defined as either a mandated tool or a preferred tool. Here, the mandated tool may be a set of hardware servers and firewalls. The mandated system might be the XYZ model K product from a specific vendor plus a list of recommended network monitoring software options.

The Big Rule here is not the standard. The very term "standards" in the IT field immediately summons up in most business peoples' minds "bureaucracy." To hear the financial control function or IS organization propose a standard is to hear the heavy tread of the technology thought-police. Business units want, reasonably enough, to match their technology and safety procedures to their own market, organization, and processes. They fear that standards are an intrusion on their autonomy.

That's a relic from the past. Effective standard-setting ensures a combination of central coordination and local autonomy, not one at the expense of the other. Firms have paid a huge price because of the yo-yoing from one extreme to the other in the technology field over the past decade. The old data processing monopolies of the 1970s through mid-1980s imposed standards as technology bureaucracy; they controlled investment decisions to the extent that purchases of PC hardware and software that amounted to a few hundred dollars often had to get "Corporate" approval. In the late 1980s, the pendulum swung to the other extreme; business units chose their own hardware, software, and local area networks (LANs). The result was multitechnology chaos—a proliferation of incompatible systems, immense overload in terms of support and administration, and a conflict between the central IS organization that saw—correctly, in retrospect—the vital need for a coordinated enterprise infrastructure but business units who saw IS as a barrier to fast and cost-effective deployment of the systems they needed.

In the information services field in large organizations, chief information officers (CIOs) are struggling with the costs of complexity, variety, and customization that the era of "let a thousand flowers bloom" has created. One CIO of a leading financial services organization recently told one of the authors that a survey showed that the firm maintains the following combinations: four different personal computer operating systems, seven types of LANs, five database management systems environments, three network management systems, eleven incompatible major transaction processing systems, fifteen data communications networks, and six e-mail systems. That amounts to 4 x 7 x 3 x 11 x 15 x 6 combinations or, in his words, "30,000 different ways something can go wrong and probably will." He argued strongly and successfully that there be a Big Rule prohibiting laptop access to the network over public dial-up phone lines, not because he does not view this as a good business opportunity, but because it adds even more combinations of complexity and weak points. For him and the executives involved in the planning of EC, this is important enough to require a Big Rule.

This same CIO encourages diversity in other areas. For example, there are no standards for commerce servers. The only Big Rule is that whatever specific server is adopted—an IBM packaging of hardware and software, a Unix-based product, a Microsoft offering, and so on—it must be able to connect to the firm's main internal data network. IS recommends the IBM option as a preferred but not mandated system. It offers incentives here by promising full support for preferred tools (and takes responsibility for mandated ones) but not for others.

This example is very typical of the collaborative to and fro and give and take that are needed to combine service with safety, flexibility with efficiency, and local needs with enterprise coordination.

The Link Between Big Rules and Standards

The above discussion highlights what may be a very new style of working together for financial control and audit staff, business relationship managers, and IT professionals. This is discussed further in Chapter 8. Note how it gets away from the standard as the purpose and makes it a vehicle for meeting a business need. Safety in EC is impossible without "standards" and "procedures." So, get rid of the terms, because they carry so much historical baggage. Instead, define Big Rules. These are the very small set of policies with teeth that *simultaneously* foster coordination of enterprise infrastructures and local unit autonomy. Examples of Big Rules that accomplish this in everyday life are:

1. driving on the right
2. debits and credits

It really doesn't matter which side of the road cars drive on, but a Big Rule is essential. Logically, of course, they should drive on the left, as is the Big Rule in Britain; that came from the historical necessity for a knight on horseback to have his sword arm free as he passed by another knight. The British suspect that the only reason for other nations adopting the historical rule of driving on the right is that the French do the opposite of their trans-Channel neighbors (and, of course, it's the English Channel). The serious point here is that the adoption of a nonnegotiable policy provides coordination of the traffic system but leaves car makers free to design features into their products, just as the de facto standard of the 8 1/2 x 11-inch standard for paper size gives makers and users of photocopiers and computer printers full autonomy within the standard. The established Big Rules for accounting—debits on the left, credits on the right—do the same. They don't impose rules about account codes nor restrict a firm from generating what may be termed its own Little Rules, such as choice of depreciation method (e.g., LIFO versus FIFO).

We take such standards for granted, and no one would seriously attempt to invent a four-dimensional new accounting convention that has credits on the left, followed by, say, microaccounts, and intellectual capital debits, then cash flow debits. That would merit the term "crazy." The basic rules of debits and credits liberate creativity, coordination, comparability, and integration of information. Let's do the same for EC.

Big Rules in the IT World

Just as Big Rules imply standards, so too do standards imply Big Rules. In the field of IT, the core question is which standards are Big Rules and which Big Rules require which standards. It's a very, very complex issue in that the volatility and pace of change means both that standards emerge very rapidly in some areas, whereas in others, it's almost impossible to predict which will win. In the area of EDI, standards have largely emerged through collaborative agreements; ANSI's X12 committees and such industry associations as AIAG (auto industry) and VICS (retailing) are examples. When telecommunications was a tightly regulated set of international monopolies, international committees controlled the standard-setting process. CCITT, for instance, defined the standards for ISDN, the ambitious effort to define the blueprint for the integration of telephony and computer communications for the twenty-first century, a blueprint that is already obsolete.

Today, competition, not committees, drives IT standards. Microsoft's DOS and Windows operating systems became de facto standards at the expense of Apple's Macintosh for this reason. Even though the Mac is in many ways far easier to use, with a customer loyalty that borders on passion, firms gradually adopted Windows and thereby reduced multitechnology chaos because this ensured that PCs could link to the corporate telecommunications networks and information resources, and that the firm could obtain economies of scale in purchasing software and equipment and in providing help desks and support. The issue here is not that Windows is better than the Mac, any more than driving on the left is somehow better than driving on the right; it's just that, first, there has to be a "standard" that is more than just a "pretty please" request and that everyone gains in some way. The Big Rule that all PCs must be Windows-based doesn't require business units to buy specific machines; they can choose, safely choose, laptops from Toshiba, desktops from several hundred providers, and printers from any vendor that supports Windows—that is, every vendor in the market. They may choose to define their Little Rules, such as requiring that laptops be bought from Dell and that the standard desktop printer be, say, an HP Laserjet. This may be to take advantage of volume purchase agreements and simplify support and maintenance.

Determining Compelling Reasons for the Big Rules

The art form for IS and for the audit and control function is to come up with the *minimum* set of Big Rules that combines the advantages of enterprise coordination and business unit autonomy. The key word here is "minimum." The rule is that if there is a Big Rule, it is organizational law. If there is no Big Rule, units are fully free to define their own Little Rules or to simply go their own way. The Big Rules must have a compelling business rationale. Otherwise, they will be seen as just bureaucracy.

Here are some general candidates for Big Rules for ensuring safety in EC, together with their underlying compelling business rationale:

- No outside individual or organization will be able to access the firm's systems except through a specific ABC firewall (where ABC is either a vendor or a hardware/software complex of tools). The compelling business reasons here are the obvious need for protection at the network entry point, the less-obvious value of having just the single ABC system to install and support, and the nonobvious advantage in cost and administration of being able to distribute just one set of software upgrades electronically and as needed. Stated as a bureaucratic standard that "All units will install the HyperSecSonarSentinel 665.3" or some such requirement, the Big Rule looks like IS or Financial Control imposing unnecessary costs and procedures. Spell out the business reasons, and it should be clear that the business units in fact gain cost and administrative advantages.
- All intranets must use servers that are interoperate with Microsoft Windows NT. To adopt this as a Big Rule would mean not allowing the use of the Unix servers, which remain the hardware of choice for many high-end servers. That means there had better be a really convincing business reason. That reason might be the following: "The choice of NT-interoperable servers ensures desktop integrity across our enterprise platform and reduces the costs of supporting business units' intranets, LANs, and PCs. In addition, it reduces security costs and network management costs for both the company and the intranet managers."

- The PQR encryption software (PQR is just some hypothetical supplier) will be the standard for any EC application that involves transactions that either update the firm's databases or involve payments. Applications that just handle one-way information flows, such as product information and contact names, may use the weaker RST encryption software, with shorter keys.
- EC transactions that involve any form of payment, such as via credit card, will be processed offline. The compelling business reason here, if this Big Rule were adopted, is that the cost of ensuring security is dramatically reduced if there is no online payment processing that can be tapped into or tampered with.
- Before any EC application, including intranets, goes "live," the business unit responsible for it must demonstrate that it includes comprehensive online audit logs and that the outstanding security weaknesses are addressed, tracked, and accepted by senior management. There should be an expiration date on these outstanding weaknesses so that they get revisited.

If there is no compelling business rationale, there should be no Big Rule, only a recommendation. If there is a Big Rule, the four policy enablers listed earlier must be provided. A clearly assigned responsibility for following the Big Rule: Policy is ineffective unless there is no absolutely clear statement of organizational accountability and authority, backed up by appropriate monitoring procedures.

1. A single point of contact for organizational support: The best incentive for business units to willingly cooperate is to provide incentives, not demands. The two main incentives in IT are volume purchases and organizational support. If the IS organization establishes a system or standard as mandated, then it must provide total support for it: help desk, expertise, crisis management, and vendor relationship management.
2. A clearly defined process for dealing with exceptions: Inevitably, there will be situations where even the soundest Big Rule either cannot be followed or is not appropriate for some unusual and unanticipated reason. There needs to be some forum/mechanism for handling the equivalent of variances for building permits.

Questions for the Big Rule

The three managerial questions here are: Who owns the Big Rule? Who ensures that the organizational resources needed to make it effective are available? (and who pays for them?) What's the organizational mechanism for handling exceptions?

A sample answer to the questions for the Big Rule that all intranets must be interoperable with Microsoft's NT operating system might be:

Who owns the Big Rule? IS is responsible for ensuring that the Rule is followed.

Who ensures that the organizational resources needed to make it effective are available? IS guarantees to provide expertise and support for all aspects of NT installation and operation. It maintains a list of recommended vendors and products. It will provide assistance in obtaining volume discounts for those products and troubleshooting; however, it takes no responsibility for help and support for products not on the recommended list.

What's the organizational mechanism for handling exceptions? The case for special exceptions must be made to Financial Control, which will review the request.

Choosing the Big Rules

The main principles here are: first, ensure clear central coordination and second, offer support and incentives for local autonomy. In this very typical instance, the Big Rule clearly specifies that the corporate IS organization is the coordinator; that gives it authority and accountability. It also offers incentives to cooperate by providing a list of recommended products for which it offers support, troubleshooting, and volume purchase agreements; it makes no offer for other products, which business units are free to choose as they wish.

The choice of Big Rules demands very, very careful decisions. The goal is to define the *minimum* set that achieves the dual goals of coordination and autonomy. The historical tendency of IS and financial control units is to overspecify standards and impose what are, in effect, regulations. In our experience, there is rarely a need for more than a dozen Big Rules. Our recommendation is to zero-base the decision—start by throwing out *all* rules and standards and then make the case one by one for a Big Rule. For instance, begin with no rule whatever for encrypting messages sent over the firm's networks; let this be a business unit choice as to whether or not to encrypt, and if encryption is to be used, let the unit pick whatever method, hardware, and software it wants. This is an issue of cost and convenience only, not one of policy.

It should take less than 10 seconds to reject the no-rule approach here. Of course, encryption is policy, not option. There *must* be a Big Rule. It need not be an absolute one, however, that demands the use of a single strong encryption method. In the example above, the Rule requires that PQR encryption software will be the standard for any EC application involving transactions that access and update the firm's core systems and databases, but that simpler, and hence cheaper, RST software be the standard for systems that just handle one-way information flows. The compelling business reason is pretty obvious here: the vital need to ensure the integrity of the firm's systems and protect them from intrusion and tampering (PQR) and the equal need to minimize business unit costs for applications that do not pose such a danger (RST).

Discipline and Innovation: The Dynamic Tension

There are no "right" Big Rules, no "correct" standards. There are only sensible business decisions, best estimates, and professional judgments. Sometimes a rule may be the equivalent of a coin toss to choose between two equally acceptable alternatives; the analogy here is, as mentioned earlier, driving on the left- or the right-hand side of the road. It really makes no difference, but everyone had better be on the same side! Equally, it makes no difference which suite of software that business units adopt for spreadsheets, word processing, and presentations—Microsoft Office and Lotus Smart Suite are both excellent products. Why not let units pick which one they want? There's no EC safety implications here, are there? Or are there? Who's in the discussion group about this? Is one of them overlooking something the others know about?

There's no general or obvious answer to these questions, but even though the Microsoft and Lotus suites are about the same in terms of cost, quality, and features, when all the parties are really together, there's a very strong case for adopting just one that minimizes support demands: the complexity of the help desk's role and needed knowledge, electronic distribution of software updates, and desktop computer configuration. Working together, the EC business group, IS, and safety team might well decide that the firm needs a single desktop environment that can be fully protected with a common server, antivirus software, and encryption method. If so, they will need to go through the steps outlined above, the key one being to provide the compelling business rationale for the recommendation that this become policy.

RELATIONSHIP DESIGN . . . .

The policy decisions discussed above relate to the coordination of the firm's overall technology resource. They define the firm's safety infrastructure. They are largely application-independent. Many of them relate to the systems defense element of safety. Business enhancement shifts the focus to the EC relationships. There are two main relationships here: business-to-business EC and consumer-to-business (we include business-to-government as a subset of business-to-business). Within these relationships, there is a very wide variation in the sophistication of partners, in terms of technical knowledge, their own EC safety mechanisms, equipment, and experience with EC, as shown in Table 7.1.

Table 7.1 EC Relationship Profiles

	Unsophisticated	Expert
Business-to-Business	Basic PC access to standard services No in-house security expertise Unwilling or unable to implement complex procedures and systems	Trading partner agreements in place for main EC relationships Fully knowledeable about safety needs and mechanisms Strong in-house expertise
Consumer-to-Business	Makes many mistakes in use of technology Oblivious of many risks Wary of technology Unable or unwilling to invest in new tools and procedures Worried about security of credit cards and privacy	Very safety conscious Willing to invest in safety Working knowledge of basics of safety technology Expects encryption of credit card transaction data

The four profiles cover the full range of EC relationships. The business-to-business component is the fastest growing, and there are many companies with strong expertise and experience. For them, EC is about sophisticated business process innovation, trading partner agreements, extension of simple procurement and basic customer–supplier transactions to cover more and more of the logistics and supply chain. Any player at this level already knows a lot about safety. But what about new players? Despite the growth rate of EDI and corporate applications of EC, most estimates are that there are less than 200,000 firms out of millions using it in North America. Who should take the lead in helping them and helping them help themselves? The same question applies for the far-less-mature field of consumer-to-business EC. This is in its infancy; its pace of growth depends heavily on consumers' sense of safety. Who's responsible for ensuring it?

Each of these categories clearly requires a different relationship safety strategy. Here, the focus on safety from the organization's own perspective, which is embodied in the policy and Big Rules, has to be carefully meshed with the business partner's perspective. For example, the unsophisticated consumer wants simple procedures, is unlikely to have antivirus software on his or her PC, uses dial-up phone links, and makes only occasional EC transactions via the Internet or America Online. Such people don't know much about security but are very cautious about giving their credit card information over the network and are reluctant to fill out e-forms that ask for personal data. By contrast, the sophisticated consumer will be very sensitive to security and will know about encryption techniques, be more likely to download volumes of information, use high-speed modems and communication links, such as ISDN, and run complex software. He or she will be looking to use online securities trading services, perhaps home banking, certainly electronic shopping and electronic catalogs, and large volumes of e-mail. How can you provide relationship safety for both types of consumers within the same technology infrastructure and inside the same EC application? There's no straightforward answer here, and each major EC service—Internet shopping, electronic payments, software downloading, and so forth—may need separate consideration. *The key business issue is to enhance the relationship.* Here are some principles for doing this:

Unsophisticated consumers. Here, safety is *totally* the responsibility of the firm. It must be kept "transparent" to the user and require no specific software or hardware. The firm must also assume that the consumer's PC is wide open to viruses and very vulnerable to "crackers." The obvious tools here are firewalls, firewalls, and more firewalls, with standard encryption methods in place. The consumer should not be burdened with information about security but offered the simple warning messages that are standard on Internet EC services such as Amazon.com, which alerts buyers to when the communications link is not fully secure.

Expert consumers. Here, safety is a shared activity, and expert consumers can be invited to adopt software and procedures that enhance security. They will understand the nature and risks of "cookies," for instance, and of such safety mechanisms as eTrust. They are likely to accept offers from the firm that add to their own protection. These can be provided through an optional menu, perhaps called "For Your Extra Safety," which the unsophisticated consumer can ignore.

Unsophisticated businesses. These pose the biggest relationship safety challenge. They need a lot of hand-holding. They are likely to be small businesses, where there is no in-house IS function and where accounting is outsourced. They will use software packages and have limited expertise for configuring and fine-tuning systems. They depend on their PCs and LANs, and as they adopt EC in, say, EDI for procurement and online inventory management, that dependence increases to the point that when the system is down, so is the business. They benefit from well-defined procedures, informative manuals, and access to a help desk where they are not put on hold for an hour or so. They will in general follow recommended procedures but will not fully understand the mechanics underlying them. They are very cost-conscious and will balk at being expected to pay a premium for safety, in terms of hardware, telecommunications, and software costs, added procedures, or record-keeping.

Expert businesses. For these, safety is as much a priority as it is for your own firm. The prime mechanism here is the trading partner agreement that lays out in full detail the assumptions, responsibilities, liabilities, and handling of special situations. They expect to share expertise and information with their trading partners.

Reputation and Performance in an Online Relationship

There are several general safety issues to consider that apply across all types of relationships, whether business-to-business, consumer-to-business, expert, or unsophisticated. Safety translates into reputation. Failures in security are failures in meeting the implicit or explicit commitment in the relationship. It is very hard in an EC environment to tell the difference between fraud and incompetence; this makes impeccable operations essential. If there is an error in, say, processing my electronic payment, I generally will have no idea what caused it. It may be that the system is poorly designed and is a software error. It could be a network problem. It could be a failure caused by a service agent giving me incorrect information. Something could have gotten lost. Someone may have "hacked" into the system and stolen my credit card. Who knows?

EC services generally are "up" 99.9% of the time, and errors are both few and far fewer than the manual processes they replace; EDI typically halves error rates. A 1% error rate, say, and 99.9% up time—less than 10 hours out of service in an entire year—look great. They're not. They translate into hundreds, perhaps thousands of botched or missed transactions and hundreds or thousands of customers who see incompetence and worry that they may have been ripped off—that is not at all a paranoid reflex in the era of the Internet. The starting point for relationship safety is simply operational excellence.

The foundation of EC relationships is continuity. The goal is over time to move more and more of the routine customer-supplier operations and internal logistics online. That requires mutual confidence. In the business-to-business area of EC, both sophisticated and expert trading partners demand this, and failures show up quickly and have fast impacts if repeated—victims will take their business elsewhere. In consumer-to-business EC, there are slightly different expectations. The field is too new for most consumers to rely on it; they may make occasional transactions to buy, say, books or CDs, but only a very small fraction of the growing Internet user community have committed their banking, shopping, and other service relationships to the Net. Many firms are betting that they will and are investing heavily on that basis. Safety is a requirement for success, and confidence is the determinant of consumer willingness to enter this new style of relationship. It took many years for people to be confident about using ATMs, credit cards, and cell phones, and there is no reason to believe that they will not over time come to take EC for granted in the same way and to the same degree.

It's up to the business to earn that trust.

The Perfect EC Relationship

From the perspective of the business partner, whether it's a consumer or business, the following list defines the features of a "perfect" EC relationship—it's an ideal, of course, in that no relationship can achieve all the items on the list, and if it did, it would probably go broke trying to do so, but the list indicates the target that firms should aim for. Safety mechanisms must enhance, not detract, from the features. The EC relationship should be:

1. **Simple:** That is a paramount requirement and one that ironically is harder to provide for in many EC applications than in more-complex interactive PC systems. The irony is that EC, a relatively new area of application that should be able to exploit the best of modern input and display tools, is often heavily dependent on older software—"legacy" systems—that were built on an entirely different technology base, that was generally based on screen displays that were inflexible in terms of displays and procedures. If you peek over the check-in counter at an airport and glance at the screen of the reservation system terminal, you will see a vestige of this tradition. The airline reservation systems are also a reminder of how difficult it can be to move these systems into a modern design environment. Even though simplicity of use is not the responsibility of safety professionals, it is so important an element in EC relationships that it *is* their responsibility to make sure that system features that handle security, auditability, and controls do not add to complexity, especially in legacy systems.
2. **Convenient:** EC is part of the emerging world of just-in-time everything, with more and more systems and services operating 24 hours a day across the world. That is essential, of course, for Internet EC. Again, safety should not add inconvenience. In many existing systems, there are security and audit features that require the use of specific equipment, software, and telecommunications links. Many large-scale business-to-business EC transaction processing applications require, for instance, that the user's software run under a specific operating system and implement database management software.
3. **Always available:** Nor should the system be out of service at the customer's or business partner's moment of value. "Moment of value" means when the customer wants, from where the customer is now. This aspect of EC service will strain systems defenses in the coming years because, of course, increasing convenience and availability means increasing access and decreasing control. When interactive TV and wireless telecommunications become an integral part of the EC base, which seems inevitable in the long term, then control will be exponentially more difficult than it is today.

4. **Error free:** This demands operational excellence as a *relationship* priority, not just as part of efficiency and productivity.
5. **Effortless:** There should be nothing to learn and remember, no screens to scroll through, no extraneous information to provide, and no waiting. This is a feature of the best Web pages, but, alas, the obverse is far more common on the Web.
6. **Free:** The Web has established a strong expectation among consumers that EC services will be if not free, then at least priced at a low fixed cost per month (as is the case for most Internet access services, America Online, and cellular phone equipment) or at a predictable and fair usage fee.

Many of these features are beyond the control of the people in a business who deal with security, procedures, accounting, and network management. That's why it's easy for them to forget that the purpose of EC is to build relationships of mutual value, satisfaction, and trust between the parties. For that reason, we strongly recommend that *all* plans that address the formal element of relationship safety be checked for their contribution to or detraction from the relationship dimension of value.

FRONT-ENDING

One of the strongest and longest established principles in modern systems design is that the interface *is* the system—in other words, the EC application is defined for the user by the front end of the system. For instance, for millions of consumers, America Online is "the Internet," though, of course, it's a gateway into the Net, employing a browser that handles the links and disguises many elements of network access. The World Wide Web is not a system in itself but an interface that makes use of many long-established Internet building blocks, such as Telnet, which were hitherto very complex and intimidating. Netscape Navigator and Microsoft Explorer, have grown to be more like an Internet operating system than just the original Web "browser" that Netscape launched a few years ago.

In all these instances, the front end does the work for the user, determines ease of use and access, and minimizes complexity. The same principle needs to be applied to EC safety, in terms of both systems defense and business relationship enhancement. The goal should be user-friendly security and "elegance" in audit trail design as well as in Web page design. A basic principle of safety should be to use the front end to include as many elements of security as practical, where those elements are part of the user relationship rather than aspects of network management. Obviously, security, logging, and control features will be placed along the entire interface to the EC processing chain, with firewalls, servers, automated network management and monitoring tools, virus protection, and so on. Many of these will be placed in "middleware," software that sits between client and server. Our personal view is that it is at the interface that the safety opportunity lies, for three reasons:

1. It is here that the dialog with the user takes place and where the user's perception of the system is determined—call this the Web versus Telnet distinction.
2. The earlier that potential problems are trapped in the communication and transaction flow, the easier they are to block and resolve, so that embedding them in the interface link—the literal front end—adds substantial protection.
3. The interface handles the dialog with and feedback to the user; we suggest that many aspects of safety can be handled as part of the relationship dialog, alerting users to risks, requesting and recommending they follow specific procedures, and so on.

BUSINESS ENHANCEMENT

Our approach to safety design and implementation—business enhancement—is a complement to, not a substitute for, systems defense. It mainly requires a shift in focus and a shift forward; that shift is toward the front end and toward the electronic relationship that the front end defines and coordinates. We view traditional security and related safety mechanisms as an opportunity to add value to the relationship rather than to control the system. Most of the procedures, standards, and tools discussed in other chapters are just as applicable to the relationship perspective on EC as is the defense and protection perspective. We are advocating that security be an integral element of business design in EC, part of the trust chain between user and system/service. We hope that this chapter gives you a different and value-adding complement to existing and more traditional approaches.

Recommendations for managers:

1. *Think relationship, not transaction or system:* Examine the design of audit and control procedures in terms of the customer-business interaction, expectations, and mutual needs.
2. *Don't become overfocused on the traditional elements of security and audit, but don't neglect them either.* Complement the systems defense approach with business enhancement.
3. *Build dialogs;* get the business planners and EC process operators, information systems designers, financial audit and control, and technology in the same room with the same agenda.
4. *Focus on Big Rules* as the key to ensuring coordination and local flexibility and range of choices.

8

Auditing for a New Age, New Purpose, and New Commerce

As we all know, things change. It isn't just EC that causes this. Change is the basis of the human condition. Sometimes, though, change is harder on some people, or professions, than on others. There are many professions that have become out-of-step with the times, and in some cases that has meant the demise of that profession. Take the blacksmith, for instance. As the invention of the automobile and mass production of metal goods came into full force, the blacksmith found himself out of a job—not just as a worker but as a part of the fabric of society.

This is true of many of the skills that technology has made obsolete. Morse code was the dominant standard for electronic information exchange over a century ago and facilitated the use of the telegraph. Very few people know how to use Morse code today (other than the SOS signal from the Titanic). As technology and its use evolve, so too must the infrastructure around it. This is true of blacksmiths, Morse code operators, and perhaps the audit profession.

Auditors, since the beginning, have suffered from a poor public image, which technological progress has done little to improve this view. This poor image tends to stem from the traditional behavior of auditors acting as the organization's double checkers and watchdogs, not a role that is seen as "friendly" or helpful to many business units.

The unfortunate part is that this negative image is largely perpetuated by the auditors themselves—believing that they are there to bear the brunt of negativity in order to ensure there is accuracy and correct process in the organizational structure, be it financial, operational, or technical. The public rarely see auditors in a value-added role, contributing to the profitability and success of their organization. This has to change. Otherwise, organizations will seek other ways to ensure that the company's assets are protected and the stakeholders are being looked out for. Technology in the electronic business arena can, in fact, easily supplant the dull process of checking, which, unfortunately, is still viewed by the public as the auditor's main job.

In the era of EC, auditors must be positive participants in the business, technological, and organizational dialog to assure that customers and companies are not at risk. Managers must encourage this dialog as well.

This chapter clarifies the changing role of auditors; not just how auditors can change their approach to their business, but how they must change if they are to be seen as a valuable part of the future infrastructure of business and not as the blacksmiths and Morse code operators of the future. We illustrate how an auditor can contribute to the safety and soundness of EC processes and activities. Throughout this book, we use the broad term "safety" to cover a full range of security, audit and control procedures, software, standards, firewalls, audit trails, and the like. Moreover, we provide the manager with the insight and process on how to better control and manage the new EC-driven organization as a business function, even further strengthening this change-or-die edict.

THE CHANGING ROLE OF THE INTERNAL AUDITOR

In recent years, increasing regulatory, cost, and competitive pressures, rising public expectations, and clear technology trends toward distributed and user-oriented processes have all prompted the audit profession to rethink the way its duties are performed. It has now become evident that auditors must anticipate customer needs, continuously improve, proactively involve themselves with the business units, and use emerging technologies in discharging their duties. In today's business environment, the auditor cannot afford to simply focus on the unit or component they audit without proper attention to their organization's new business relationships, processes, customer needs, and the broad perspective outside of the immediate control environment. This changing role is summed up in the Institute of Internal Auditors (IIA) new definition of internal auditing. On June 26, 1999, the IIA Board of Directors unanimously approved a new definition of internal auditing as "an independent, objective, assurance and consulting activity designed to add value and improve an organization's operations. It helps an organization accomplish its objectives by bringing a systematic, disciplined approach to evaluate and improve effectiveness of risk management, control, and governance processes." (www.theiia.org.) EC is the mainstay of this change for the future and needs to be included in the sphere of knowledge that the audit professional has at his or her disposal.

Recent research and development in the broad concept of control and internal controls and in current audit thinking have stimulated positive changes in the profession's profile. Public expectations have also helped define the auditor's emerging and expanding role. Clearly, a new role for auditors is developing. Auditors are now expected to be change agents, facilitators, and control consultants who anticipate emerging issues and work with their clients on measures to prevent problems before they occur. Already, the profession is working toward "just-in-time" auditing so they don't miss the boat. When executives are asked to sum up the role of audit, many are quick to point out that they want auditors to be involved up front in requirements development rather than in after-the-fact criticism. They also want to see auditors as an unbiased sounding board on company issues and a vehicle for cross-unit validation of good control practices.

What follows is the current framework of control that has influenced, and will continue to influence, management style and audit approaches and practices, and in turn, influence the way EC is managed and audited. The latter part of this chapter will demonstrate how this control framework can be effectively applied to the audit of EC processes and activities.

INTERNAL CONTROL: TRENDS AND RECENT DEVELOPMENTS . . . .

Control is a fundamental business objective and is crucial to the success of business. This concept, until recently, has been narrowly associated with the controller, within the accounting and audit departments. Prior to the 1990s, few directors of companies would have felt that they were directly responsible for the internal control structure of an organization. Now, with a new focus on corporate governance, directors are expected to understand their organization's internal control structure and to report this to the stakeholders as the need arises. In fact, stakeholders are holding directors accountable for the gaffs and mistakes the company makes—creating a liability to them on a personal level. What options do directors have? What are the key issues that can help a director ensure that they are not sitting on top of a time bomb of poor control or worse?

Four recent developments in the area of internal control have significant implications for management in general and for auditors in particular. These form the baseline for evaluation of controls in EC and can help managers ensure that they are not going to find unpleasant surprises in their business. These developments are structured under the following headings and can provide much-needed insight into control management.

Internal Control: Integrated Framework, 1994

This report, issued by the Committee of Sponsoring Organizations of the Treadway Commission (COSO) in the United States in 1992, and revised into two volumes in 1994, identifies five interrelated components of internal control:

1. **Control environment:** its people and the environment in which they operate.
2. **Risk assessment:** an integrated view of the risks an organization must deal with and mechanism to identify, analyze, and manage the related risks.

3. **Control activities:** policies and procedures established and executed to help ensure that risks are appropriately managed and control objectives are effectively carried out.
4. **Information and communication:** ways and means for the organization's staff to capture and exchange information needed to conduct, manage, and control its operations.
5. **Monitoring:** a way to react dynamically, to change as conditions warrant.

At a glance, there is nothing new about these classic management pronouncements. However, the noteworthy component of this framework **stresses that internal control is a process that should be integrated with ongoing business activities.** It also clarifies the roles and responsibilities of the board of directors, management, internal auditors, and everyone in the organization, sending a strong message that control is everyone's business. This removes the common view of the past that, even though the control process is important, it shouldn't be allowed to slow down the business process. Now, control is being viewed as part of the business process, and managers need to take a proactive view of these elements.

At the same time, audit and control professionals, both inside and outside the organization, need to participate in the requirements setting and design phase of any new EC-focused business. This is not to suggest they give away their impartiality; rather, it places the burden of establishing control criteria for this business process *before* the project is launched.

Implications of COSO in the EC Context

There are some additional insights to be gleaned from the COSO framework as well. Because internal control is process-centered, EC and audits (which are part of the business process), must also be process-centered. Process reviews require that management and auditors understand EC end-to-end: from customer to network, and from network to the organization and back. Therefore, it also makes sense to follow the spirit of COSO and map out the roles and responsibilities (directors, management, auditors, et al.) for specific control issues in EC.

Guidance on Assessing Control, 1999

Following the publication of *Guidance on Control* in 1995, the Criteria of Control Board (CoCo) of the Canadian Institute of Chartered Accountants (CICA) issued its third guidance on control-related document. *Guidance on Assessing Control* offers eight principles of assessment and clearly spells out the responsibilities of the board of directors, the chief executive officer, and the people appointed to conduct the assessment, including internal auditors. It also provides generic questions for each group of control assessors to use as a platform for customizing their own control questionnaires.

Guidance on Assessing Control can be viewed as a second-level book on control evaluation, a companion piece to *Guidance on Control.* This control model is an excellent primer for assessing the EC control environment (see next section). Because this book explicitly states that the control assessment is viewed from the perspective of an organization as a legal entity, we have to be mindful not to lose sight of inter-organizational issues. That is to say: (1) EC is global in nature; (2) with the amount of EC outsourcing, cosourcing, and joint business arrangements with external entities, the legal entity approach can only offer a piece of the big picture; (3) whether it is business-to-consumer or business-to-business commerce, EC is relationship-based, not entity-based; (4) like EDI, interenterprise management effectiveness cannot be fully assessed using the eight principles alone, unless we pay special attention to studying the external environment which must be monitored constantly, and appropriate changes made where necessary. As a matter of fact, the *Criteria on Assessing Control* contains special recommendations on the last point.

Guidance on Control, 1995

In 1995, the Criteria of Control Board of CICA issued its first *Guidance on Control* for the board of directors, governing bodies, senior and line management, owners, investors, and lenders as well as auditors. Simply put, this document is for anyone who is responsible for, or concerned about, control in organizations.

Commonly referred to as the CoCo report, this document broadly defines control (not internal controls) as those elements of an organization, that *taken together*, support people in the achievement of the organization's objectives. CoCo is about relationships between components of an entire organization. Internal controls, in CoCo terms, are narrowly defined as those checking, comparing, analyzing routines designed to provide assurance that processes operate as designed. For example, compliance with aircraft maintenance routines and their documentation is only one component of airline safety, but it is not by itself sufficient to generate the assurance that the airline is in control. This is the same argument we put forward in the SET analysis in the Appendix of this book that SET is only part of the EC solution. To establish reliability, CoCo introduces 20 control criteria as basis for understanding control in organizations and for making judgments about their effectiveness. These criteria are grouped into four components:

1. **Purpose:** provides a sense of the organization's direction.
2. **Commitment:** provides a sense of the organization's identity and values.
3. **Capability:** provides a sense of the organization's competence.
4. **Monitoring and learning:** provides a sense of the organization's evolution.

CoCo framework is very broad based, future oriented, and offers maximum flexibility on how control is to be implemented.

Implications of CoCo in the EC Context

As far as its applicability to EC is concerned, the following concepts may be useful:

People throughout the organization participate in, and have responsibility for, control. We encourage those who are entrusted to manage EC to self-assess the state of control surrounding their organization's EC processes. As control self-assessment is a new discipline to many organizations, and is highly recommended by regulators and governing bodies alike, it is an opportune time for EC managers to consult their auditors in this exercise.

CoCo places more emphasis on the people aspects, such as commitment, capability, mutual trust between people, and periodic challenge of assumptions. It suggests, even with an impressive set of internal controls in place, that losses may still occur because of mixed messages from senior management, unethical acts of employees, or simply poor business judgment. The 1995 Barings Bank fiasco demonstrated that it is not the "rogue trader" that brings down the bank; it is the lack of management supervision. As discussed in Chapter 7, it is very hard in an EC environment to tell the difference between an intentional event, such as fraud, and sheer incompetence. Perhaps high-caliber management can make it a little easier, but still the risk remains. While EC is heavily technology dependent, it does not relieve the need for the usual due diligence and management supervision.

The CoCo definition of control includes the identification and mitigation of the risks of failure to maintain the organization's capacity to respond and adapt to unexpected risks and opportunities. Considering that we only see the tip of the EC iceberg, this concept (not found in COSO) deserves some serious attention. EC can be viewed as a potential new risk and an opportunity. A proactive risk and control assessment involves an understanding of the new environment and its control dimensions, to be cross-validated by specialist and auditors.

Control Objectives for Information and Related Technology, 1998 (CobiT)

The Information Systems Audit and Control Association (ISACA) in the United States recently developed and refined the *Control Objectives for Information and Related*

Technology (CobiT) to serve as a framework for IT control. CobiT, which is also concerned with corporate governance, distinguishes itself from COSO and CoCo by taking a three-dimensional view on IT control as the interaction between IT processes, information criteria, and IT resources. Thirty-four control objectives are organized into domains, processes, and activities, all of which are linked to business requirements for information. Four domains are identified in CobiT:

1. **Planning and organization:** covers strategy, tactics, and is concerned primarily with the identification of the way IT can best contribute to the achievement of the business objectives.
2. **Acquisition and implementation:** refers to the need for IT solutions to be integrated into the business processes. We should give CobiT the credit for preaching "business drives technology."
3. **Delivery and support:** describes the usual IT activities.
4. **Monitoring:** domain states that all IT processes should be subject to regular assessment of their quality and compliance with control requirements. Monitoring is a recurrent theme in COSO, CoCo, and CobiT. Contrary to popular belief, the monitoring function is neither the exclusive domain of auditors nor their raison d'être. Because monitoring has to be ongoing, auditors, who mostly perform period-in-time or point-in-time audits, are not suited for this function.

IT professionals will find the various processes listed in CobiT to be all too familiar. The value of CobiT does not reside in its full catalog of IT processes but in the highlights of the control objectives associated with each process, and the means to achieve them. Another good source of IT control guidance is CICA's *Information Technology Guidelines Third Edition* (1998). But to find specific control guidance for Internet-related processes, we will have to wait for ISACA's upcoming publication, *Control Objectives for Net Centric Technology*, expected to be released at the end of 1999.

To support additional manageability of the IT control objectives, the *CobiT Third Edition*, planned for availability in April 2000, will include a Maturity Model, Key Goal Indicators, Critical Success Factors, and Key Performance Indicators for each of the 34 high-level control objectives. These performance measures will increase the appeal of CobiT to IT management and general user management, by providing the means to evaluate performance and progress against established goals, and will also provide the IT auditor with a more pro-active set of tools in defining and managing the IT control objectives.

Implications of CobiT in the EC Context

Of particular interest to EC professionals are the three control criteria that CobiT refers to as business requirements for information:

1. **Quality requirements**
2. **Fiduciary requirements**
3. **Security requirements**

CoBiT further expands the above three reference models to include seven information criteria requirements to manage their 34 high-level IT control objectives. These include: effectiveness, efficiency of operations, reliability of information, compliance with law and regulation, confidentiality, integrity, and availability. All of these features are essential in designing EC controls.

The CobiT framework is built on the premise that controls exist to satisfy business requirements. It is a theme that resonates throughout this book, particularly in Chapter 7. **Controls exist to enhance business. Controls are part of the business enhancement strategy, not just defense strategy.**

We believe an understanding of the multiple control framework or models presented in COSO, CoCo and CobiT is the first step to the development of an effective, customized control framework for EC. These concepts and documents reflect the changed thinking of management, users, and auditors in the context of today's business reality. In the next section, we will use the relevant COSO, CoCo, and CobiT concepts and integrate them in a blended control framework to audit EC processes. Even though this proposed control framework is applicable to many EC processes, it goes without saying that EC in the financial services environment will require a closer examination of each of the following control categories. For this reason, the control framework here and in Chapter 9 are written with financial services EC concerns in mind.

A comparison of COSO, CoCo, and CoBiT and the implications for EC is presented in Table 8.1.

AN INTEGRATED CONTROL FRAMEWORK FOR EC . . . .

CoCo, COSO, and CobiT concepts are designed to be broad based so that they are sufficiently flexible in their application in most business environments. Our objective is to find context for all this control material, so that we are not looking at an arm or a leg, but at the total picture. Classic internal controls applicable to EC will not be elaborated here, as they are found in many related books on the subject. In the following sections, we will focus on the new control landscape toward management, IT professionals, and auditors, and use it as a backdrop for control self-assessments by business units and nonauditors engaged in various aspects of EC activities. Regular control self-assessments and reporting of the risks and controls by management is an effective way to inspire customer confidence and ensure customer safety. An auditor's role is to independently evaluate management's assertions on the state of control. Harmonization of these two roles is critical for the success of the enterprise.

The EC Control Environment

Controls are exercised in relation to risk. An organization's risk management and control structure generally exhibits the following characteristics: board oversight; risk policy and risk identification by senior management; and evaluation and monitoring by operations management. The audit function spans this control structure. Its role is to provide an independent assessment of the risk and control processes. The introduction of EC into an organization does not change this control structure. What has to change is the audit approach. Instead of just looking within the organization for the necessary controls, the auditors now have to find out if their EC trading partners' control structure is in place and is consistent in practice. When double control standards exist, we have to challenge and be satisfied with the rationale for the discrepancy.

We encourage the auditors to share the results of their EC risk and control assessment with management. Sharing information with the audit clients narrows each other's expectation gap. It is a practical way to ensure that the EC business objectives and control objectives are synchronized.

Business objectives: In the EC world, where everyone can be potentially commercially connected to everyone else via the Internet, the business requirements of trust and accountability are obvious. This requirement will in turn drive technology to deliver information that can fulfill CobiT's quality, fiduciary and security requirements of business. The fiduciary requirements, in particular, are twofold: In case of public companies, they exist to protect stakeholders' interest; in all other cases, they can be viewed as an ethical way to take care of customer safety, which in turn will inspire public confidence, maintain the trust bond, and ultimately take care of business relationships.

Control objectives: Control exists to fulfill some key business requirements. Five classic control objectives can be applied to meet EC business objectives: (1) management control; (2) reliability of information; (3) security; (4) monitoring; and (5) timeliness, availability, and recoverability. Risk assessment begins with an understanding of the threats to meeting these objectives.

Risk Assessment

Risk assessment begins at the planning stage and is an ongoing exercise as dictated by the environment. It begins with an understanding of the entity-wide business objectives and whether or not the objectives for engaging in EC are consistent with corporate objectives.

Risk management is an essential element of effective control. It is about how worthwhile it is to take risk or to avert it. Take the sailboat metaphor. In sailing from point A to point B, there cannot be absolute assurance that the boat will arrive at point B. All the necessary preparation may be done, from selection of engineer, boat design, safety, fuel, and so forth, but the boat may never arrive. This may be due to a storm, faulty navigational equipment, or that the boat anchors at the wrong harbor. The only assurance that can be given is one of "risk worthiness;" that is, after taking all into account, the sailing is sufficiently risk worthy, and that there is sufficient assurance that destination B will be reached. At this point in global EC development, we find three of the seven risk models/choices introduced in CICA's 1998 publication *Learning About Risk: Choices, Connections, and Competencies* most relevant: In launching EC initiatives, you are making (1) **strategic choices** that involve (2) **operational risk and choices**, and by (3) **choosing to be aware** of the external and internal environment, you are better prepared for the unknown and better positioned to recognize opportunities and act on them.

We are interested in the potential risks in the new environment (refer to Chapter 2). In reviewing EC-related business initiatives, a management study of the external environment will position senior officers of the organization to make strategic choices. A detailed assessment of the new risks in the business cases, and a high-level discussion on how they are to be addressed, will set the stage for making operational and control choices. CoCo stresses the people aspects of control. Choosing to be aware is most appropriate in an environment where the ability to see and interpret changes in various stages of EC processes is a key control in itself. It goes hand in hand with the "information-seeking" mind-set.

Risks may reside in areas outside of a business unit's immediate sphere of influence or core EC process/activity. We need to review upstream and downstream activities as a continuum so that control gaps can be identified. From a financial institution's perspective, events such as operational changes to the existing merchant sign-up process and the merchant support procedures regarding Internet point-of-sale service must be adequately considered, as these events may affect changes to an organization's security policy and ultimately to its safety infrastructure. Refer to the SET analysis in the Appendix of this book.

Profiling EC risks is not a standalone exercise. It requires a broad understanding of the external environment and the future place of EC in the organization. It is more fun treating the risk assessment as a risk-seeking exercise. Refer to Chapter 2 for EC-specific risks and select those that are likely to be faced by your organization, then proceed with an assessment in concert with sales, production, marketing, financial, operations, and technology groups.

Some technology risks and vulnerabilities are common to most EC environments, and some are industry specific or transaction specific. The Web sites for these industry groups, user groups, and lobby groups may be consulted first for initial direction; and then test for relevance.

EC is about business relationships. The meaning of due diligence now extends to taking care of these relationships as well. If the risks and exposures are outside the domain of the existing organization's control policy and standards, then all EC trading partners should start a dialog to address these risks jointly.

EC is global in orientation. Regulatory requirements may vary in different locations and jurisdiction. The regulatory risk of noncompliance can be averted with periodic review of new rules and regulations in locations where EC business is conducted. Failure to do so may incur loss of license, fines, and invite negative publicity.

Control Evaluation

Management

As we have said previously, it is management, not auditors, who are responsible for control in an organization. When designing EC solutions or products, we need to build controls up front as part of business enhancement, not simply because auditors want them. Challenge auditors' rationale for their recommendation so that only those controls that add value to business are included as part of the solution. Increasingly, auditors are seen as catalysts and change agents who make things happen by diligently following up on key control issues when management attention is slipping.

Policy compliance. With the introduction of EC into the organization, certain IT policies may have to be revisited. Existing policies related to the following are a likely subject of reexamination:

1. *New regulatory announcements:* A visit to their Web sites is a first step, to be followed by queries in the context of your organization's EC initiatives. (Refer to Chapter 9 for more on this topic.)
2. *Protection of proprietary information:* There are business-to-business transactions and business-to-consumer transactions. Identify and assess all the EC transaction types to ensure that the Big Rules still make sense in the new environment, and that the various levels of protection can be afforded without breaking the rules.

3. *Privacy:* Information protection, security, and privacy go hand in hand. Refer to Chapter 4 for background to this safety infrastructure for EC. Organizations, especially financial institutions, have extensive privacy policies communicated to the general public. In the event that clarification is necessary as a result of new EC product introduction, communicate externally and internally on a timely basis.
4. *Security:* Security policies that govern IT are your terms of reference. In EC, most of the software and hardware components and services deployed are vendor supplied. Unfortunately, not all vendors and suppliers understand and respect your organization's security policies. The rule of thumb is to compare the third-party's policy statements against your own organization's. The relationship between your organization and vendors is analogous to a contractor and the subcontractors. The ultimate responsibility for ensuring policy compliance rests with the contractor.
5. *Outsourcing:* Refer to Chapters 2 and 4 for new awareness in this area.

Relationship management. There are two types of relationship management:

1. *Internal relationship* between the three parties to EC systems development—business managers, IT professionals, and the control function: Management effectiveness is assessed based on how well they work together. Decisions on matters of safety come from the business managers with independent opinions and input from the other two parties.
2. *External relationship:* If it is business-to-business, the slant is to favor mutual reliance on good control practices. Unlike EDI, which demands a previously established relationship, in many other types of EC relationships, you may not know all your partners. If it is a business-to-consumer relationship, then the consumers have an expectation to know what has been done to address their concerns. A regular and timely communication to resolve their founded or imaginary concerns goes a long way in boosting consumer confidence.

Current and up-to-date knowledge. Tune in to the changes affecting EC. Issues in international law, taxation, security and interoperability standards, privacy, and transborder data flow are constantly refreshed on various Web sites. Also, EC publications are growing rapidly and are a great source of information. Business managers, IT professionals, and auditors need to be familiar with the latest trends and directions that affect their business, function, and product offerings. This knowledge is needed to regularly test the relevance of their EC business and control objectives. In Chapter 10, we make a few predictions. Of all the technology innovations and tools relevant to EC, software agents are, in our view, the single most important topic for security and audit specialists to be concerned with.

Capability and Commitment. One important aspect of control stems from using the right people and right skill sets from line, business, and technical areas. This is not to underrate the need for competence, ethical values, and integrity, all time-honored soft management attributes for any successful business venture. Fiduciary requirements outlined in CobiT complement these with considerations in terms of effectiveness and efficiency of operations, reliability of information, and compliance with laws and regulations.

Reliability of Information

At the transaction level, many of the controls prescribed for electronic funds transfer (EFT) and financial EDI (FEDI) are applicable to EC. Like these earlier forms of EC, the focus is on preventive controls that secure and confirm transactional integrity. Instead of reinventing the wheel, review application and environmental controls recommended for EFT and FEDI first, especially those that satisfy the control objectives of accuracy and completeness, processing integrity, proper reporting of status, errors, exceptions, and resolutions.

The key difference between EFT, FEDI, and the EC business environment is the ubiquity and anonymity of the customer-consumer. Evaluate the effectiveness of safety measures from the point of view of the consumer, merchant, financial institution, service provider, and trading partner, and the dynamic interaction between them.

Security

This is the most discussed aspect of the Internet these days, and its application to EC, by extension, constitutes the most-written-about topic. The security control objectives of confidentiality and integrity are classic IT control objectives that must be satisfied, in proportion to the risks and complexity of the system and transaction. CobiT includes availability as a security requirement. It may be relevant in light of the risks brought by denial of service attacks. At this point, a visit to Chapters 2 and 5 is recommended.

The following are new control considerations to satisfy EC integrity and confidentiality:

- Communication to staff and the public about any revised security policies and practices as a result of EC and framework for building public confidence by way of constant reinforcement of these practices.
- Rationale and use of the various layers of protection: firewalls, dedicated Web servers, virtual private network (VPN) servers, dedicated lines, secure Internet tunnel, public key infrastructure (PKI) or appropriate encryption, authentication, and certification authority.

- Security relationships with vendors and suppliers: State your security requirements upfront.
- Assess security from several perspectives: e.g., merchant messaging, accounting, payment and authentication devices; peer-to-peer payment software; customer registration and authentication process; and the client browser, server application, and the service provider.
- Assess security at any point during transmission over the Internet between send and receipt.

Monitoring

Auditability is more than just the logging of Web server and Internet server activities and a review of the associated reports. Information is auditable when it can be substantiated by tracing it to source, electronic or otherwise, or when reliance can be placed on a proven and continually monitored control process. The audit trail is a prime component in the monitoring process. Audit trails do not have to be historical and "after-the-fact." Continuous monitoring using automated tools cuts down on the need for extensive logging for investigation purposes. Context-sensitive triggers can better enhance operational control than can historical audit trails.

When designing audit trails, keep "ease of use" in mind. Audit trails are not designed for auditors alone. They facilitate problem management and allow tracing from incident back to the root cause. When used properly, they are an effective operational control tool. Make sure that audit trails are not turned off without justification. CobiT recommends that audit trails closely work with change management, availability management, and configuration management; that is, with all the delivery and support staff.

Timeliness, Availability, and Recoverability

Obviously, service availability is a key business requirement. From a control standpoint, sufficient redundancy has to be built into the EC infrastructure to help ensure uninterrupted systems operations. This requires the identification of mission-critical EC processes and documentation of any single points of failure.

All EC applications are supported by a network or networks that have varying processing priorities among the organization's applications. Make sure that the existing network hardware and software infrastructure can support the organization's EC business objectives, both now and in the long term. Ensure that there is redundancy for the critical application servers. If not, ensure that the organization's renewed contingency plan includes the recovery for these servers and systems on these servers.

The Payoff Idea

One of the key concepts in the evolving business model for EC is that information sharing is an essential part of the success of any business that wishes to exploit this technology. It is this thinking that is making companies like Wal-Mart the dominant entity in their industry. This applies to control information as well. EC control guidelines that are good enough for the auditor should also be good enough for the IT manager. There is no reason at all why the audit guidelines and the IT manager's guidelines do not follow similar paths and, in fact, focus on similar results. Management's role is to ensure that the controls are properly built into the EC system up front and that they continue to operate as designed. Auditors, on the other hand, provide an independent assessment of the effectiveness of these controls and ensure that they are incorporated into the EC system and the related management activities.

Guidelines for IT Managers

Design control policies and procedures early as an integral part of the IT organization, its business objectives, and interrelated control elements, resulting in coordinated decision making. Include safety rules (see Chapter 7) in business policy for EC. *There should be sufficient front-end planning for building safety into the basic design.*

Be familiar with the subjects that are EC significant: regulatory pronouncement, protection of proprietary information, privacy, and security. When it is regulatory requirement, all efforts must be made to comply.

EC processes are highly dependent on many external vendors and suppliers, from the acquisition of Web-based hardware/software services to contracts and agreements with intermediaries, such as VANs, ISPs, and network carriers. Discuss the organization's existing IT policies governing EC with the external parties at an early stage, and obtain an opinion from the legal department whether the policies can be complied with. In EC, the most common concern is privacy with respect to the custody and use of customer information at a vendor location. If the vendor is not subject to regular external audit review, *negotiate a right-to-audit clause to be included, and before the contract is signed, clearly spell out who pays for the audit engagement.*

Control self-assessment (CSA), a discipline that is gaining increasing acceptance, is a way for management to communicate its responsibility for control and report on the state of control affairs. We encourage IT managers to highlight and document the key risks and controls in EC by using this control framework. A succinct documentation on CSA goes a long way. It is an efficient and effective way to communicate to management, internal and external auditors, and the regulators, who are all interested in the control dimensions of EC.

Communicate internally and externally. Chances are the concerns that one IT manager faces are similar to those of another manager across the street. Although information is available on the Web sites, the best resource is always your counterpart in another organization or the manager you have an EC relationship with. Like EDI, IT managers are developing cooperative systems and must look beyond their own organization's boundaries for win/win solutions.

Aim high at attaining a cost-effective EC relationship. In Chapter 7, we describe a perfect EC relationship as simple, convenient, always available, error free, effortless, and free. Depending on the type of EC application, some of these features are more important than others. Regardless of how the manager ranks them, the security and safety mechanisms that are built into these relationship are there to enhance, not to distract from, these features.

During an EC implementation, there are times when a recommended security or control measure cannot be applied for various valid reasons. *Compensating controls may be adequate as an interim solution, but as the EC business grows or current technology is replaced in future years, these alternate controls may be ineffective.* Use a security issues tracking document to track all less-than-satisfactory solutions. Make sure that they are subject of periodic reassessment as the EC environment changes. When a security solution is non-compliant with the organization's policy, either revisit the policy or refer the matter to senior management for appropriate action.

Involve the auditors early in the EC development project. Auditors have the opportunity to see EC in action across functional or business units. They can bring forward the good control practices from one division to be considered in the next division and cross-validate them. The areas where auditors can best contribute are security, auditability, and control.

Guidelines for Auditors

This section focuses on the IT auditor's role in auditing EC. The interdependencies of the financial, operational, and technical elements of EC (therefore the coordination and sharing of findings among the auditors) require a complex and more comprehensive set of controls.

To provide an objective opinion on the state of controls in EC, the auditors must independently evaluate and verify the control assertions made by management. The control framework presented earlier in this chapter is our point of reference. Here are some suggestions:

Capitalize on existing knowledge and audit guidelines from the earlier forms of EC such as EFT and FEDI. EC will not drastically change these guidelines. It just adds a new dimension—the Internet—to the existing infrastructure.

Internet audit guidelines are not synonymous with EC audit guidelines. EC puts the usage of Internet in a particular focus. Here, the business context takes precedence. *The auditor must first understand the prime business issues affecting EC before applying the Internet guidelines.* The audit drivers are not network, PKI, encryption, authentication, or browser/server security and the like. These are only drills of different sizes. The actual audit drivers are business requirements, holes of different shapes.

Focus on the new risks and new controls. Make a list of the new risks and controls and include them in the CSA. From this list, build a risk and audit profile of the EC system or process. Profiling is a top-down approach and requires an overall view of EC as an integral part of the entity-wide business objectives. Confirm this understanding with the business and IT managers.

Some of the risks of EC exist outside of the organization's span of responsibility and control. External vendors and suppliers, and outsourced operations are common in EC. To assure that no hands-on controls are lost, *there may be a need to verify the management and controls surrounding these third parties. Obtain an independent report on service organizations.* (In the United States, it is commonly referred to SAS 70 report; in Canada, the Section 5900 report.) The right-to-audit clause allows the organization's auditors to independently audit their safety and soundness procedures and processes.

EC audits require a multidisciplinary approach. The lead auditor should validate the findings with the organization's business and IT managers, lawyers, compliance officers, and security experts—as the need arises.

There is a wealth of information in recent management publications on the concept of control to enhance corporate governance. The good news is that they all sing the same tune: control must be business driven; control exists to satisfy business objectives but not vice versa. Creating the belief that everyone in the organization is responsible for control, from the board of directors to individual work units, has universal appeal. By building controls during front-end planning and viewing each design as a step toward their organization's business enhancement strategy, the EC practitioners are able to better align business objectives with control objectives. This EC control framework will serve as a proactive guidance toward building quality operations that combine security for business and safety for customers. In other words, this is how trust and relationships are built. Ultimately, this will also protect the global citizens in the new electronic age.

Table 8.1 The Nature of Control: A Comparison: COSO, CoCo, and CobiT

	COSO	CoCo	CobiT	Implications for EC
Audience	Management	Applicable to all members of the organization, including the board of directors, management, employees, and other stakeholders.	Management, users, auditors	IT managers are members of an organization's management team. They should have a high level understanding of these pronouncements.
Definition, scope	Viewed as a process entitywide	Concerned with the organization as a whole in achieving its objectives. The interconnectedness and relationships between all business units and the external environment are considered key.	Viewed as a process, focus on IT control function.	EC should be viewed as a process first, to be integrated with on-going business activities.
Underlying concepts	Internal control is affected by an entity's board of directors, management, and other personnel designed to provide reasonable assurance regarding the achievement of stated objectives.	Control is about the future and the achievement of the mission and the vision; CoCo is based on the philosophy that the organization as a whole is greater than the sum of its parts and that the whole has characteristics that neither of the parts individually has. Organizations are considered to be dynamic organic systems that continually change, adapt, and learn, as opposed to the mechanistic, deterministic, and static view.	Control in IT is approached by looking at information that is needed to support business requirements and the associated IT resources and processes.	Controls in EC should be approached by assessing information that is needed to support the EC requirements.

(continued)

Table 8.1 (continued)

	COSO	CoCo	CobiT	Implications for EC
Control objectives	Effectiveness and efficiency of operations Reliable financial reporting Compliance with laws and regulations	In the first instance, achievement of the organization's mission and vision. In striving to achieve these, there are subordinate objectives that fall into one of the following categories: Effectiveness and efficiency of operations. Reliable internal and external reporting. Compliance with laws, regulations, and internal policies.	Effectiveness Efficiency Confidentiality Integrity Availability Compliance Reliability of information	Control objectives and business objectives are the same. The attributes on the left all contribute to establishing accountability and trust in EC.
Control components	Control environment Risk assessment Control activities Information and communication Monitoring	Purpose: being guided by the mission and vision. Commitment to the purpose. Capability of organization to achieve its purpose. Monitoring and learning to adapt and change as required.	Planning and organization Acquisition and implementation Delivery and support Monitoring	These components can be used to form an integrated control framework for EC.
Responsibility for control	Management	Corporate governance function. Everyone in the organization has a governance function. The ultimate responsibility is the board of directors, but they need to mobilize the entire organization in this regard.	Management	By extension, everyone in the organization. The control dimension is not to be overlooked.

(continued)

Table 8.1 (continued)

	COSO	CoCo	CobiT	Implications for EC
Judgment of effectiveness	Reasonable assurance that the stated objectives are met	Using 20 criteria grouped within the four control components as a guideline. The criteria are not minimum standards and are relevant in nature.	Satisfies stated objectives	Same: satisfying stated business and control objectives of EC.
Control period reported	At a point in time	Concerned with the organization's future nimbleness to achieve its mission and vision.	For a period of time	It is recommended that EC control self-assessments be reported over a period of time.

9

External Audit Requirements and Regulatory Compliance

OVERVIEW

There is no doubt that the future of EC, both in terms of its growth and its ability to generate new ways of doing things, is assured. Experts all over the world predict that in the foreseeable future, the number of businesses of all sizes involved in EC will grow substantially, and business-to-business Internet commerce will explode. This view is reconfirmed in PriceWaterhouseCoopers' Winter 1999 issue of *Risky Business*, and Deloitte Touche Tohmatsu's 1998 publication, *The E-Business Tidal Wave* by Trevor R. Stewart.

However, as early as 1995, a Deloitte Touche Tohmatsu International study forewarned that EC is an emerging area of concern and "will become the key control challenge for the international financial community in the next five years." This is not to say that EC will be limited by these control concerns, rather, that thought and efforts need to be focused on providing realistic solutions to the emerging control issues that seem unique to EC.

The implications of the above are significant: (1) these forecasts come from the major accounting firms that are also responsible for many of the external audits of EC in large corporations who would turn to them for expert advice; (2) these firms have positioned themselves to take on the challenge and are offering various EC consulting services to meet the growing demand; (3) the potential EC reach to every segment of business and every type of consumer has already raised the attention of regulators and governments alike; EC will be high on the external auditors' and regulators' review agenda; and (4) because EC is a new deployment of existing and emerging technologies, EC organizations should communicate expectations (whether they are safety related or service related) clearly and regularly to instill public confidence.

What needs to be clarified is: Who performs what role—and under what circumstances—and how can the business managers position themselves to be out of harm's way, should a problem or concern arise? This suggests that an analysis of the key issues and audit groups that are interested in them will be immensely helpful. We have categorized the key audit roles and issues as follows to provide a clear path of understanding, these somewhat mysterious elements.

THE EXTERNAL AUDITOR'S ROLE . . . .

The external auditor is often responsible for providing an opinion on the well being of the company, usually for the benefit of shareholders in the case of a publicly owned company, or for financial organizations who have taken some risk in that organization. To accomplish this assurance process, external auditors will perform a statutory audit.

In a statutory financial audit, the external auditor has a mandate to periodically perform an audit, and to express an objective opinion regarding the fair representation of the financial statements of the reporting legal entity. The external auditor's opinion is based on an independent review and a review of the internal auditor's work to arrive at a reasonable, but not absolute, assurance that the financial statements are free of any material misstatement. Generally Accepted Auditing Standards (GAAS) is applied in conducting such audits. GAAS is a set of rules acknowledged as those by which auditors can measure performance and by which others can measure it as well. These rules can be either written or unwritten and have been established by a variety of groups, including government, professional or standard setting bodies, courts, and practitioners. Typically, these standards include both a series of tests of controls and substantive procedures as appropriate to the entity being audited. In the United States, they are found in the Statement on Auditing Standards (SAS) issued by the American Institute of Certified Public Accountants (AICPA). In Canada, pronouncements regarding GAAS are found in the Canadian Institute of Chartered Accountants (CICA) Handbook. In the United Kingdom, it is the Statements of Auditing Standards, issued by the Auditing Practices Board, which contain, *inter alia*, the basic principles with which auditors are required to comply.

What External Auditors Look For

External auditors, like internal auditors, must fully appreciate the total impact that EC will have on an organization's business and the extent to which the technology will be integrated with the organization's application systems. It means that they will not just review security as a standalone issue simply because it has been overhyped as the number one public concern. Adequate business knowledge of EC includes an understanding of EC end to end: from customer to network and from network to the organization and back, including a fair understanding of the flow of transactions beyond organizational boundaries. It also means that their audits will be process centered rather than input-output centered. Process centered reviews allow the auditor to see the big picture and to discern linkages between EC participants from the top down. Browser-based interfaces in EC arguably will become the area that will draw more attention than the traditional "input-process-output" types of reviews.

Theoretically speaking, there should be no difference in risk assessment and control objectives in the work of the external auditor compared with that of the internal auditor. Depending on their objective and scope, the external auditors rely on the work of the internal auditors as their first source of information regarding the state of control in EC. This chapter will walk through the control review process through the eyes of the external reviewers and to illustrate how their requirements can be satisfied through documentation of key controls, verification procedures, and reporting and managing of control deficiencies. In a typical audit engagement, the external auditor goes through a similar planning process as the internal auditor.

Risk Assessment

After obtaining a bird's eye view of the EC environment, the external auditors usually begin with the assessment of the inherent risks of a transaction stream or account balance, and changes to the business nature of transaction processing such as high volume, the speed of processing, low human intervention, the effect of reduced balance sheet amounts, shrinking of working capital due to JIT inventory and implications of electronic audit trails. The increased dependence on ISPs, multiple network carriers, VANs, and software and security vendors will be high on their agenda because consequences of poor vendor operations or poor security are not limited to a single victim. Request for due diligence reviews on behalf of the outsourcing clients will grow. Chapter 2 contains many pointers to risk assessment used by external as well as internal auditors. At the end of the day, the same fundamental principles apply to EC as to any other business process. What's always needed is an intelligent assessment of the facts, constraints, assumptions, and the associated risks.

Evaluation of General and Processing Controls

External auditor's classic control objectives will have to be satisfied through a variety of techniques. These include confirmation that a recorded transaction is real, properly valued, reflected in the proper accounting period (timely), correctly classified, summarized, and posted. Assuming that outbound transactions are governed by corporate policy regarding confidentiality, inbound transactions will be subject to greater scrutiny than outbound ones due to the risk of compromised data sources. In addition, they will likely look beyond the individual transaction and focus on interorganizational issues and the dynamic EC technology environment.

Testing of Key Controls and the Use of Advanced Audit Software

Increasingly, external auditors need more powerful computer-assisted audit techniques (CAATs) and more technology-dependent tools to do their job. Traditional "after-the-fact" batch controls will not be sufficient for their purposes. They may need to develop their own EC control databases and query programs to confirm interorganizational transactions almost as quickly as they are created. Instead of seeking assurances from internal sources, they may be more disposed to obtaining larger electronic samples of evidence from outside the organization, such as the EC consumers at large via direct surveys and questionnaires over the Internet.

Transactions That Affect the Organization's Financial Statements

External auditors are primarily concerned with the nature of the transactions entering into an organization's accounting system. Any EC application that directly or indirectly affects the organization's financial statements would naturally become a prime candidate for independent review. It makes perfect sense for management to document all new EC implementations and significant changes since the last external review and highlight such aspects as the relative materiality of the transactions processed, the volume, infrastructure, systems interfaces and interdependencies, and the level of technical sophistication in each EC environment. Failure to produce such documents may prompt the external auditor or the regulatory examiner to perform a more in-depth review than is normally warranted.

Control Self-Assessments

As mentioned in Chapter 8, control self-assessment (CSA), when properly designed is an excellent process that allows management to identify and define the control objectives they must fulfill. In Canada, the filing of an annual self-assessment report by deposit-taking financial institutions is mandatory (see The Regulator's Role). For some organizations, it may be an option, but others are making it a "must do" exercise. SETCo, the company set up by Visa and MasterCard to oversee compliance matters, require their SET Payment Gateway Service Providers to perform "self-audits." The AICPA/CICA Web Trust^{sm} Principles and Criteria also provides a "Self-Assessment Questionnaire" for use by EC service providers in documenting their EC business practices, disclosures, and related controls.

CSA is a proactive way to tell auditors and regulators that you are well positioned to conduct business in EC. It saves a lot of explaining to the external reviewers and ultimately saves management time. We have provided all the pointers for CSA in the earlier chapters of this book.

The Findings in the Last Internal Audit Report on EC

One of the key documents an external auditor requests is the most recent copy of the audit report on EC and the changes that have taken place since that time. Major control deficiencies noted in the audit report and the lack of follow-up or resolution increase the EC risk profile. Many organizations have factored the results of the recent audit into their risk assessment. We stress that the findings in the last audit report are relevant only if the management, environment, business activities, and processes have not changed since the last audit. The external auditors would want to know the state of affairs at the time of their audit and determine whether or not those findings are still relevant. Any consultants' report or regulators' review report will be of particular interest to them.

Outsourcing and Joint Business Arrangements

Due to the increased dependence on third-party products and services used in EC applications, many of the controls have migrated to the suppliers' organizations. EC management should be in a position to articulate the following to the auditor:

- the process of managing the supplier
- supplier compliance with company's Big Rules
- confidentiality, security, privacy, and regulatory requirements
- coordination of business resumption planning and testing
- special arrangements with international suppliers
- due diligence reviews of the supplier organization
- data protection and records held by third parties, ISPs, and VANs

THE QUESTION OF CORPORATE GOVERNANCE: THE REGULATOR'S ROLE

Although the attention given to internal control in recent years was born of regulatory pressure and an increased focus on corporate governance, the basic tenets regarding control remain unchanged: (1) everyone in an organization is responsible for internal control; (2) the board of directors provides governance, guidance, and oversight; (3) management is accountable to the board of directors. To assist all levels of management in appreciating and implementing internal controls, the regulators in several continents have also communicated their expectations. Because of its global reach, EC will touch on cross-border and international rules and regulations in a large scale. IT managers, auditors, and business managers with EC responsibilities should have a fair appreciation of the regulators' control outlook and incorporate this into their EC control self-assessments.

The difference between the regulator's review and that of the external auditor is the level of detail reviewed and the use of hands-on techniques. Whereas the external auditors may run diagnostic tools to evaluate the effectiveness of security and other controls, regulators do not perform hands-on activities. Rather, the regulators would interview management about the independent tests that have been conducted by the internal and external auditors or other consultants and review the results and follow-up action. The scope of the regulatory review is generally of a high-level nature and employs a risk-based approach. The examiners focus on those activities that present the greatest risk to the health of the regulated institution. This approach is consistent with the internal and external auditors' way of doing things.

Here's the good news. Many regulators have communicated their requirements and expectations on their Web sites. These sites are easily accessible for questions and clarifications. The Federal Deposit Insurance Corporation (FDIC), for example, has a corporate Web site (www.fdic.gov) where all examination manuals, policy statements, rules and regulations, and guidance letters are provided. The site is designed to meet the information needs of both consumers and bankers. They even have a section for consumers to conveniently report on, or locate, suspicious Internet banking sites by using their search engine. Our experience with a few federal examination specialists has been most rewarding. They exemplify the new breed of independent reviewers who are there to help when the public needs them.

The following highlights some of the public sectors' pronouncements relevant to EC.

FDIC Electronic Banking: Safety and Soundness Examination Procedures, 1998 (U.S.)

FDIC is the insurer of all U.S. banks and thrifts, and supervisor of all U.S. chartered banks that are not a member of the Federal Reserve System. This set of procedures will eventually be included in their Division of Supervision's Examination Manual. FDIC's definition of EC is broad. It refers to "activities involving the exchange of goods and services over a computer network or automated system." For purposes of this discussion, we will focus on the examination procedures for payments over the Internet, as other payments mechanisms are not new, and the associated risks and controls are classic.

This document segregates electronic capabilities into three levels, reflecting progressive processing sophistication: (1) information only systems, (2) electronic information transfer systems, and (3) electronic payments systems. Levels (1) and (2) have been the subjects of many Internet books, but the lively debate on the use of the Internet as an alternative payment channel continues. In all cases, this manual maintains the view that trust and confidence are the cornerstone of EC: "trust in participants . . . and confidence in the process are crucial to a particular system's acceptance and survival." Our entire book is devoted to the ways and means of building trust and confidence in EC, with a focus on the payments area. We have also taken the regulators' requirements seriously throughout this book.

FDIC also published *Security Risks Associated with the Internet* in December 1997. A new guidance document, *Risk Assessment Tools and Practices for Information Security*, was issued in July 1999. The potential areas of security vulnerability have all been addressed in Chapter 5.

Independent Report on "Electronic Commerce and Canada's Tax Administration," 1998

Published in April 1998, this report to the Minister of National Revenue from the Minister's Advisory Committee on Electronic Commerce is Canada's first step in grappling with the complexities of EC in the new compliance and tax administration areas. In September 1998, the Minister responded to his Advisory Committee with overwhelming support that the "time is right to move beyond principles and implement a Canadian EC strategy by year 2000."

We encourage EC project managers to familiarize themselves with the tax implications and regulations and to design the legislative requirements into the system in their front-end planning. A close follow-up of these developments is necessary. The following are some salient control-related issues discussed in this report.

Build Trust into Electronic Marketplace. The report recommends that Industry Canada set clear policies on the recognition of digital signatures, the use of encryption, and the protection of consumers' rights and personal information, all of which have been addressed in Chapters 4 and 5.

Increasing Risk of Noncompliance with the Tax System. The report recommends developing compliance programs and "Webcrawler" software to trace nonfilers to complement existing programs. This software could be created to search for merchants' Web sites that point to Canadian residence. The software would be similar to existing software for indexing Web pages, counting the number of hosts, and others. Although we still don't know the exact specifications of the "Webcrawler" software, we can safely assume that the fundamental principles are similar to that of electronic audit trails, discussed in Chapter 3.

Policy Related to File Servers. This is intended to ensure that EC transactions are fairly allocated between locations. From a regulatory perspective, the knowledge of the location of the servers where online commercial activity records reside matters more than the location where the company records are kept and maintained. Permission is required to maintain books and records outside Canada. These issues are discussed in Revenue Canada's latest Information Circular IC78-10R3, which is also available at www.rc.gc.ca. This circular also discusses retention of electronic records and rights of inspection.

Encryption of Records. Where the taxpayer does not provide the decryption key or access to the decrypted records, the report recommends that those records be treated as nonexistent. In addition, the Government is advised to clarify what a business must do regarding the transmission, receipt, and storage of electronic documents, and to publish criteria for acceptance of digital signatures, in the absence of any legislative or other requirements. An area to watch out for.

Record Retention. Transaction managers should be required to provide Revenue Canada with the electronic records of a taxpayer being audited.

As a result of the above recommendations, four technical advisory groups (TAGs) have been formed in 1999 in response to the recommendations in this report.

Readers can also turn to a 1999 discussion paper entitled, "The International Taxation of Electronic Commerce," published by the Certified General Accountants of Canada, available at www.cga-canada.org.

There are similar developments in the international front. The following Web sites are a backdrop for the discussion on EC from the regulator's or government perspective:

- *www.ncsl.org* (National Conference of State Legislatures, United States)
- *www.fdic.gov* (See FDIC Electronic Banking section of this chapter)
- *www.ato.gov.au* (Taxation and the Internet, Australia)
- *www.govt.nz/news* (Guidelines to Taxation and the Internet, New Zealand)
- *www.oecd.org* (Taxation Framework Conditions, Organization for Economic Co-operation and Development)
- *www.rc.gc.ca/ecomm* (Canada)

CDIC Standards of Sound Business and Financial Practices: Internal Control 1994 (Canada)

The Canadian Deposit Insurance Corporation (CDIC) provides insurance for depositors against the loss of eligible deposits held by CDIC member deposit-taking institutions. The CDIC set certain conditions of insurance called its Standards of Sound

Business and Financial Practices covering eight areas. Only the one on Internal Control provides some insights on conducting business electronically. Because the importance of internal control has been heightened by the increasing attention given to corporate governance, internal control is now considered a vital element of corporate management. The scope of CDIC Standards encompasses the management of and effectiveness of IT. The well-publicized security attacks and breaches on the Internet are a constant reminder that it is the organization's responsibility to prove to their regulators and the public that it is safe to transact using the Internet.

Of interest to auditors, control designers, and IT managers is the CDIC's standards self-assessment criteria for internal control, which is similar to the COSO or CoCo criteria described in Chapter 8. The difference is that the CDIC requires each deposit-taking member to file an annual report in accordance with their Standards Assessment and Reporting Program (SARP). Essentially, this report on internal control (one of the eight areas of businesses to be reported), is the CDIC member's assertion that prudent and sound policies on internal controls are in place, and that they have been adhered to, for a period of time. Included in this report is a description of IT controls in operation since the last report date, the deficiencies uncovered, and the actions taken or being taken to address those deficiencies. A copy of the report is provided to the institution's regulators. The regulators will require adequate documentation to support the assertions made in these self-assessments to enable the examiners to reach a conclusion on adherence and report to the CDIC. Inadequate documentation may not permit the examiner to reach a conclusion.

Our experience with SARP suggests that a self-assessment report usually begins with a statement on significant changes in the control environment since the last report to the CDIC. It is prudent business practice for CDIC members to document the key risks, mitigating controls, and procedures of any EC applications using the established criteria. Companies that do business with these financial institutions can also use the SARP criteria as a reference tool.

Financial Aspects of Corporate Governance, 1992 (U.K.)

In 1992, the Code of Best Practice issued by the Cadbury Committee (*Financial Aspects of Corporate Governance*) recommends that listed companies include information on corporate governance issues in their annual reports. Although mandatory only for listed companies, the code helps to establish the key governance issues for all companies. This code places great emphasis on the role of nonexecutive directors, audit committees, internal control systems, and back-to-back reporting by boards and company auditors about their respective and complementary responsibilities. The Cadbury Code was endorsed by the London Stock Exchange through requirements that listed companies' reports on their compliance with the Cadbury

Code. In 1994, the Toronto Stock Exchange (TSE) issued a similar report (*The TSE Governance Report*) entitled *Where Were the Directors*? It basically resonates the Cadbury Code.

In 1994, in response to the Cadbury Report, a working group organized by the accounting profession in the United Kingdom issued guidelines entitled *Internal Control and Financial Reporting: Guidance for Directors of Listed Companies Registered in the U.K.* The good news is that the working group's guidelines are very similar to those found in the COSO report.

What does all this mean to business and IT managers? First of all, these publications provide good insights into the scope of the work of the auditors and regulators. If your company is listed, most likely the control criteria reflected in these best control practices are the yardsticks that independent reviewers will use to measure the effectiveness of internal controls.

Both the Cadbury Report and the TSE Governance Report guidelines are sufficiently generic and universal in their applicability. With the growing number of listed high-tech companies engaging in EC, the shareholders of these corporations should demand that their management refer to these guidelines as a fundamental measure of trust.

The new guidelines issued by the Turnbull Committee, intended to replace the Cadbury Report, will be released shortly. One of its main requirements will be that directors of a company will have to ensure that they have undertaken an internal control review.

For the year 1999, it will suffice to be able to declare that one is putting in place the necessary procedures for such an internal control report. From the end of the year 2000, company directors will have to demonstrate the results of such an internal control review.

EXTERNAL REQUIREMENTS HARMONIZATION . . . .

The Common Ground

From a survey of the requirements of external auditors and regulators, some best control practices emerge. We suggest that business and IT Managers consider these practices as their contribution toward corporate governance and as a value-adding exercise to business enhancement. Here are a few common denominators:

- Board of directors, CEO, and management are responsible for control.
- Auditors independently review and assess the effectiveness of organization's system of internal controls.
- Control criteria are established to fulfill management objectives.

- A call for formal management reporting on the status of risk and control.
- Best practices can be derived from the control criteria established by the various professional, regulatory, or standard setting authorities (many of these are covered here and in Chapter 8).

ACTION ITEMS FOR CONTROL DESIGNERS . . . .

"Control designers" is an emerging professional specialization. A specific focus of control designers is to assist management and organizations who are required to, or have chosen to, report on the status of control and risk management against a set of established control criteria such as COSO, CoCo, Cadbury, or CDIC. These professionals provide training and tools to management to facilitate formal reporting to regulators and/or the board of directors on the adequacy of the organization's control environment. Control designers and consultants who provide enterprise risk and assurance services already have a broad-based knowledge on best practices in control self-assessments and generally accepted control criteria. They need to consider the following additional points when evaluating EC controls.

Apply Safety Tools

This action item is not restricted to the new breed of control designers. It is placed here because the technical project team is expected to be familiar with the usage of the tools discussed in Chapter 3. Control designers may need to question the relative strengths and limitations of the tools to be used in order to determine if there is a "good fit" between the control framework and the tools for particular applications. Cost-effective controls are not always available. In some cases, compensating controls may have to be used. As discussed in Chapter 3, the speed of processing and high volume of transactions have rendered traditional manual controls ineffective, if not irrelevant. The ability to observe the state of control becomes more distant, as the controls are no longer exclusively resident in your processing center or call center. They may be in the outsourcing company, or with the ISP, and/or your trading partner on the other side of the globe. As indicated throughout this book, EC is a complex arrangement of business relationships. For those EC partners critical to your business, check out how compatible their control environment is. This is a prerequisite toward an effective control design. The higher the volume, the more data is to be analyzed. Control designers may consider the creation of a segregated EC database for real-time or off-line analysis of credential-based, policy-based, and audit-based information. Such measures will increase the level of trust.

Add New Control Self-Assessment Topics

As EC expands, we will see more nonbanks involved in financial activities that are traditionally within the banking domain. EC is a prime example of potential competition from the nonbank sectors, where control self-assessments will be particularly useful and where control designers can help in a big way. Banks are heavily regulated. They are also familiar with their fiduciary responsibilities. The newcomers may not have the necessary discipline and control mindset. Using the classic control self-assessment model as a base, control consultants, when advising these organizations on EC controls, may want to add the following items to their existing design framework:

- briefing on the control and audit dimensions in their business proposals (not just security alone!)
- factoring in regulatory requirements and Big Rules
- external relationship management control process (suppliers, regulators, external reviewers, outsourcers)
- new indicator/measurement tools for the Internet environment
- outsourcing controls
- advice on the relevance of COSO, CoCo, and CobiT
- design of safety features (again, not just security!) into customer surveys

Promote Quality Documentation

Promote *quality* documentation, not just any documentation. Control designers can advise on how to document the significant changes introduced by EC to the enterprise risk profile, risk, and control assessments performed; evidence as to how the controls are tested; control deficiencies uncovered; action and follow-up action plan; and how residual risks are managed. Traditionally, documentation is the area that receives the lowest priority in an IT shop. Control designers are in the best position to sell to management the importance of good control documentation, especially for "immature" products and services like EC.

ACTION ITEMS FOR EC PROFESSIONALS . . . .

Do not reinvent the wheel of controls. This book focuses on EC that results in payments via the Internet. There is the retail type of funds transfer, and there is also the business-to-business type of payment settlement. The latter activities are similar to those involving EDI trading partners, so review the risks and controls for EDI as a start. Granted that the financial risk of the individual, consumer type of EC transactions is relatively lower than business-to-business EC, the anticipated high volume, when considered in aggregate, may pose a potentially higher risk. These transactions have similar business properties as retail electronic funds transfer (EFT) and point-of-sale (POS) transactions. Existing control procedures for EFT and POS are great reference points to be reviewed first for their applicability in the new environment.

In the United States, the *1996 FFIEC Information Systems Examination Handbook* suggests that examinations of retail EFT facilities "focus on the potential large scale risks of a given product." EC products that have similar characteristics as EFT and POS should be assessed using this approach. *A word of caution*: Although we can treat consumer EC products as part of the retail EFT and POS family, the assumption is that EC risks are EFT and POS risks intensified.

Concentrate on the new features. Prepare an EC list of "things to consider." Trust and confidence aside, the customers will likely evaluate Internet payments based on a number of criteria that they are accustomed to when transacting in EFT and POS. These are: user privacy, transaction legitimacy, security, nonrepudiation, systems dependability, efficiency, cost, and convenience, all of which have been discussed throughout this book.

In the Appendix, we will present an analysis of the application of SET to credit card purchases over the Internet and review their "potential large-scale risks." This analysis will illustrate how the financial institution, the merchant, the consumer, as well as third-party service providers can participate in the same risk management program to design safety and soundness requirements of the regulators to achieve the internal control objectives of the organization. Whether we are concerned with a consumer-to-business or business-to-business EC, transacting on the Internet is not as mature or as proven as retail or wholesale EFT or POS. The common EC infrastructure and de facto standards, though emerging, are still lacking in universal application.

Use "four eyes." Follow the classic management control of using "four eyes." When there are significant decisions to be made in EC, involve at least two individuals. This is an issue that regulators will consider. It is specifically spelled out in Annex II of the Bank of England's consultative paper: *A Risk-based Approach to Supervision*, March 1997.

Check out what the financial institutions have to say. It is reasonable for the public to expect the financial institutions to continue their traditional fiduciary role into the EC territory. The public should look to them to lead the way in the design of appropriate EC control and security. These days, financial institutions are all prepared to reach the public in a personable way. Customers have the right to be satisfied that the appropriate safety features are built into the EC applications they use and demand a clear statement of their efforts to establish reliability for EC transactions.

Seek the Advice of Experts. EC environment is dynamic. It is impossible to be fully in tuned with every aspect of EC on the domestic front, let alone international developments in the field. The issues that regulators will always consider include quality and skills of management. The Bank of England, for one, specifically includes the appropriate location of "mind and management" in the above-mentioned consultative paper on risk-based approach to supervision.

No organization engaging in EC builds its EC components from scratch. A well-designed EC product is the result of the efforts, knowledge, experience, and expertise of many disciplines. There is no one expert in the field of EC. As mentioned earlier, EC will never be configured with a single operating environment or an established protocol, or a set of universally accepted standards of security hardware or software. The configuration of all these components will in turn add complexity and vulnerability to the implemented product. Even though EC suppliers are touting interoperability and full scalability in the open systems environment, remember to test the connections at the seams. This is where experts may have to be called to certify that the integrated EC application, not just the built-in component controls, operates as designed. In the FDIC's *Electronic Banking: Safety and Soundness Examination Procedures*, their examiners are urged to consult specialists at critical junctures in their review before finalizing their findings. It makes good sense to those who have responsibility for EC to follow a similar approach, and seek technical review or assistance from the experts before the EC system is implemented. Some of the areas that require expert advice are: enforceability of digital signatures, contingent liabilities in international EC, taxation, outsourcing outside of the country of domicile, and cross-border data transmissions.

Assign a relationship manager. Besides the three key players internal to the development of EC—business managers, IT professionals and the control function—the EC relationships extend to EC suppliers and service providers, outsourcing companies, regulators, external auditors, and international governing bodies. This integration role will oversee that the perfect EC business relationship is actively pursued. This relationship manager will work closely with the project and product team to ensure that the EC is simple, convenient, always available, error free, effortless, and free! (See Chapter 7.)

How does one establish a relationship? How does an organization convince a new relationship to believe that it will be worthy of their trust? An example of this can be seen in the emergence of the large Dutch bank, ING, who has established a virtual banking beachhead into the Canadian market. ING DIRECT tells you they are a member of the deposit securing agency, CDIC, and follows the rules and guidelines of the banking industry regulator, OSFI. They also refer to how secure your money is in terms of the quality of their relationship with highly respected financial institutions, including MasterCard International, and Interac Association. The same is true of Security First Network Bank (SFNB) of Atlanta. When it first came to market, its primary marketing message was that it was the first U.S. virtual bank to be FDIC approved, identifying that the regulator was an integral part of designing trust.

Design controls upfront. The cost of retrofitting controls into the implemented EC system is high. Identify and involve qualified staff to participate in the design phase. Auditors can be called on to act as control consultants when they are not performing audits. These days, audit professionals are working toward the so-called "just-in-time" auditing. Their timely participation as needed at various stages of the EC project prior to implementation is a case in point. When outsourcing arrangement is a major EC component (especially where processing is outside of the country of domicile), it is prudent to check with EC lawyers and regulators whether special safeguards are necessary. Adequate design is only the first step. **Controls must be fully tested to confirm that they actually work!**

Involve the auditors early in any new EC initiative. Invite them to present their views on the EC project they plan to audit. This open forum goes a long way toward building relationships and mutual understanding of the control requirements. Like management consultants, auditors have a broad-based perspective on control issues and are in a good position to bring cross-unit best practices to the table. When expectations are communicated up front, there is less challenge to the audit findings and recommendations at the end. This is true for both internal and external auditors.

Repair control deficiencies sooner than later. An audit may result in the report of control deficiencies of various degree of seriousness. Major control deficiencies must be immediately corrected. These are usually the ones that would cause material financial loss or expose the organization to undue risk, some of which is not quantitative (e.g., reputation). Depending on the nature of the control weakness, auditors do not expect every minor finding to be addressed with the same exigency. In some instances, compensating procedural controls may suffice.

Be diligent in follow-up and report on the disposition of control deficiencies. It goes without saying that when major deficiencies are uncovered in the prior audit period, auditors will follow up more diligently. Experience has shown that when unfavorable audit ratings are given, audit visits become more frequent. The most efficient and effective way to manage the auditors is to timely report on the disposition of the findings and the status of the implemented recommendations. Instead of waiting for the independent reviewer to knock on the door, issue a timely report to the examiner or auditor, clearly evidencing the improvements in control before their next visit.

Equipped with these good control practices, the auditor, the regulator, and the EC team together will put the trustworthy stamp on EC.

10

Trends to Follow and Opportunities to Take

This final chapter is about the future—that means it's about uncertainty. Our goal is to help you make change an ally, not a threat, by focusing on what we see as the most likely developments in EC over the coming years. "Likely" does not mean "definite"; it is close to impossible to predict anything in the field of EC, though, of course, there's a growing industry of expert opinions and forecasts, especially concerning the growth of Internet commerce.

Predictions made by respected experts over the past several years about the size of the Internet market in the year 2001 range from $1 to $3 trillion. All we can be sure of is that the market will be somewhere between zero and infinity. Add to this the wildly optimistic and inaccurate forecasts made in the early 1990s about the coming explosion of interactive TV as a mass market, the failure of many early Internet shopping mall ventures, plus the as-yet tiny fraction of retail sales made electronically, and there's plenty of reason to doubt the many claims about consumer-to-business EC that scatter the pages of the Internet and IT trade press. To read *Wired*, the magazine of Internet utopians, you'd believe that Internet EC was already in the trillion-dollar range and has taken over the mainstream of business; it hasn't, and total revenues are as yet well under a billion dollars.

That said, look at business-to-business EC on the Net. Here, a number of companies are handling a billion dollars or more of transactions. Cisco, the manufacturer of network equipment, is one. GE has made the Internet the base for its billion-dollar-plus of procurement bids. Business-to-business EC is close to being a requirement for being a well-run firm. In 1990, it was fully practical to be well run, making only limited use of PCs, fax machines, and 800 numbers. Now, it's pretty dumb. We're within a few years—five at most—of it being dumb not to make EC a foundation of business logistics. So here is a prediction we can make with confidence and plenty of supporting evidence: EC will be the base for next-century logistics, supply chain management and enterprise resource planning. The paper invoice, accounts receivable, and related documents will become the exception, not the norm. This won't happen in a flash, but it will happen quite soon.

It's not that clear what will happen in the consumer sphere. So far, none of the hype has been matched with results. Internet advertising, retailing, and financial services are still a miniscule fraction of total business and there are very few profitable firms on the Net. That could change quickly; anyone who—like us—is skeptical that consumer EC on the Internet will be in the mega-billion dollar range in 2001 must, of course, accept that a massive increase in EC cannot be ruled out. The World Wide Web shows that; after over a decade of slow but sustained Internet growth, this relatively simple but astonishing innovation moved the Net from a specialized corner of the network world to its very center, with growth in users and volumes that were so large and so rapid that Internet statistics are out of date the moment they are collected and are very unreliable. The Internet is as embedded in the fabric of everyday life as is the cell phone (and used by very much the same demographic groups as those who own mobile phones) and that ensures that consumer-to-business EC is as sure to come as ordering pizzas over a cell phone.

Obviously, EC is on an overall growth path, and that growth path will be a steep one well within the next five years. Although, it may take time for consumer-to-business EC to get up speed, as it did for business-to-business EDI and electronic payments, once that happens, the minimal growth rate should be the 15–20% that has marked EDI for over a decade. That adds up to a doubling every five years. And that's at the bottom end of the growth rate. What other areas of business in this time of immense competitive stress offer that opportunity?

The faster the rate of growth, the more important safety will be, in terms of both systems defense and business enhancement. Technology risk increasingly means business risk. It also means relationship risk. EC is part of the emerging Trust Economy described in Chapter 1. It's completely dependent on relationships. It changes many of the basic rules of business. That means it will change many of the basic rules of security, accounting, and financial control. That's a pretty obvious statement, to which the equally obvious response is "Which ones? When? How?" The honest answer here is "Dunno." Any other reply is either dogma—the *Wired* ethos of Apocalypse Soon—or ungrounded prediction. The challenge is to plan when you can't predict—there is, in our view, no prediction that can reliably guide any firm along the growth path of EC.

HOW TO PLAN WHEN YOU CAN'T PREDICT . . . .

In this chapter, we take up the challenge. We make no direct predictions, though we give our own best estimates of trends. We do this so that we can highlight opportunities for you to look out for and assess their implications for security, audit, and control. We classify these trends in four categories of likelihood: inevitabilities, strong probabilities, possibilities, and unknowns. We add a second dimension of assessment: time horizon (near-term, medium-term, and unknown).

The likelihood categories are as follows:

- **Inevitability**. Here, all the evidence points toward this being a certainty, *at some point in time*. We add that last emphasis because in technology so often the issue is not "if" but "when." Thus, it's very easy to be sure that interactive television will at some point in time become a major element in EC. Billions of dollars have been invested on the basis of that inevitability, with many trials and pilot projects, great expectations and even greater financial write-offs. As one expert commented in the late 1980s, EC via interactive television will be a $60 billion business—the only question is whether that will be $60 billion of revenues or losses. That statement is as applicable now as then.
- **Strong probability**. Less than certain, but more than just a possibility: These are often the developments that rest on market forces rather than technology, whether a critical mass of users adopts them and makes them a de facto standard. They are thus not "sure things" but have plenty of factors and forces moving them forward.
- **Possibility**. There's enough evidence that this has a more than 50% chance of happening. There are so many of these in the market and on the horizon that many will move quickly from possibility to probability to inevitability and others will slide down the likelihood scale.
- **Potential "wham."** This is a possibility that could relatively suddenly become a bandwagon; it's something to watch for and think about but there's as yet no basis for factoring it into business planning. The World Wide Web was a "wham." It took off so fast that much of the IT industry was taken by surprise—Microsoft in particular. In 1996, intranets were a wham application; even though most experts expected them to become a routine component of corporate telecommunications and computing, few predicted the massive explosion which, if 1996 was the year of the Internet, made 1997 the year of the intranet and 1998 the year of the extranet.

For the time-horizon dimension of our matrix, the categories are as follows:

- **Near term**. This indicates that the technology or application should become a force or factor that will be part of mainstream EC, and hence part of business planning, within the next 3–5 years. Three to five years ahead is the time frame for innovation; the company has time to build policies, skills, and procedures *now* to be positioned when demand takes off.

- **Medium term**. Five to eight years. This is the practical long-term horizon for business planning and for addressing infrastructure needs. It's too early for the firm to make specific moves and investments but not for it to begin to assess business opportunities and technology needs. Beyond this period, it's close to impossible to make assessments. We recommend a strong focus on the near term as a necessary base for strategic planning and a more relaxed assessment of the medium term as the base for strategic brainstorming.
- **Unknown**. Here, no one knows, and there will be optimists who see it as the "Something of the Future" and realists who point to the optimists' last urgent predictions and recommendations. Here, our recommendation is to periodically update your mental map, looking for where and when "unknown" starts looking like "coming soon." An obvious example here is digital cash. It could be 20 years away from becoming the mainstream of EC, but it's not too fanciful to see some force jump-starting the so-far experiment—perhaps Japanese consumers, a very trend conscious society, making the Mondex smart wallet the next equivalent of the 1997 Tameguchi fad.

The resulting likelihood/time horizon matrix is shown in Table 10.1, with examples that we review in more detail later in this chapter. The examples are based on our own conclusions from experience, research, and the opinions of the experts we most respect. Some of our assessments will inevitably be incorrect, and there will be many surprises that no one can reliably anticipate. For instance, had we filled out this matrix in, say, 1990, Java would not be on the list for the obvious reason that it did not exist. In some areas, our opinion is far less optimistic than that of many experts in the technology field. We strongly feel that, for example, e-cash—electronic cash, digital wallets, Mondex, cybercash, microcurrencies, and the like—will take many years to build to a critical mass; we classify it as an inevitability in the unknown time horizon category.

By contrast, we are more sanguine than many commentators about the likelihood of network appliances and network computers reaching a critical mass—strong probability—within the near term. You may disagree. That in no way invalidates the assessment, ours or yours, as the aim is to examine the implications for the central topics of our book: safety for EC. If you think that, say, e-cash is a near-term strong probability, then it should move up on your learning and planning agenda. If you believe the network appliance is no more than a medium-term possibility, then you can simplify your agenda and have one less item to worry about in this time of constant technology change.

We thus suggest that you develop your own matrix and keep it updated over time. The goal is to make change your ally, not a threat, and to be alerted to the implications of trends, so that if, say, the death of copyright—a potential "wham!" with an unknown time frame—should relatively suddenly move to, say, a strong medium-term probability, you have at least a broad sense of the opportunity, problems, and challenges it implies and can map these into the business enhancement strategy of business policy, relationship design, and front-ending that we presented in Chapter 7.

Table 10.1 The Likelihood/Time Horizon Matrix

	Near Term	Medium Term	Unknown
Inevitability	Component software as the mainstream of EC application development Rapid growth in intranets, extranets The triumph of ANSI X12	Widespread use of credit cards on the Internet by consumers	Digital cash Total dematerialization
Strong Probability	Network appliances Standardization of EC secure payments Growing use of software agents	International regulation of EC Consumer protection laws for EC transactions Full implementation of "strong" encryption Widespread adoption of EC in business-government transactions	Shortage of expertise needed for EC safety Emergence of established third-party trust industry Interactive television succeeds—at last!
Possibility	Widespread adoption of Microsoft's EC standards and tools	Disappearance of VANs as major EC force Growing use of wireless telecommunications for EC	
Potential "wham"	Massive litigation as a fallout from the Year 2000 date problem	Sustained Internet breakdowns The Internet as "cracker" heaven	The death of copyright

THE NEAR TERM

The near-term scenario we outline in Table 10.1 is:

- **Technology**. Component software like Java will become the mainstream computer programming language for EC applications (inevitable); network appliances capture a significant fraction of the corporate market (highly probable); at the same time, Microsoft's standards and tools become de facto standards for merchant systems and secure electronic payments (possible). Software agents become a powerful element in all aspects of information technology application—and a major problem for safety (highly probable).
- **EC standards**. ANSI's X12 becomes the central framework for more and more aspects of EC (highly probable).
- **Organizational applications**. Intranets and extranets grow very rapidly, far faster than Internet EC (inevitable).
- **Business environment**. The Year 2000 problem creates a nightmare situation (a "wham" potential).

This scenario assumes no technology surprises in the next few years and also assumes no major legal or regulatory moves in such areas as consumer protection, privacy, taxation, and strong cryptography. What does it imply for EC safety professionals? The obvious answer is that they will need much sharper and more focused knowledge of technology than they now do. Currently, there are three main technology issues that they must address: PCs, and mainframe processing "engines," both of which handle EC transactions, and corporate databases and large scale telecommunications networks, ranging from corporate private networks to industry VANS to the Internet.

Transforming the Nature of Security with Agents

If the scenario we sketch out above is an accurate broad picture of key emerging trends, then it defines a very different technology environment for EC safety professionals to apply their expertise and accept their responsibilities. Most obviously, the combination of Java, agents, and network appliances has the *potential* to transform the nature of security. We emphasize "potential" because there remain some skeptics of the claims that Java is inherently more secure than alternate programming languages. It almost certainly is, because its basic design principles provide for "applets"—mini-applications—to be self-contained and self-monitoring, with built-in protections against viruses. Given how new component software is, it may take another year or so before the language is backed up by the tools needed to fulfill its promises, but that seems sure to happen.

Change Through Component Software—An Observation on Java

The combination of Java and applets marks a major shift in the very nature of IS in general. It is no exaggeration to say that we are rapidly moving from the era of applications to the era of agents. Basically, an agent is a small piece of mobile software. Once activated, it can move across networks and computers, carrying out its function with no direct supervision from the application that launched it. Agents are already widely used in such areas as telecommunications network management, where they roam the network looking for problems and monitoring performance. Commercial uses include agents searching the Internet to locate bargain air fares. Several Internet search engines employ agents to locate, classify, and index new information sources.

Change Through Cookies

Cookies are a form of unlicensed agent. They are routinely used in Internet EC to store information when a PC user makes a hit on a Web site. They are stored on his or her hard disk; when the user next hits the site, the information is accessed to either speed up processing, customize offers and information flows (Bank of America uses them to display a screen that shows additions and changes "since you were last here"), or to capture information about the customer. They can be seen as either adding value to the business-customer relationship or as a dangerous invasion of privacy. Many people do not realize that their surfing of the Web is in effect monitored and information is collected that can be misused. This concern led to the eTrust certification service, which displays a Web site's policy about cookies: A guarantee that it will not give the information to other parties and will store the cookie only for a short period. This is the highest level of certification. Browsers like Netscape Navigator allow PC users to be alerted when a site tries to download a cookie and to accept or refuse them.

Cookies are a signal of massive coming change through agents. Obviously, they are a relationship safety issue. At least cookies have a direct link from a Web site to a PC. Agents, once launched across the Internet, are independent of either. They may be anywhere and may arrive at a site or PC at any time. They may stay for just a few milliseconds and then move on, leaving no trace. This challenges the traditional system defense approach to security and will demand creative ways of handling the potential flood of tiny, speedy movements of an unknown volume of agents whose functions range from the harmless and trivial to the consequential and risk-loaded.

Change Through Network Computer Growth

Network appliances (NAs) will speed up the growth in agents. There are many other names for them, network computers and Internet computers, for example, but the underlying principle is the same: to shift processing and storage from the PC hard disk to the network. A stripped-down processor uses a Java compiler and minioperating system to access applets on an as-needed basis. In the words of the chairman of Sun Microsystems, the firm whose staff invented Java, "the network is the computer." There are many skeptics about NAs, which are, to a large extent, a counterattack on the stranglehold that "Fortress Wintel" (Microsoft and Intel) has on the PC market; they may not become the mainstream of Internet usage, but there is plenty of evidence that businesses will adopt them to reduce growing PC costs and complexity of operation, and that they will be a substantial niche product in the consumer and education markets. Again, this poses challenges to the traditional approach to security. The very idea of an audit "trail" looks less and less sustainable, given the dynamic and volatile nature of the flow of agents, the lack of any fixed location of the flood of Java applets that the NA downloads, and the loss of traditional application controls. These are all challenges to be turned into opportunities. That requires that security professionals adopt the perspective we recommended in Chapter 7: a focus on relationship safety and on front-ending.

Of all the technology innovations and tools relevant to EC, software agents are, in our view, the single most important topic for security and auditing specialists to be concerned with.

ANSI and Internet/Extranet Growth

In our near-term scenario, we see two obvious organizational and business trends: ANSI X12 as the core of EC standard-setting and the continued growth of intranets and extranets. Both of these strong trends largely simplify relationship safety, given appropriate business policies and Big Rules. The main danger is that intranets may lead to the same ad hoc and localized developments that marked the early days of the PC revolution, where little, if any, attention was paid to safety; Big Rules are essential to avoid that happening with intranets. However, intranets resolve many of the worries concerning the Internet itself. They can be far more easily protected, through firewalls and gateways, and policies more easily defined and enforced—virtually *nothing* can be enforced on the Internet. Extranets are an extension of intranets.

We have included as a potential "wham" in our short-term scenario the nightmare possibility—inevitable in many experts' opinion—of the Year 2000 date problem generating massive breakdowns across the business supply and relationship chain. We do not discuss this in detail, and it is not in itself a security issue, but it will surely take much of the time and attention of just about everybody involved in EC.

THE MEDIUM TERM

In our near-term scenario, the main issues concern technology. We see this shifting in the medium term—5–8 years out—to the consumer side of EC: payments, protection, and regulation. We anticipate a rapid growth in the use of wireless communications, to the degree that there is quite a strong possibility that it will become the mainstream of telecommunications. That will obviously make strong encryption a vital issue.

Already, there is a rapidly accelerating convergence of Internet technology, consumer electronics, and wireless technology. Here were just a few recent innovations of 1998:

- *The Nokia 9000I digital cellular phone*: This device was the first of a growing flood of hand-held tools for which there is no term as yet: a digital cell phone, pager, Internet browser, and fax machine.
- *Palm Pilot*: This small personal digital assistant (PDA) sold well over a million units in its first year. It includes reliable and simple handwriting recognition, calendar management, scheduler, address book and notepad. The newer versions added a wireless modem and Internet browser.
- *Cars*: Ford announced that it will offer Internet and e-mail wireless capabilities in its year 2002-model cars.
- *Iridium*: The long-planned satellite-based service that makes the entire world a local phone call went live (and in 1999 declared itself insolvent).

All of these have the same basic features: mobility plus Internet access plus the standard consumer electronics price curve. That price curve virtually guarantees a takeoff in consumer EC at some point: Whatever the initial price of a device, it ends up costing around $300. The Palm Pilot was announced in that range, and the new versions added processing power and features for no additional cost. The Nokia 9000I came on the market at around $1,200. Ericsson's and Canon's offers pushed the price down in the very same year to the $600 level.

Wireless EC opens up many new opportunities—and new safety challenges. It's an area to watch.

Safe Payments

Safe payments are the single key issue today for the growth of Internet EC, and there is also a whole host of proposals for new forms of digital currencies that will charge small fees for services and make information cost effective. Basically, there are three issues that must be resolved:

1. **Security**. That's basically a matter of encryption and adoption of standards for payment processing. It's an area of intense activity and innovation. PKI seems to be leading the way.
2. **Perceived safety**. That is *the* issue that will pace progress in consumer EC.
3. **Regulation**. EC on the Internet poses many new problems of warranties, taxation, privacy, liability, and contract. So far, there has been little intervention by governments, but we see a strong probability of this changing.

Nowhere is the distinction between security and safety in EC more marked than in the area of credit cards. Using a credit card in an Internet transaction is far more secure than in most everyday routines. People have no concerns about giving their card number over the phone, faxing it, or leaving it on file with a travel agent. Internet credit card fraud to date is tiny in comparison with cellular phone theft, for instance. But most people simply don't as yet feel safe using their cards on the Net. That will surely change over time; the only question is, how soon? We take a conservative position here. We see mass use of credit cards as being over five years away. We expect it to be moved forward by the diffusion of strong encryption techniques and tools, such as PKI, with DES gradually eroding. There will be more initiatives to ensure consumer protection. Internationally, there will almost surely be a flood of regulatory moves. Already, the United States government is attempting to extend its legal authority to cover one of the fastest-growing areas of EC: gambling over the Internet. Antigua, a small Caribbean nation that has made support of the gambling industry a cornerstone of its economic planning, with a government Minister overseeing it, is challenging that attempt. There will be many similar arguments between nations about which laws apply where and to whom. It's likely that there will be increased cooperation in the end. That cooperation will center on the problems of pornography, fraud, and consumer protection—safety.

Taxation

Much of the conflict and cooperation between governments will address consumer protection and privacy, but one major driver will also be taxation. That is a topic that accounting professionals involved in EC need to track carefully and continuously, because it may demand very new and very complex record-keeping and tracking systems. In the United States, the government has to date avoided imposing new procedures or taxes; the priority has been not to impede the innovation that has marked the Internet and not to make any moves that may slow down the take-up of EC. That won't be the case abroad. The European Commission, centered in Brussels, has been dominated by centralist and restrictive policies in most areas that come under its jurisdiction; it's a regulation machine. It is targeting EC on the Internet as a growing concern. The basic issue is, where is tax paid on purchases? The United States wants it paid at the point where the goods are sold; there are some problems to resolve here about where that point is when the transaction is handled by a server in State A, whose customer service operations are in State B, and the goods are delivered from State C—but these are manageable. The European Union wants tax paid in the country of purchase. The reason is that goods such as books, records, and computers are generally much cheaper in the United States than in France, Germany, or Belgium. Thus, there are far fewer purchases by U.S. consumers from European sites. That means there will be a tax imbalance; the European Union doesn't want it to be in the favor of the United States.

The Effect of "Crackers"

One element we include as a potential "wham" in our middle-term scenario is very difficult to assess: the Internet becoming cracker heaven. "Cracker" has increasingly replaced "hacker" to describe those who view the Internet and computer systems as a domain for play, experiment, mischief, and profit. Hackers include good guys; crackers are definitely bad guys. That there are criminals and saboteurs in cyberspace is not new; for decades, all large organizations have had to protect against efforts to intrude into their systems. Every year, a company with experience and expertise in security suffers from a break-in. The Internet makes it easy for them to get into where the goodies are—Web sites—and opens up massive opportunities for them to do damage.

What has to be of most concern is that the sophistication of crackers is growing rapidly as are the tools they have access to and the clandestine electronic communities they form, which anonymously share tips, software, and strategies. Even relatively unskilled crackers can cause plenty of damage. What stands out in a 1997 book, *@Large*, which reviews "the strange case of the world's biggest Internet invasion," is how easily the Phantom Dialer was able to intrude on hundreds of highly "secure" university, military, business, government, and bank systems even though he was a neophyte. In addition, the book reveals how unprepared and short of expertise law enforcement agencies and the FBI are in facing off against the cracker community. The original design of the Internet is in the public domain, so that many crackers are totally familiar with its weak points. It was never intended to be secure; in the pre-Web days, security was Big Brother and the antithesis of the open and sharing community of researchers who formed its early user pool.

It's quite possible that in the medium term, there will be a retreat from the Internet as EC base and that intranets and extranets will take over. It seems close to certain that there will be new legislation and regulation. We expect this in the medium term rather than the near term because of the long lead times and political maneuvering required for what is sure to be controversial and widely opposed—trying to "control" the Web—and because there are as yet no clear principles for defining new laws and even fewer principles for making them work.

Obviously, computer crime and hacker/cracker activities are a matter for constant vigilance, and many of the well-established tools and procedures firms now use to secure their networks and systems will still apply and will, of course, evolve. But the challenge gets tougher and tougher to meet. Our own concern here is to emphasize that the priority remains business enhancement of the EC relationship *plus* system defense, not one at the cost of the other.

THE UNKNOWN TIME FRAME

We've highlighted in our matrix just a few trends, all of which have major implications for relationship safety.

Digital Cash

The first is digital cash; this seems an inevitability *in the long term*, but for all the claims, hype, and proposals, there has been little activity to date. From the perspective of safety, just about all the main schemes offer immense improvements over existing payment mechanisms in terms of security and privacy; Mondex and CyberCash are the leaders here. (Governments, of course, are more anxious to limit privacy and security when it's a code phrase for tax evasion and money-laundering.) Our personal view, however, is that they will take far longer to reach critical mass than their proponents expect, for two main reasons: (1) Existing mechanisms work pretty well, and (2) the organizations that operate them have a major investment to protect.

Changes in Payment Mechanisms

Checks, debit cards, and credit cards are the main payment mechanisms of consumer commerce. The main requirement for them to remain so in electronic transactions is relationship safety and, more important, users' confidence and trust that they are truly safe. For business-to-business EC transactions, firms have a wealth of experience and tools to draw on: financial EDI (FEDI), electronic funds transfer, electronic cash management, and others. All of these can evolve to meet the needs of all parties in the EC chain.

Changes in payment mechanisms and forms of currency have been very slow over the past decade. An example is the smart card, which has been widely promoted for well over a decade. It offers many advantages over credit cards, in terms of security, features, and storage of information and currency. Its use has remained very limited in the United States, though it is more widely employed in Europe and Asia. Only in the past 2–3 years have stored-value cards, a far simpler technology, become widely distributed, mainly for phone calls. Debit cards are increasing rapidly in use but, again, this is a simple and very dated tool.

One continuing barrier to the adoption of smart cards, debit cards, and stored-value cards has been the self-interests of players in the traditional market. Visa and MasterCard throughout the 1980s dabbled with smart-card pilot programs, each watching the other warily; the strategy seems to have been to make sure that, if smart cards took off, they would not be left behind, but at the same time not to move ahead until there were a clear opportunity or competitive necessity. They have taken the same tack with smart wallets. The credit card system works very well indeed and is global in span. Why change it?

Checks and currency work well, too, and meet most routine needs. Government treasuries have a large vested commercial interest in their continuance, too. The U.S. Federal Reserve Bank is a check-processing factory system, with massive warehouses and an entire fleet of aircraft that manage their sorting and sending to banks. The dollar bills and coins in our pockets provide what is termed "seignorage," a fancy term for the earnings the Treasury gains—around $70 billion a year—for what is a form of float, the interest on the currency it has issued and that is indeed floating around the financial system. A $100 bill hoarded in Russia is a contribution to seignorage. There are about $450 billion of U.S. currency bills in circulation. Of these, $150 billion is held outside the United States, in the form of $100 bills. In countries with financial instability and inflation, the $100 bill is the modern equivalent of gold bars, and more portable and convertible. When inflation in Bolivia reached rates of hundreds of percentages a *day*, the street dealers traded in dollars. They are a primary savings and storage vehicle in Russia.

Why on earth would the Treasury rush to eliminate all this, especially by encouraging new forms of electronic currency that make tax collection more difficult and money-laundering far easier?

We don't discount digital cash in our likelihood/time-horizon scenario. Indeed, we see it as an inevitability over the long term. We believe, though, that developments will be evolutionary and incremental—and relatively slow paced. Credit cards, checks, and cash will still be the trusted mainstay of commerce in general and will adapt to the demands of EC.

The Death of Copyright

There is one element in our evaluation of trends that has such huge implications that we can only guess at how it will play out. This potential "wham"/unknown time frame is the death of copyright. Digital technology, multimedia, and the Internet are fairly rapidly pointing to the loss of documentable "reality." Desktop publishing tools allow for forgeries of such accuracy that one German counterfeiter of U.S. $20 bills complained in court that he had had to lower his aesthetic standards because of the poor quality of the design. There can be no guarantee that any photograph has not been tampered with. Almost every day, there are published reports of e-mail hoaxes. Information accessed over the Web can be cut-and-pasted, plagiarized, and stored elsewhere. Multimedia makes it easy to "morph" a picture and so totally transform its details that it is unrecognizable from the original.

Most of the topics we have reviewed throughout this book relate to security and control of messages and transactions. We speculate—and it is only speculation—that there will be growing attention in the future to the *content* of what is to be kept safe. That will include protection of intellectual property and ways of certifying the documentable "reality" of, say, a picture or document; this is an extension of authentication, where instead of authenticating the sender of a message and ensuring that it has not been tampered with, the process authenticates that this is a "real" photograph or the "true" document. There will need to be new information accounting mechanisms that may include electronic watermarks and other ways of preventing alteration of information content. If copyright is to be kept alive, ingenious ways of identifying and tracking information sources and movements must be designed. Personally, we doubt that they can be.

The main implication for today in this scenario is simply that safety strategies will move from validating, protecting, and tracking transactions and messages in EC to validating, protecting, and tracking the *information* content of transactions and messages.

RECOMMENDATIONS TO MANAGERS . . . .

Whatever happens in any area of technology, business, government, and society relevant to EC, the need is to be there when demand takes off. Our recommendation is skeptical brainstorming:

- Make sure your firm tracks IT, EC payments, legislative moves, and the like.
- Don't fall for hype, but ask where's the evidence, who's actively behind this and can make it all happen, and how likely are EC customers to adopt this? When?

- Be alert to breakouts: when a previously niche aspect of EC or technology suddenly starts being discussed by businesses rather than just vendors, the IT trade press, and "gurus."
- Build a strong network of contacts in your region, industry, and professional field. Get out and meet them, through local universities, well-focused conferences, and associations.
- Subscribe to relevant publications outside your own field: IT, international business, EC in general, and ones that cover your industry. Skim them, looking for patterns. Very often, you will see a topic that's been around for years in, say, IT, suddenly start showing up in articles about banking or manufacturing. This may sound heretical, but read *outside* rather than *inside* your area of expertise. If you read about a topic you know, well, it will just tell you what you already know or, if it's news, a colleague will bring it to your attention—"Hey, did you see that article on . . .?"

Our final recommendation: View EC as the inevitable mainstream of business and look to make a major contribution to how your firm exploits the opportunity.

Appendix

Electronic Commerce in Action: The Case for Secure Electronic Transaction (SET)

Since the first recorded use of money in Mesopotamia 3,000 years ago, payment systems have been developed and adapted to support traditional commerce. How else can the business transaction be satisfied? Today, these methods include cash, checks, charge cards, credit cards, debit cards, prepaid cards, bank notes, physical tokens, and script. This has not always been the case. Instruments of value carry many attributes that identify them and allow them to perform their function in society. Whether the item is a rare sea shell or a low-value piece of metal with an identifying stamp on it, the key attribute of all of these forms of payment is the inherent level of trust that was created in the payment tool.

For some forms of money, the money itself carried the worth, through the fact that it was made of a precious metal like gold or silver. Even then, the skill of assaying and other verifications were needed to validate the money (remember the custom of "biting" coins—this was to see if they were soft enough to be made of real gold and that the gold had not been alloyed to a lower content). Fraud and counterfeiting have been part of the money process from the beginning.

In more-developed societies, it was not the token of value that made money worthy, but rather the knowledge that the backer was identified and different techniques were used to prove the veracity of the money. In the case of some forms of money, counterfeiting carried the penalty of death. In others, technologies such as metallurgy or clever stamping techniques made the money difficult to replicate. Even today, with paper money, the use of special technologies such as holograms, special threads, and watermarks have made counterfeiting difficult, but not impossible.

EC provides an attractive channel for the sales of goods and services over public networks. However, for EC to succeed, it must be complemented with a suitable payment system. Furthermore, a critical adjunct to the payment systems is an intrinsic ability to deliver trust and security. How is this trust created? More important, how is it maintained? What happens if counterfeit money is as good as the real thing?

Today, buying on the Internet is becoming more widespread. The convenience, selection, and easy access to products and/or services are among some of the main reasons for the popularity of EC. However, there are potential security risks associated with shopping and performing financial transactions online. Many companies, in recognizing the risks associated with the Internet's unsecured environment, are taking the necessary precautions through the encryption of these transactions.

Taking a cue from the Mesopotamians, several ways of conducting payments across the Internet have been devised to solve this problem. There are two main approaches, both variations based on procedures and protocols for transaction confidentiality and encryption to conceal individual credit card numbers.

The first approach involves retrofitting the currently used credit card process. By extending and complementing the current legacy approach with encryption technology, the confidentiality of credit card numbers and the integrity of the process are protected. The second approach involves the creation of a new form of token-based currency known typically as *cyber-dollars*, electronic credits that can be redeemed for real money with authorized merchants. So far, the use of an electronic token has not seen much success. Issues such as technological compatibility, brand identity, and potential regulatory issues have created barriers for this scheme's success. We see the use of the credit card as the dominant form of payment for the more basic forms of EC and, as a result, have provided an outline of the process as our most likely scenario for the near future. Our view was shared in the recent article in *American Banker* (July 1999), "Concern About Transaction Fraud Revive Movement to SET Standard."

1. WHAT IS SET?

The Secure Electronic Transaction (SET) protocol is collaborative specification involving groups such as MasterCard, Visa, American Express, GTE, IBM, Microsoft, SAIC, Terisa, and VeriSign, among other companies. SET made its debut in 1995 and proposed a standard that would allow:

- easy integration into existing legacy credit card payment systems
- safeguarding the established trust in existing legacy systems
- cost-effective implementation
- highly secure transaction integrity, privacy, and confidentiality
- strong industry alliances and buy-in to increase the success of a global SET implementation (e.g., the formation of the Joint Electronic Payment Initiative (JEPI), responsible for defining future protocols, is an excellent example of the industry commitment to SET)

The whole point behind SET is to build a mechanism that would allow the buyer and the seller to validate each other and to design trust in the electronic payments process. In order to succeed, SET must achieve three things:

1. It must be easy, both to use and to set up and maintain. People tend not to want to take on significant levels of maintenance and support, and to expect this would be a major detriment to SET's success.
2. It must be simple. As opposed to easy, the need for the user to understand the process and the implications must be quite clear. For example, to try and describe a PKI would not be valuable, simply because most people just don't need to know this level of complexity. However, to use an analogy for the complexity of the cryptographic process, such as the concept of a trusted third-party who knows both parties and can act as a vouchsafe for them, needs to be continually reinforced.
3. It must be cheap, meaning that the costs associated with the use of the SET approach must not be significant, or for that matter, even needing discussion. Designing trust is predicated on ensuring the belief that a safe and reliable environment is in place. The value of secured processing is directly related to fear, and if people fear the process, they will use cost as a reason not to participate.

Typically, a SET-based transaction process would work quite simply, as follows:

1. A SET-compliant cardholder visits a cyber-storefront via a browser. Cardholders may range from casual shoppers to businesses conducting some form of procurement.
2. The cardholder begins to select goods and services to be purchased. This may occur in a secured or unsecured manner. Although confidential banking information isn't being exchanged during this phase, some advocate the entire shopping experience be conducted in a private manner.
3. Once all required items have been selected, the cardholder is presented with an order form indicating all items and associated prices and total price including shipping, handling, and taxes. If the cardholder agrees to the terms, the merchant considers the order form to be active.
4. The cardholder is requested to select a method of payment. Because SET is merely an electronic representation of a plastic card, it is entirely possible that a cardholder has more than one SET "credit card" (that is, SET certificate).
5. The merchant creates a unique transaction identifier so the transaction can be identified and tracked. Furthermore, the merchant sends this identifier to the cardholder along with two digital certificates, which are required to complete the transaction of the specific method of payment.

One certificate identifies the payment gateway, an electronic gateway to the banking system that processes online payments on behalf of the merchant, and the other certificate identifies the merchant itself.

6. The cardholder sends the completed order form along with payment instructions to the merchant. The order form is digitally signed with the cardholder's digital certificate.
7. The merchant decrypts the order information and sends a confirmation to the cardholder that the order has been received.
8. The merchant then proceeds to create a request-for-payment authorization from the financial institution. The merchant digital signature, transaction identifier, and payment instructions are included in the encrypted request sent to the payment gateway of the acquirer.
9. The payment gateway decrypts the message and uses the merchant's digital signature to determine that the message is from a valid merchant. The payment gateway then uses the payment instructions to send an authorization request to the bank that issued the cardholder's bankcard.
10. If the bank approves the authorization, the payment gateway sends a digitally signed and encrypted message to the merchant. The merchant confirms the payment gateway's digital signature and ships the goods or services to the cardholder.
11. Once the transaction is completed, the merchant requests payment from the bank. The merchant creates a capture request that includes all the pertinent payment information and digitally signs it with the merchant's digital certificate. The information is encrypted and sent to the payment gateway.
12. The payment gateway decrypts the message, validates the merchant's digital signature and sends a request for payment to the bank, using the bankcard payment system. It receives a message confirming payment and sends the confirmation to the merchant.
13. The merchant confirms the message sent by the payment gateway and stores the information for reconciliation purposes.

For such a process to occur, a number of participants must be involved, each with relationships to some degree with one another (see Figure A.1). These are:

- *Cardholder*: The cardholder in the world of EC is a consumer or corporate procurement agent with a payment card issued by an issuer. SET maintains the confidentiality of the information sent to and from the cardholder and the merchant. Furthermore, SET authenticates the validity of the payment card used to tender payment.

- *Merchant*: The merchant is a Web storefront that offers goods and services in exchange of payment. SET secures confidential customer information from the merchant allowing for secure electronic interactions. Merchants that accept SET payments must have a relationship with an acquirer.
- *Issuer*: The issuer creates accounts and offers payment cards to cardholders. Users of the payment are guaranteed payment for authorized transactions.
- *Acquirer*: Acquirers are financial institutions that establish accounts with merchants and process payments on their behalf.
- *Payment gateway*: A payment gateway processes merchant payment messages. Typically, payment gateways are owned and operated by acquirers.

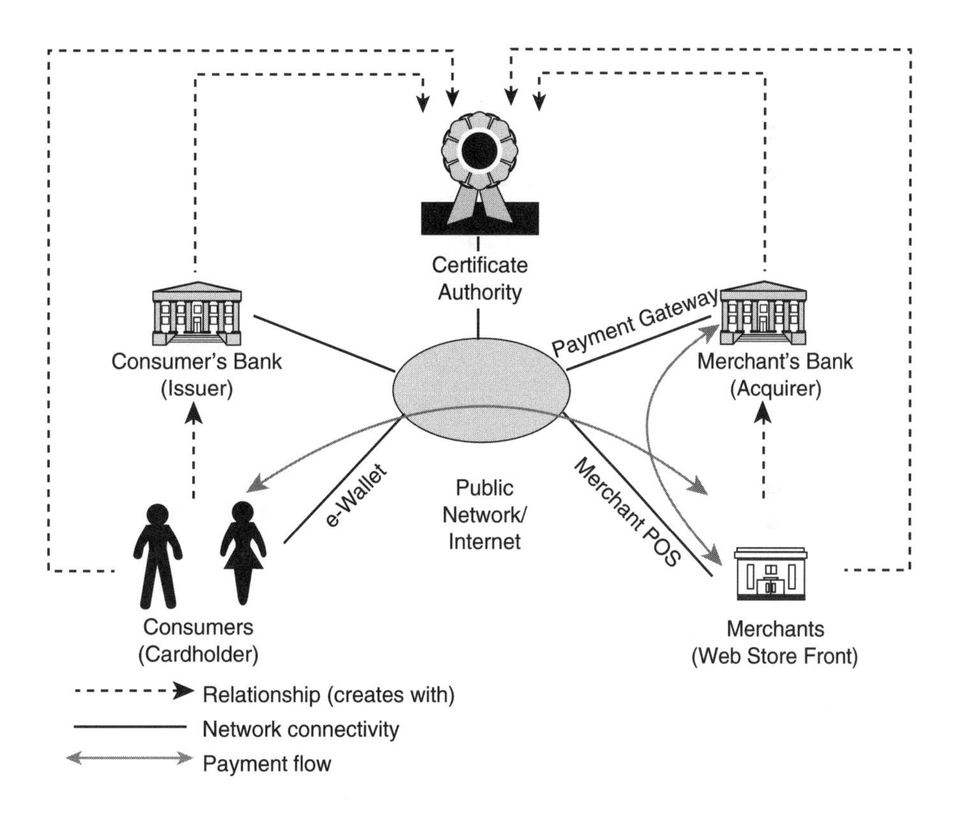

Figure A.1
Relationships established with SET partners.

2. WHY SET AT ALL?

Organizations, financial institutions, and merchants are looking to SET as a means of replacing the current, unsecured manner of transmitting account information in EC. The main concerns that SET is intended to address are:

- confidentiality of information achieved through the use of message encryption
- integrity of data achieved through the use of digital signatures
- merchant authentication achieved through the use of digital signatures and merchant digital certificates
- cardholder account authentication achieved through the use of digital signatures and cardholder digital certificates
- interoperability achieved through the use of SET, a common protocol and message format

This is not to say that unsecured transactions have no place in the EC matrix. They do. In fact, unsecured credit card transactions are generally quite safe—and are not subject to the widespread theft and counterfeiting that the doomsayers first thought. Rather, the use of SET is intended to increase the ability to develop a broader offering for transactions that need more security. In other words, there is always the need for more choice, and in order for these choices to be viable, there has to be consensus on how they are applied.

3. RISK PROFILE WITH IMPLEMENTING A SET PAYMENT SYSTEM

Each of the participants involved in the SET payment system utilizes technology and must abide by some process or set of guidelines. The degree of risk at each level varies substantially.

SET Payment Cardholders

Cardholders must protect their SET payment certificate just as they would with their present-day plastic credit, corporate, or procurement cards. The key difference being that today's SET payment certificates tend not to be very transportable, residing on PC disk drives. This will change over time with the greater proliferation of smart cards; however, in the mean time, cardholders are responsible for maintaining some form of logical controls on the computer systems containing the SET payment certificate (datafile) itself. Just as today's credit cards include a reference to cardholder agreement on the flip side of the card, SET payment certificates similarly make reference to agreements indicating cardholder responsibilities. The risks are relatively low at the consumer level, as cardholder agreements protect against fraudulent activities, and the value of any one SET payment certificate is relatively low.

SET Merchants

Merchants are a consumer's first and only point of contact to the SET payment system. For any transaction to take place, the consumer must implicitly trust the merchant or the process. Merchants can look to the hierarchy of trust established from a PKI as one level of reassurance to the consumer of their legitimacy. However, the merchant does represent a hub of activity that, if not carefully safeguarded, could be compromised, and in turn compromise the integrity of the payment system. Merchants are also subject to a merchant agreement indicating standards that must be adhered to. These standards involve some measure of logical and physical controls.

First, merchant Web sites must comply with the SET protocol to ensure effective and accurate exchange of information. Merchants can look to many off-the-shelf products, typically known as *merchant servers*, to deliver such functionality. Microsoft Merchant Server, Netscape's CommerceXpert, Open Market's Transact E-commerce, and other competing vendors, including: Ariba, Commerce One, Harbinger, and a variety of other niche players. EC organizations, such as BCE Emergis, AOL, Microsoft, and others, have taken it several steps further by offering totally secure environments based on such technologies for customers visiting their services. Second, merchants must ensure that their digital certificates are not compromised in any manner whatsoever by applying appropriate local security policies as well as technical and operational security policies. It is the merchant's responsibility to ensure they have applied all the necessary levels of security should they wish to maintain the consumer's trust.

SET Payment Gateways

The SET payment gateways are transaction hubs tying together EC payment systems and legacy payment systems. Acquirers or processors for the systems that process authorizations endorse payment gateways by issuing them gateway digital certificates. Payment gateways, much like merchant servers, are software components that adhere to the SET protocol. Several vendors, such as IBM, Tandem (a division of Compaq), VeriSign, and others offer such software. Most of the products perform the same function, adhering to the SET standards, with the exception of some value-added services. Acquirers or processors of authorizations must undergo a selection process to determine which of these products best suits the needs of their organization.

Payment gateways act as intermediaries, simplifying the number of relationships required by both merchants and processors. Hence, payments gateways establish many bilateral relationships between merchants and processors. Given this responsibility, it is imperative that payment gateways have very stringent controls protecting the service's environment and processes.

Although SET is an essential component in the trust design at the transactional level, it is the compliance with SET specifications, self-audits, and the adoption of best business and IT practices that reduce the risks surrounding the use of SET. As noted above, SET is *not* a complete EC solution, but a integral part of it. The new component not found in existing credit card payments system is the PKI and the issuing of digital certificates as a way of reinforcing trusted relationships.

4. THE TRUST DIMENSION: THE PUBLIC KEY INFRASTRUCTURE . . . .

To achieve the level of trust necessary between all of the participants, trusted relationships need to be established. SET, in it of itself, does not offer trust. However, through the use of what is known as a public key infrastructure (PKI), a hierarchy of trust can be constructed. The PKI is a hierarchy of trust where each SET certificate is linked to the signature certificate of the entity that digitally signed it (see Figure A.2) The idea is that following the tree to a known trusted party, one can be assured that the SET certificate is valid. This level of trust is not achieved by SET but rather through what is known as a PKI.

5. SET IMPLEMENTATION ISSUES . . . .

Vendor Products May Not Be Fully Certified at Time of Implementation or Self-Audit

SET vendor products, whether for the consumer ("e-wallet"), merchant, acquirer ("payment gateway"), or certificate authority, are very new. Many of them are at various stages of pending approval by SETCo, the company set up by Visa and MasterCard to exclusively oversee that products are SET compliant. As of September 1999, less than half of the vendors listed in the Vendor Status Matrix have earned the SET Mark, SETCo's seal of approval. Financial Institutions (FIs) that have been using the payment gateway products are faced with two new challenges. (1) Many

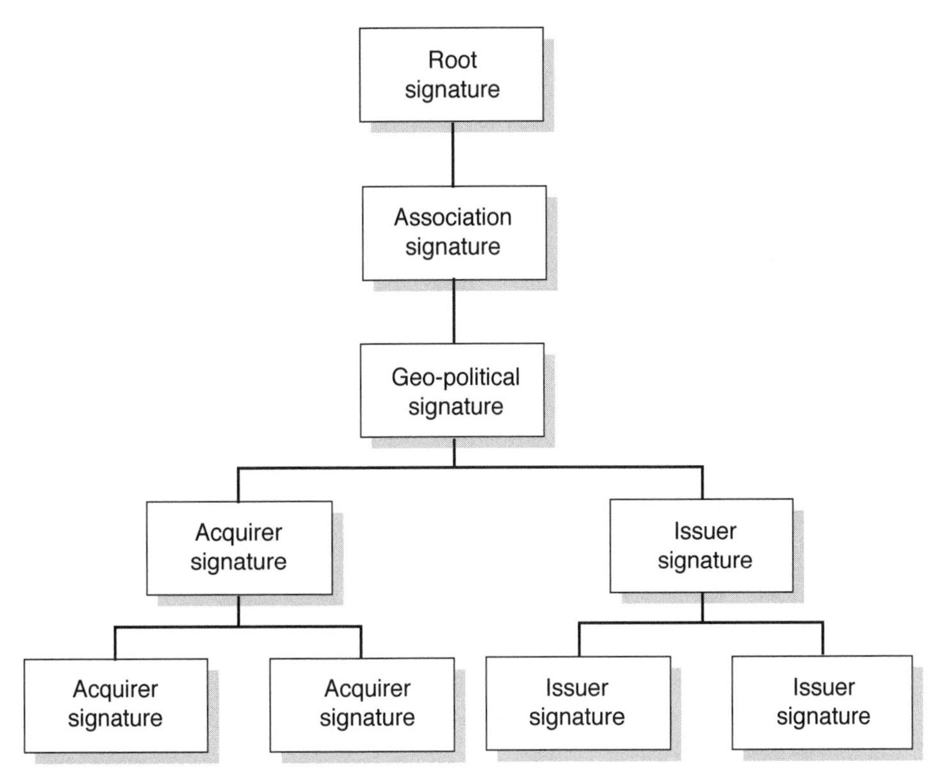

Figure A.2
Illustrative SET public key (certificate) infrastructure.

of the vendors have not fully earned their SET Mark. FIs have to rely on SETCo's vendor summary status reports to be assured of the software quality of the vendor they have selected. Choices are not that many, and vendor track records have yet to be established. (2) Interoperability among payment gateway products is still an issue, which in turn limits their potentially wider selection of vendors and indirectly the merchant's selection of POS software. Such scenarios have prompted FIs to adopt a staged approach to SET implementation, with the objective to gain technical and operational experience and to position for future delivery of enhanced SET. Monitoring the certification status and progress of your vendor is a necessary step in SET project management. Information on vendor testing status is available on SETCo's Web site. The Vendor Status Matrix is updated weekly.

Although checking the certificate status of the payment gateway service providers is a convenient way for FIs to obtain a level of assurance, to the general public, the ultimate hallmark of trust is the strict adherence to Visa and MasterCard's requirement of mandatory filing of Payment Gateway Security Standards Self-Audit Compliance Statement (see the Self-Audits and Independent Audits section later in the Appendix).

Merchant Sign-Up Process Change

Visa and MasterCard have introduced new operation regulations for handling Internet transactions. These regulations will affect the existing merchant qualification and monitoring process. Considering that credit card payment services are now extended to a new breed of merchants with only "virtual" storefronts, the approval process of accepting merchants into the Internet POS and merchant agreements must be drawn up to reflect these new regulations and the FI's own security policy for such services.

In addition, there is a major difference between the SET merchant software and the traditional POS terminal services. SET merchant software can be installed in any computer with an authorized license, where as a POS terminal is a physical device with serial numbers. FIs have well-established procedures for the deployment of POS terminals to merchants. POS terminals can be thought of as minicomputers with the necessary hardware and software to execute merchant transactions. Included with these POS devices are encryption keys to secure the transaction between the device and the FI. FIs use sophisticated hardware (self-destructs if tampered with) and techniques (encryption key injection) to controls the integrity of these devices. FIs now have to establish similar distribution and inventory control procedures for the SET merchant software.

Certificate Management

Visa and MasterCard have a detailed approval process for the payment gateway service providers to follow in order for them to obtain brand certificates from their CAs. FIs must use a service provider that has successfully completed this approval process. Effective certificate management is crucial to managing the trusted relationships forged in the SET payment process. Issuers and recipients of SET certificates will likely involve themselves in many, if not all, of the following domains of certificate management: issuance, revocation, changes, recovery, publication, and archival. Each of these domains requires attention at various levels of security policies, including local security, technical security, network security, and operational security.

Performance

In a November 1998 white paper from Gartner Group, a SET comparative performance analysis with SSL, the researchers find that there is a near term impact in high-end payment gateway applications and a very minor difference between the investment required in a server that supports SET and the one that supports SSL. Gartner's conclusion is that the benefits of additional security and trust from SET outweigh the additional cost.

Although performance is not a key issue at this stage of EC growth, a plan to identify the performance objectives for transaction throughput and response time using end-to-end scenarios will be useful for future reference and fine-tuning. It is also worth considering a cryptographic hardware for SET encryption and decryption in the future to improve transaction throughput and to reduce CPU loading. These are now enhancement items for SET 2.0.

Backup of SET-Sensitive Files

While backup and recovery processes for the SET environment are no different from those in use in any computer processing center, the backup tapes for the payment gateway server contain restricted data, such as the cardholder credit card information and the FI's digital certificates. With these backup tapes, someone could set up a bogus Web site to process these POS Internet transactions on behalf of the FI. It appears that stricter control procedures are needed to handle such tapes. The contents of these tapes must be destroyed at expiration. We encourage a constant dialog between the FI and the payment gateway service provider to come up with an effective off-site backup storage arrangement.

Managing Vendors and Outsourcing Partners

New EC is heavily reliant on purchased or licensed software, and the outsourcing of development efforts to consultants and specialists is very common. What are our criteria for selecting one CA instead of another? What kind of assurances are we getting: third-party control reviews? SET Mark? Self-audits? Independent auditor's report? These issues have been discussed in Chapter 3. Andrew Shapiro, in his 1999 book, *The Control Revolution* goes further to suggest that we could draw on the interactivity and flexibility of the Internet to inform users who they can trust. The absence of the SET Mark, for instance, can sometimes be a more-valuable indicator to the user than its presence. It prompts the user to ask probing questions as to why the vendor is not able to obtain an established trust bond in the interim. Ultimately, failure to obtain a SET Mark is not a tenable business proposition.

SETCo has very astringent certification requirements for testing vendor products before they can earn the SET Mark of approval. They also practice "clean management," requiring these service providers to rectify under various conditions and timeframes. Visa and MasterCard also have their own specific requirements for these SET service providers and self-audit programs to continuously monitor them. Project managers do have a readily available independent source of information about the quality of these products and services. Because the SET technology is still evolving, these vendors also provide vendor summary reports on their status of compliance. We need to treat these reports as our own internal reports, as the safety and soundness of SET transactions very much hinge on how well these suppliers meet specifications. Managing the vendors and outsourcing companies is like managing an extended enterprise.

Self-Audits and Independent Audits

Self-audits as applied to payment gateway service providers and CAs are similar to control self-assessments (CSAs) discussed in this book. They are a way for an organization's work units to demonstrate that internal controls are in place and working as designed. The self-audits required by Visa and MasterCard to secure EC is a much higher control requirement than the usual CSAs. Compliance with their standards is nonnegotiable. The service provider must complete an individual exception for each statement of noncompliance. The form must be certified by an independent auditor.

CSAs and self-audits, whether they are SET-related or not, are useful tools to communicate to all interested parties that management has a sound basis to establish trust and maintain relationships as a going concern.

The independent auditors who have to confirm the payment gateway service provider's assertions on their completed self-audit report must be qualified and technically competent. They are like trusted intermediaries and we value their perspectives in their review of SET certificate revocation, key management and security policies, and procedural controls. In this highly specialized area, the auditor's "questioning" skills are just as important as the auditor's "listening" skills to elicit the evidence needed.

6. WHAT SET DOES NOT COVER . . . .

As mentioned earlier in our analysis, SET is not a total EC trust solution. It provides transactional-level security and technical trust through the use of a PKI, but it does not cover aspects such as relationship management or how the consumer may choose to use them. The main issue with any form of secure processing is: Although everyone says they want it, few will pay for it, and no one wants to be inconvenienced by it.

Our observation about SET is that it forms the basis of the trust platform for the use of credit card transactions in EC. However, more attention is being spent on the technical infrastructure than on the relationship and user needs—and this is a concern; not because this is an insoluble problem, but rather that the solution seems to be to throw more technology at it: a higher level of encrypting bits, different algorithms, and faster and more physically secure hardware and software. Yet we think someone is missing the point. The most critical element for the successful use of SET will ultimately be its ease of use and value as trust agent for EC, not how many bits are used for encryption.

It is clear that the credit card has a major role in the success of EC, whether as a transaction settlement process for the consumer or for the corporate user. Even more important, if the credit card begins to define the way payments will evolve in EC, at least in the short term, what can be the role for the token-based payment process if secure and trusted credit card transactions cannot be established?

SET is, first and foremost, about developing relationships between potentially unknown parties. This is the essence of the problem for EC in the future and the reason that all this activity is happening. As long as it is difficult to establish a trusting relationship, EC will struggle. When these issues are resolved, it will flourish. In fact, there are trusting EC relationships today—without SET or PKI, or, in fact, any real level of technological security. These are supported by rating systems (as in the case of eBay), brand identity (as in the case of Amazon.com, Charles Schwab, and Barnes and Noble) or direct personal experience (such as in the use of e-mail to order goods or services from a familiar party).

SET needs to be seen as part of this overall relationship support environment in order to be truly valuable and relevant to the EC trust equation.

Index

A

B

C

D

E

F

G

H

I

J

K

L

M

N

O

P

R

S

T

U

The Authors

Peter Keen

Peter Keen is the founder and Chairman of Keen Innovations (formerly known as The International Center for Information Technologies). He has served on the faculties of Harvard, MIT, Stanford, with visiting positions at Wharton, Oxford, Fordham, the London School of Business, Stockolm University, and Duke University. In 1994, he was profiled by *Forbes* magazine as the "consultant from Paradise." In 1988, he was named by *Information Week* as one of the top ten consultants in the information technology field.

A prolific writer, Peter Keen is the author of many books that have strongly influenced the business-technology dialogue, starting with *Decision Support Systems* (1978), which introduced in the early 1970s the concept of IT as a support to managerial judgment. Consequently he published *Competing in Time: Using Telecommunications for Competitive Advantage* (1986), the first book to anticipate the immense impact of telecommunications on the basics of business, and *Shaping the Future: Business Design Through Information Technology* (1991), a book addressed to senior executives that has been translated into many European and Asian languages. His *Every Manager's Guide to Information Technology* (1995), now in its second edition, and *Every Manager's Guide to Business Multimedia* and *Online Profits: A Manager's Guide to Electronic Commerce* were published in October 1997, *The Business Internet* was published in 1998. Another one of his titles, *Process Edge: Creating Value Where It Counts* (1997), looks at business processes as invisible financial assets and liabilities to be managed as a portfolio of capital investments targeted at increasing shareholder value.

Dr. Keen has worked as a consultant on a long-term basis and as an adviser to top managers in helping them fuse business choices and technology decisions. Examples of companies that Dr. Keen has worked with in this capacity include: British Airways, British Telecom, Citibank, Glaxo, IBM, MCI Communications, Royal Bank of Canada, Cemex (Mexico), Sweden Post, Unilever, World Bank, IATA, CTC (Chile), and many others. His work with these companies has generally included the development and delivery of senior management education programs for action (rather than just "awareness") as a lever for taking charge of change and making IT part of everyday planning and management thinking.

Craigg Ballance

Craigg Ballance is a Partner with E-Finity Group Inc. in Toronto, Canada. He is recognized as an expert in the area of EC, EDI, and Financial EC and is the author of two books: *Electronic Commerce and EDI in the Financial Industry* (Lafferty Publications, 1996) and *On-Line Profits: A Manager's Guide to Electronic Commerce* (Harvard Business Press, 1997).

During his previous twenty-year career in the financial industry, Craigg was responsible for the development of a variety of progressive EC systems including the Canadian national ATM system called Interac and the debit card POS system. He was the creative force behind the Canadian Financial EDI initiative and chaired the Audit and Control task force of the development committee.

Craigg has provided consulting to numerous corporations and financial institutions around the world, including such places as Ireland, Chile, South Africa, the Caribbean, and Mexico, as well as in Canada and the U.S.—helping them effectively apply EC principles to their businesses. His specific emphasis is on e-business technologies, such as EC, the Internet, payment systems and ACH, audit and control applications, EDI, and card-based delivery systems and implementations.

Sally Chan

Sally Chan, MA, CMA, is the Manager of Information Technology (IT) Audit of Internal Audit Services of Royal Bank of Canada. She is responsible for the IT audit of Royal's Corporate and Investment Banking Systems worldwide. Before assuming her present position, Ms. Chan was the Audit Manager of Corporate Banking Systems, responsible for auditing and reviewing all Royal Bank's EDI systems, which included both purchasing and payment functions.

Ms. Chan was chairperson of the EDI Study Group that wrote *EDI for Managers and Auditors*, published by the EDI Council of Canada in 1991. The second edition of this book was published by The Canadian Institute of Chartered Accountants in 1993. Ms. Chan is also the co-author of two other books: *EDI Security, Control and Audit*, published by Artech House in the U.S. in 1993, and *EDI Control, Management and Audit Issues*, published by AICPA in 1995. She is a member of Revenue Canada's Technical Advisory Group on Electronic Commerce.

Ms. Chan's previous experience includes systems and consulting in design and project management for the manufacturing, insurance, educational, and banking sectors. She was also a part-time community college instructor for five years.

Steve Schrump

Steve Schrump is the Chief Technology Officer for Basis100 Inc., a leading provider of global business-to-business EC solutions for the financial services sector. He has held senior positions at three major EC startups.

Steve has more than ten years of experience in the delivery of solutions to the market in the banking and technology sectors, and possesses an extensive understanding of Application Service Provisioning and Internet EC. Prior to Basis100 Inc., Steve was Chief Technical Architect at Cebra Inc., a Bank of Montreal subsidiary company that specializes in EC for financial, health care, insurance industries, and government.

He is known for establishing high-integrity philosophies and strategies, such as instituting risk mitigation quality assurance programs like the Software Engineering Institute's Capability Maturity Model and ISO 9000. His focus on the maintenance of a strategic vision for best-in-class software solutions that offer technological superiority stimulate demand and exceed customer expectation.